Praise for *Grassroots*

"Have you ever wanted to make a difference but didn't know how? *Grassroots* is the book you've been waiting for. Using examples drawn from progressive and feminist campaigns all over the country, veteran activists Jennifer Baumgardner and Amy Richards explain how to organize your friends, your community, and most important, yourself."
— Katha Pollitt

"One need not be a vegan, tree-hugging, 'round-the-clock meeting-goer to be an activist. Instead, Baumgardner and Richards offer anyone interested in improving the world small but significant ways to effect social change . . . Would-be agitators look no further for the sass, savvy, and skills you'll need to begin."
— Eleanor J. Bader, *Library Journal*

"A booster shot of inspiration, *Grassroots* reaches out to activists of all generations. Baumgardner and Richards have not only shared the secrets of their and others' success— just as important, they've recorded the mistakes they've made. I related to so much of it—especially the mistakes— and by showing the fits and starts of real-life activism, *Grassroots* will help readers to both sustain their enthusiasm for social justice work and be more effective as a result."
— Rosalind Wiseman, author of *Queen Bees and Wannabes*

Jennifer Baumgardner
and
Amy Richards

Grassroots

Jennifer Baumgardner is a former editor at *Ms.* and writes for *The Nation, Glamour,* and National Public Radio. Amy Richards is a member of the advisory board at *Ms.*; a co-founder of the Third Wave Foundation, an activist group for young feminists; and the author of *Shopping in New York.* They are the co-authors of *Manifesta: Young Women, Feminism, and the Future* (FSG, 2000) as well as the founders of Soapbox, Inc., a speakers' bureau representing outspoken experts with a progressive take on current events and culture.

Also by Jennifer Baumgardner
and
Amy Richards

Manifesta: Young Women, Feminism, and the Future

Feminist Classics (Jennifer Baumgardner, Series Editor)
The Female Eunuch by Germaine Greer
The Dialectic of Sex by Shulamith Firestone

Grassroots

Grassroots

A Field Guide for **Feminist Activism**

Jennifer

Baumgardner

 and

Amy

Richards

Farrar, Straus and Giroux

New York

Farrar, Straus and Giroux
19 Union Square West, New York 10003

Library of Congress Cataloging-in-Publication Data
Baumgardner, Jennifer, 1970–
Grassroots : a field guide for feminist activism / Jennifer
Baumgardner and Amy Richards.— 1st ed.
    p. cm.
Includes index.
ISBN-13: 978-0-374-52865-2
ISBN-10: 0-374-52865-9 (pbk.)
1. Feminism.   2. Social action.   3. Social justice.   4. Women
social reformers.   I. Richards, Amy.   II. Title.

HQ1154.B333 2005
305.42—dc22   2004010306

Designed by Patrice Sheridan

www.fsgbooks.com

3   5   7   9   10   8   6   4

For anyone who has ever wondered:
How can I get more involved?

Contents

Acknowledgments

We were lucky to have a near constant stream of young, smart, stylish, and hardworking women who reached out to us to be interns. Our gratitude goes to Jackie Arcy, Tara Brindisi, Sarah Taylor Cummings, Anna Davies, Jenny Egan, Jessica Hatem, Elizabeth Maki, Elizabeth Masuhr, and Mikki Pugh.

A great debt is owed to all of the people who have ever written to Ask Amy, including those who call her a feminazi and provide a reality check that we don't yet live in a feminist world. We are grateful for the thousands of letters we have received over the years and to everyone who has approached us in towns large and small across the United States to problem-solve. Thanks to everyone whose story ended up in *Grassroots*. You not only shared your experience, but worked with us to make it a model for others.

Farrar, Straus and Giroux remains the publisher of our dreams. We are especially grateful to Denise Oswald, our strict, funny, and intelligent editor (who suggested the title);

to Sarah Almond, her intrepid assistant; and to Elisabeth Calamari, our memorably named and highly effective publicist.

Jill Grinberg, our agent, neighbor, and friend, initially pushed us to turn our "activist idea bank" project into a book. We owe her thanks for that and for her graceful assistance on many other fronts.

Thanks to Mia Herndon, Elizabeth Birdsall, David Brotherton, Liz Maki, Sarah Taylor Cummings, Jessica Baumgardner, and Gloria Steinem for insightful readings of a probably embarrassing draft. Merci to Julie Felner and Irad Eyal for brainstorming titles when we still were calling the book *Recipe-tested*.

Most of all, we thank our friends, families, and Gordon and Peter, for their support and belief in us—we also thank our sons, who were born during the writing of *Grassroots*.

Introduction

by Winona LaDuke

I have spent my entire adult life as what you might call a political activist. I have testified at hearings, demonstrated at countless protests, and been involved in litigation. I've worked in a number of Native communities across the continent, and founded the White Earth Land Recovery Project (WELRP) on my home reservation. With our work here, we've been able to recover more than seventeen hundred acres of our land and create a land trust, while we work toward recovery of more of our own birthright. We also continue to work to protect our wild rice from genetic modification and ecosystems from contamination by pesticides, and to stop clear cuts of the forest. From inside my own house, we roast fair-trade and organic coffee. I have written books about the environment, run for vice president twice (as Ralph Nader's Green Party running mate in 1996 and 2000), and been arrested because I don't think that a thousand-year-old tree should become a phone book.

The perception of me, or of any well-known activist, is probably far from reality. Activists, the thinking goes, must be organized, focused, always working on the next strategy.

My real life, the one in which I conduct all of my activism, is, of course, messy. If you came over, you might find my five children, ages four to sixteen, three dogs, fifteen horses, a few cats, several interns from around the country, and many friends who double as coworkers helping with WELRP's work. The 2000 veep campaign was conducted with me breastfeeding my newborn son before and after each stump speech and during many an interview. I still coordinate the sustainable food projects central to the White Earth Land Recovery Project literally from my kitchen table at the same time as I figure out meals for my kids, take coffee orders for Muskrat coffee company, and pop in videos for my youngest to watch on TV. I talk to Native community leaders from across the country as I cook meals and clean up (sort of an endless job). I write books at the same table where I make rawhide ornaments for sale as part of WELRP and help with maple syruping in the spring season, and my house is filled with labels that spell out the Ojibwe words for "bed," "book," "cupboard," and "table" as part of my ongoing commitment to indigenous language and culture preservation. My activism is simply in my life—it has to be, or it couldn't get done.

My own life as an identified activist has made me wonder at the term itself. What separates simple "responsibility" in life—motherhood, for example— from the fine line that one crosses to become an "activist"? I have been surprised and moved by encountering so many other mothers in my years as an activist: mothers in Chiapas breastfeeding their babies like anyone else, but who mask their faces as they speak with me because they can't afford to have their identifies known; Mohawk and Ojibwe mothers who face down General Motors and Potlach Corporation, knowing that if they don't, their kids won't ever know clean water, and generations ahead will have contaminated breast milk.

I have developed longstanding friendships with women who are engaged in struggles of responsibility—for their land, their own community health, and the water their children drink. Are these women feminists? That depends on who defines the term. Many of these women, including myself, are committed to the process of self-determination and believe in our inherent rights, as bestowed by the Creator, to live with dignity, peace, clean air and water, and our duty to pass on this legacy to our children and the generations to follow.

At the United Nations Conference on the Status of Women in Beijing, China, in 1995, I asked women from small countries around the world why they came all this way to participate in what was, in essence, a meeting. "I came because the World Bank is here," explained Victoria Tauli-Corpuz, an Igarok woman from the Philippines whose village is targeted for a Word Bank–funded dam. "I believe that those people at the World Bank and the IMF, those who make the decisions which will transform my life, should see my face." That sentiment applies whether you are an Igarok woman from the Philippines or Sherry Honkala from the Kensington Welfare Rights Union, challenging federal budget cuts to aid for dependent families or tending to the needs of homeless families. The message of self-determining women is the same for all people: *We want control over our lives, and we will challenge those who impose laws on our bodies, our communities, and our future.*

I believe that women move to activism out of sheer necessity. As a group, we are not of privilege—budget cuts devastated our household, the military wreaks havoc on our bodies and our homelands. The National Priorities Project reports that $152.6 billion spent on military aid in 2003 could have provided Head Start for an additional 20,211,205 children, health coverage for an additional 89,780,249 children, affordable housing vouchers for an additional

22,894,974 families, or salaries for 2,673,864 new elementary school teachers. Feminist activism, then, doesn't begin
or end with my uterus: this is about my whole body, my life,
and the lives of my children. We are women who redefine
"Women's Issues," and say all issues are women's issues. I
say: *We are the mothers of our nations, and anything that concerns
our nations is of concern to us as women.* Those choices and necessities move us to speak out and to be active.

I happen to come from a line of these women who speak
out, and I continue this work—our work. Women's work.
My grandmother Helen Peskin, a Jewish woman from the
Ukraine, recently passed into the Spirit World. Her early
years were formed by the reality of war, first the Cossacks who
overran her village and then the Nazis. With her life came a
sheer determination to not be a victim, to speak for peace, to
make a better life, and to demand dignity. Of her ninety years
on this earth a good forty were spent as a seamstress: a purse
maker, a member of the Pocket Book Makers Union in the
garment district in New York, a folk dancer, and a peace activist. *A woman's work is about economic justice, and about quality of
life.* My mother, Betty LaDuke, made her own path as a mu-
ralist and art professor, one of the first women on the faculty
of her college, and like other women, she had to do it better
than any man around because it took that much to get recognized. She has done this work in a way that celebrates life, and
celebrates the work of other women. And she has done this
work by linking with women in Eritrea, Nigeria, and Peru. *A
women's work is about creating and celebrating life.* Our parents'
struggles become our own, in our own time. We can't escape
from that history, nor can we escape from our time in it.

In the lives of women in my family, it was never about
just our own selves, it was about the collective dignity and
everyone's health and rights. This is counter, in many ways, to

Americanism. Americanism teaches individualism. My family, and indeed movements for social transformation, are not about anything as limited as the better job or the better advantage for the individual woman. Even the tragic deaths of three of my closest friends, activists all, are lessons in the urgency of change on a broader scale. Marsha Gomez, a gifted artist, was killed by her own son, who lacked the psychiatric medical attention he so desperately needed; Nilak Butler passed from ovarian cancer because she did not have adequate health coverage; and Ingrid Washinawatok El-Issa was assassinated by the FARC, Revolutionary Armed Forces of Colombia, with a gun and a bullet that came from my tax dollars in the second most highly financed recipient of U.S. military aid in the world.

The compelling reason behind activism is that our most personal lives—even the intimacy of death—are actually embroidered in the reality of public policy, foreign policy, military aid, and economics. Each day, then, I, like the women in my family before me, and like so many other woman in the world, recommit to continue this struggle for life, and to celebrate its beauty in the process. That struggle and that celebration are who we are as women, as we take responsibility for our destinies.

The book you hold in your hands, *Grassroots*, is a call to understand and undertake action. The authors, Jennifer Baumgardner and Amy Richards, have their own flawed, chaotic, and activist lives, which they share with you in an attempt to prove, as I hope I have done, that you don't have to be Superwoman to change the world. You just have to take responsibility for your life and your community—and realize that you have the power to do so, even from your own sticky kitchen table.

—White Earth Reservation, MN, August 18, 2004

Prologue:
Portrait of
an Activist

Noam Chomsky looks like an activist. He wears practical, worn clothing and eyeglasses. He's old and he clearly cares not about Prada's or Gucci's designs, just about how and under what conditions the clothing is made. A venerated professor of linguistics at MIT, he lectures around the world and has written seventy political books thus far (and at the rate he is going will write twenty more before he is through). Chomsky's beat is demystifying world politics, global economies, and the media. His specific message is that average citizens like *you* have the power to hold those huge forces accountable. When activists want to know how to protest the war in Iraq or how to dismantle the World Trade Organization, they turn to Chomsky for analysis. He always knows where injustice lies, cutting through complex worlds with his laser IQ. "You've told us what was wrong, but what can we do about it?" is a frequent question in the Q and A after his talks. "You've got to organize," is Chomsky's perennial response.

But what does it mean to organize? What does organizing look like? According to a profile of Chomsky in *The New*

Yorker, even his wife describes his "You've got to organize" response as his "fake answer," given to comfort people from his depressing predictions about the state of the world. We don't see his answer as false, but simply as too broad. As feminist activists, we are confronted with this question, too, and we've concluded that an accurate and responsible answer is different for each individual. The details of organizing vary depending on who you are and what you seek to change.

For ourselves, that awareness came slowly, but eventually we grew to understand that being an activist didn't mean adding an identity or tasks to our lives, but simply recognizing the opportunities for change that our lives (as responsible, passionate citizens) already included. We asked ourselves, "Do we have a few dollars to give, or a few friends who might help protest the execution of a young man on death row?" Our mode and expression as activists are based on what jobs we have, where our talents lie, what we care about, where we live, and other individual details. What Chomsky himself does to organize is write best-selling polemics such as *9-11*, lecture, analyze a problem clearly for others, and reveal how the media and big business work to, as he puts it, manufacture consent. Not everyone has the power of Chomsky to draw crowds or the IQ (or time) to read hundreds of pages of wire-service reports each day, but everyone has the power to impact the world—indeed, that is Chomsky's message. The problem, to which even Chomsky contributes, is getting to the next step: action. That, we realized, requires demystifying activism for those eager to be involved but confused and possibly intimidated by what that might entail.

When we sat down to write *Grassroots*, we were ambivalent about even using the word "activism." We wondered if more people would relate to the terms "volunteerism" or "charity," or something more fuzzy—like "do-gooders united." On the one hand, the word "activism" sounds so dramatic, as if this book was for people who chain themselves to trees or ruin dinner by lecturing to their families and friends about factory farming. On the other hand, we believed that social change was simple at its core and the book could be a call for people to find the activist within.

Since we ended up committing to activism as a term as well as a process, we want to make sure readers know what we personally mean by the word. The two of us define activism as consistently expressing one's values with the goal of making the world more just. We use feminism as our philosophy for that value system; that is, we try to take off the cultural lens that sees mostly men and filters out women and replace it with one that sees all people. We ask: "Do our lifestyles reflect our politics?" "How can we make sure that we all receive the same breaks—and basic necessities—traditionally awarded to white males?" An activist is anyone who accesses the resources that he or she has as an individual for the benefit of the common good. With that definition, activism is available to anyone. By asserting that anyone can be an activist, we aren't trying to weaken or water down its power. We believe that activism is by definition profound, a big deal, revolutionary. However, we are challenging the notion that there is one type of person who is an activist—someone serious, rebellious, privileged, and unrealistically heroic.

If we had to name one person who embodies our ideal activist, it's eighty-something Lois Weisberg from Chicago, Illinois. We learned about her through an article by Malcolm Gladwell in *The New Yorker*, "Six Degrees of Lois Weisberg," in which he characterized her as a "super-connector." Lois looks at her friends, family, garbage collector, neighbors, shoe-shop clerks, and co-workers as resources for her to solve problems and make the world better. As former commissioner of cultural affairs in Chicago, she created a ping-pong project (Ping-Pong tables set up all over town, inviting harried urbanites to play a game), a youth arts initiative called Gallery 37—where professional artists mentored low-income kids—and she was responsible for those life-sized painted cows ("Cows on Parade") that invaded several cities in 1999, among many other things. Though her achievements are numerous, Lois Weisberg won't go down in the history books with Malcolm X and Dolores Huerta, because she is an everyday activist. She approaches her daily life as a conduit for change, as a big game of Concentration wherein a random meeting or request can ultimately be matched with a parallel concern or solution—and in that way she is affecting the world.

Elle Woods does not immediately come to mind either when you think of a radical change-maker. She wears pink, is more perfect than Gwyneth, has more shoes than Carrie Bradshaw, and carries her chihuahua, Bruiser, in a Gucci bag. Elle was president of her sorority (Delta Nu), keeps a regular hair and nail appointment, and is unequivocally a super-activist. Oddly enough, she is the epitome of Chomsky's call to organize.

For those of you who haven't seen *Legally Blonde* I and II, we should say that Elle Woods is the charming hell-raiser portrayed by blond screwball comic actor Reese Witherspoon. In the first film, she leaves golden Bel-Air to compete with pale, Brooks Brothers grade-grubbers at Harvard Law School. Her initial motivation is to win back her WASP-y boyfriend, but she soon learns that she has an affinity for solving problems using her wits, her willingness to ask the "dumb" question, and the law. In the sequel, Elle translates her stellar record at Harvard into a job on Capitol Hill, working for a congresswoman who was a fellow Harvard alum. Elle's cause is saving Bruiser's mother and other animals like her from being cruelly and unnecessarily used for the testing of makeup. Rather than engage in the stymied and age-old bureaucracy of The Hill—bartering for votes using backdoor deals, waiting for the day that someone would owe her enough favors to hear the bill, and compromising her ethics in the process—Elle uses her particular resources to find another way.

At doggie day care, for instance, she befriends the conservative chair of the Committee on Energy and Commerce that will hear her proposed bill. She aligns with a doorman/dog walker to find out which of the representatives own dogs and would, thus, have an emotional stake in this bill, if pushed. When she can't get an appointment with a powerful Thatcher-style Texas congresswoman, Elle figures out which hair salon she goes to and talks to her in that setting. Wearing a beauty-salon robe and with her hair mid–color process, the Texas Iron Maiden is revealed to be a Delta Nu sister. Elle finds out who wears the makeup that the animals are being tested on, and makes the connection between one congressman's moisturizing gloves and another congresswoman's "raspberry macaroon" lip gloss and the abuses of animals via unregulated testing. Her bill gets a hearing, but when backdoor maneuvers threaten it, Elle needs to beat the bushes to demonstrate that there is public support. Elle turns to her sorority—an organized network of women fiercely loyal to each other—and accesses "Phone tree #255." Within a day, thousands of young, hyper women show up to march in D.C. Elle wins and what is revealed is the potential power and efficacy of the many invisible organizations an individual already has at one's disposal—resources which can be leveraged for one to become a successful activist.

Elle Woods does not exist, but the conflict—and resolution—that she illustrates does. Acknowledging that someone like Elle is an activist brings us to one of the central theories of *Grassroots*: it's not who you are but what you do. We came to this understanding through our years of traveling across the country in support of our first book, *Manifesta: Young Women, Feminism, and the Future*. One of the most popular questions we were asked points to this truth. The question almost always came from a young woman, someone who reports she has taken her first women's studies class the year before and it changed her life. "I see the world through feminist-colored glasses now. Issues make so much more sense. I am electrified!" she'd gush. "I'm volunteering at a battered women's shelter and I can't wait to do more and . . . um, I wear a thong. Can I still be a feminist?"

At first we laughed, and answered that her underwear neither qualified nor disqualified her feminism. After getting this question at several schools, though, we realized that the woman wasn't asking for clothing advice. She was saying, "Can I be myself and care about these issues?" And the questions in that vein kept coming. *Am I good enough? Am I pure enough? If I don't eat red meat, do I also have to forgo leather? Can I never shop at the Gap again? Do I have to give up my religion? I think I'm a feminist but . . . I diet. I listen to rap. I'm pro-life.* We realized that one of the main barriers to seeing oneself as someone who could truly make change in the world is that we feel trapped in our own contradictions. As Amy says, "Can I wear Nike running shoes and still protest their labor practices in Indonesia?" There is a huge fear that we'll be revealed as hypocrites so, in search of moral perfection, we're paralyzed from doing anything.

The two of us are not advising people to deck themselves out in Nike gear and get a bikini wax every week—or even to disavow careful reflection about the challenges of participating in a capitalist economy. We are advocating, quite simply, that if you wait until you are perfect and free of conflicts, you will never change anything in the world. In fact, all of our most-loved social justice superstars have lives that are riddled with contradictions. "Mother of Modern Feminism" Betty Friedan had a husband who used to give her black eyes, yet Friedan didn't complain publicly, nor did she report him to the police or leave him flat. Inspiring civil rights activist Al Sharpton took Republican funding for his radical bid for the 2004 Democratic nomination for President. Beloved feminist author bell hooks advocates a Marxist critique of capitalist society but nonetheless has been known to love her red BMW and charge large speaking fees. The filmmaker Michael Moore advocates workers' rights but we've met a few disillusioned former employees who note he doesn't apply the same pro-labor standards to his own workplaces. The Center for Third World Organizing eviscerates major corporations like Levi's in its magazine *Colorlines* and yet takes money from Levi's foundation. We're not telling people's dirty secrets but demonstrating that these accomplished, effective, respected activists still have issues to work out—just like the rest of us. Each of us has to begin where we are to address the slew of inequities that present themselves in our lives.

Once you begin to address the problems you see in your own life, you discover how interconnected all issues are. One anecdote that bears this out: in the 2004 book *The*

Working Poor: Invisible in America, David Shipler documented the story of an eight-year-old asthmatic boy living in Boston public housing. The asthma (treated medically but not improving) caused the boy to miss school and his mother to have to stay home from her much-needed job. A nurse paid a visit to his home and discovered the likely sources of the boy's intractable asthma: a leaky pipe causing mustiness as well as wall-to-wall carpet riddled with mites. The boy's mother attempted to get the landlord to fix the pipe and remove the carpet, but to no avail. Finally, lawyers from Boston Medical Center (the employer of the nurse) sent a letter to the landlord, who—under legal threat—fixed the pipe and replaced the carpet. What was the result of this one direct action? The boy's asthma cleared up almost immediately, he returned to school, and his mother was no longer in danger of losing her job. Helping people living in poverty isn't always about convening a think tank, changing a law, or writing a letter to your representative. Sometimes it is ripping out mite-infested carpet. Many issues were contained in this story—welfare to work, Medicaid, the environment, education—and the act that resolved it is one that might be accessible to any of us.

The people you will meet in this book are each addressing an issue that directly impacts their community, and we profile their process in creating a solution from the grassroots up. The point of each chapter is not the issue they tackle but the steps for change they outline. In other words, a description of how Lauren Porsch—as a college student in New York—created an abortion fund isn't just a guide to financing the termination of unwanted pregnancies; it's a plan for creating a financial distribution network. A reader in Texas might use Lauren's advice to put together a fund for the defense of murder defendants who are not provided free legal services by the state. Your fund might award scholarships to smart but low-income African American students who want a college education and have no other means of affording it. Our chapters about what high-school students and artists can do isn't meant to be limited to those demographics—the examples can apply to any skill set or any community, from carpenters and computer programmers to transgendered people and stay-at-home moms.

The real portrait of an activist, after all, is just a mirror.

Grassroots

chapter 1 Why the World Needs Another Advice Book

"How do we bring attention to [an] issue and make change, not just discuss it, not just march about it, but make change?"

—Ruby Dee, actor and activist

JENNIFER AND AMY

In 2002, New York City mayor Michael Bloomberg, a billionaire who believes in the bottom line, slashed recycling in America's most densely populated city. The mayor's office claimed it could save $40 million in crew and export costs. True or not, the city has 8 million citizens, many of whom buy several liters of coffee in paper cups and ask for it in a bag with seventeen napkins and four individual sugar packets—*every day*. Thus our city's contribution to the world's garbage problem is indisputably significant. Recycling was our one bit of moral credit, not to mention it kept

us from drowning in Starbucks frappuccino cups and
Glacéau Vitamin Water bottles. In a mere month, a ten-
year process of training New Yorkers in garbage-sorting behavior was demolished. Standing in our tiny New York City
kitchenettes tossing pounds of recyclables into the trash
made us realize how much we waste—and how necessary
the recycling program really was.

Soon many people were angry with Bloomberg and so
eager to have the service back that some were willing to
pay for it, and most assumed that somebody else (Giuliani?
Nader? Oprah?) would soon be informing us of the new
strategy. The two of us also waited for someone else to have
a plan. And waited, and waited. Then we realized that we
weren't practicing what we preached unless we took some
action ourselves. We called a colleague whose family started
the garbage removal company BFI (yes, it's helpful as an
activist to have a wide variety of friends) and attempted to
tackle the recycling problem ourselves.

One solution immediately jumped into our heads:
Since many of our friends said they were willing to pay for
the service of recycling, why not research how much it
would cost to have private contractors pick up recycling?
We knew this was how other places, such as Marin County,
California, dealt with their recyclables. On another track,
we noticed that homeless people have always acted as de
facto recyclers in the city, returning cans and bottles to grocery stores for the five-cent deposits. The fact that the garbage
was no longer sorted impeded their efforts to gather cans
and bottles for deposits. As a stopgap solution, perhaps we
could amplify the work of the homeless who recycle to make
an income. We envisioned placing giant bins outside grocery stores and on street corners as drop-off centers for

cans and bottles. Then homeless people or other can collectors could return them for the deposit.

We began gathering information. As so often happens, we started with strong assumptions about what was going on, which turned out to not be nourished by facts. We placed a call to the city's Department of Sanitation and were connected with Kathy Dawkins, their PR person. That one call yielded this important fact: recycling wasn't *abolished*, as we had thought, but merely scaled back. Plastics and glass were no longer considered recyclables, but aluminum cans, newspapers, and cardboard boxes were. Furthermore, businesses in New York were still mandated by law to recycle, a service they paid for out of pocket. Knowing that recycling was technically still in place made us even more depressed since that fact wasn't being publicized. We became obnoxious, seething at our neighbors for throwing away their cat food cans, returnable bottles, and magazines.

Our approach was shaping up to be a full-time job, including private contractors, public education, and homeless outreach. This moonlighting couldn't pay the bills, so we decided that if we could mobilize our own neighborhood, that would be a start. We reached out to our local city council representative, Margarita Lopez, who, as a vocal "out" lesbian council member, is known for being radically progressive. Our interns, Liz and Anna, called her office—many times—but never received a response to our request for a meeting. One day we just walked over to the office, knocked on the door, and were able to get an appointment to meet with the councilwoman for the next week. From this we learned that when at first you don't succeed, make a house call.

At the meeting, we learned that we were right about her

being an ally: she was the only city councilperson (of fifty-one members) to vote against the reduction in recycling. She pointed out how lucrative recycling could be and, if done correctly, the city should have a vested interest in maintaining it. Further, the program in New York wasn't actually in the red. "Even with losing money from glass and plastic," Lopez told us, "the city was making money from recycling," a point that had been kept from the council members until after they voted. We told Lopez of our desire to get our neighbors to subsidize curbside recycling, which she promptly shot down. "I represent a poor district," she said. "And having your garbage and recycling picked up is a basic service that citizens deserve." Lopez characterized the service as an equalizer—"whether you are rich or poor, your garbage is picked up." Although, at the time, it was the *lack* of recycling we were sharing equally, her point was well taken.

We left the chaotic but productive meeting, jettisoning the idea of paying for pickup, but with a plan to move ahead with public education and getting returnables out of the trash and into the hands of can and bottle collectors. Lopez also encouraged us to call the council member in charge of sanitation.

Ideally, we wanted a homeless organization to work with us. So we pursued a meeting with the outreach coordinator for the National Coalition for the Homeless (NCH), only to learn that they could not help us with our project for two reasons. First, people who go to shelters (mainly families) don't tend to be the same people who collect cans. Second, NCH prioritizes direct services for homeless families, from providing clothes and food to finding permanent housing. Recycling was not on the list.

The coordinator told us about WE CAN, a redemption

center in midtown that serves the poor and homeless who collect cans and bottles to support themselves. WE CAN has paid more than $30 million in rebates since it began in 1987. Some collectors even make a decent living. According to an article in *The New York Times*, one man who collects cans full-time made more than $35,000 a year in income. When Liz and Anna called the founder of the organization, Guy Polhemus, he said that "it wasn't a good day to talk," because they were getting evicted.* It turned out that Christine Quinn, that district's usually progressive council-woman, didn't want WE CAN there since it primarily served homeless people who, being homeless, don't have access to bathrooms and often use the neighborhood as a rustic latrine.

With WE CAN too beleaguered to help, we moved on to phoning the councilman in charge of sanitation. We assumed his office would be hostile to our calls or he would put us off as our councilwoman's office did initially, but we were wrong. Counsel to the NYC council committee on sanitation, Carmen Cognetta, called us back immediately and set up a meeting for the following Friday.

Cognetta was pro-recycling and seemed pretty shocked that there hadn't been more outcry from New Yorkers when the service was reduced. We said there had been—even the volunteers in Margarita Lopez's office were complaining about how dispiriting it was to throw away soda bottles. People just didn't know they had to direct their dissatisfaction at the Department of Sanitation rather than at each other.

Amy asked how New York City could get away with not recycling given the state law requiring it. "The law states

---

*After receiving several eviction notices, WE CAN moved locations.

that you only have to recycle if there is an economic market associated with it," said Cognetta. From him, we learned that the scaling back of recycling had been a disaster, even economically. One of the justifications for cutting back recycling had been the assumption that it would reduce the number of truck shifts the city had to pay for. But with more waste being generated each day, they had to add just as many shifts to pick up the extra garbage.

We also discovered that paper is always profitable because you can mix all sorts of paper together, plastic is less profitable, and all of those glass beer, tea, and wine bottles are a nightmare. In New York, paper is particularly viable because it goes directly to a pulping company, Visy, which pays the city $20 or $30 a ton. The problem with plastic and glass was twofold. First, the city had to pay a middle man to have plastic and glass picked up, who then sold it to recyclers—so the city saw no profit, whereas the contractor profited twice. Second, both substances were hard to clean well enough to meet industry standards for reuse. "Glass especially is very difficult to recycle: it breaks, the colors mix, and that mixed-color glass is not reusable," Cognetta told us. The main use for recycled glass is fiberglass landfill covers. (Ironically, the less we recycle, the more need we will create for recycled glass's most popular product.)

Glass is also incredibly cheap to produce, he continued, given that it's manufactured from sand, which is plentiful. It costs less to make bottles than to recycle what we have already used. While we mentally tallied all of the glass waste we had created in our lives, Cognetta told us about two forward-thinking plans to deal with the glass issue. Recycle America Alliance, a division of the garbage behemoth Waste Management, worked with the Gallo wine company to develop a glass that uses all three colors (green, clear, and brown).

Across the Atlantic, Germany has instituted a fifty-cent deposit on every bottle sold, so that it is not economically feasible to simply treat glass as disposable.

Since there was so much confusion about what could be recycled and whether there was economic incentive to do so, we determined that public education was the most pressing issue. Cognetta said that changing behavior required constant education (TV advertising, subway posters, and radio announcements, to name a few), but in New York, the media market is so outrageously expensive that only cheap PSA spots in the middle of the night are affordable. Meanwhile, you don't want to make tons of posters and booklets for a recycling campaign—all of that trash defeats the purpose. Cognetta showed us the material the Department of Sanitation created for schools—we were impressed that they had them—but they were encased in three-ring plastic binders and the city had no idea how or if the materials were being used. The one staffer in charge of bringing the recycling message to the city's public schools had been laid off.

Then, as we were formulating a public education campaign, plastic recycling was reinstated after the city received a financially viable offer from a recycler. A year and a half later, glass was phased back in. We didn't come close to resolving the city's recycling issues, but we did accomplish a few things.

1. We learned that many public servants were available to us as citizens, from our city council member to counsel for the committee on sanitation. (Don't Be Afraid to Pick Up the Phone.)
2. We learned how much we didn't understand about recycling, from the fact that recycling bottles doesn't do

much for the environment to the fact that New York City technically hadn't stopped recycling. (Challenge Assumptions. Don't Believe Everything You Hear.)

3. We learned that we shouldn't ask people to pay for recycling, because it's a basic public service. (Don't Provide to the Few What the Government Should Provide to the Many—You Only Siphon Off Those Who Are Most Likely to Pressure for Change.)

4. We learned about WE CAN and other social service agencies as well as homeless or low-income individuals who act as recyclers. (Align with Complementary Activists.)

5. Most important, we learned how to change our own personal stake in recycling. We both began returning beer bottles to the corner stores in order to get our five-cent deposits after we learned that millions of dollars in deposit nickels go uncollected by consumers and retail businesses get to keep this as pure profit. (Change Your Own Behavior Before Demanding Changes of Others.)

As we poked around our city's garbage issue, we were able to speak with more authority to our friends and community, and move beyond just complaining that our feckless mayor dismantled the panacea of recycling. The moral: trying projects, even if they don't work out, has more activist value than doing nothing.

*   *   *

I just finished reading Eve Ensler's *The Vagina Monologues* and I have to say that I've been inspired. Ever since I can remember, I have always felt unique for being a woman and if I can feel that way so can ALL women. I want to help the women in my community in any way I can but since I'm

only 17 and don't really have any money to
donate, I was hoping you could give me advice on
what I can do to help out.

—Sarah Rocha
Bakersfield, California

The above e-mail is a typical request, in its urgency, sin-
cerity—and in its vagueness. It happens to be from Ask
Amy, Amy's online activist advice column. But we hear
questions just like this all the time. We hear it when we
speak at colleges and students raise their hands and ask,
"Do you have advice for getting involved?" We hear it when
we are on radio shows and stay-at-home moms call in to
ask how to connect with other feminist-minded mothers.
We hear it when we are at dinner parties and investment
banker friends say that they want to do something besides
push paper for Citibank. We hear it from professors, retired CEOs, privileged high-school students on Manhattan's Upper East Side, and crunchy college students in
Chapel Hill, North Carolina. Like Sarah, everyone wants
to know "What can I do?"

Traveling around the country, we learned how hungry
people were for ways to change the injustice they found in
their midst. They wanted to be heard and visible. It was a
universal need, not just an interest of the marginalized people
and do-gooders presumed to attend feminist events. Sometimes questions were more urgent in specific regions—such
as people in Portland, Oregon, talking about transgenderism and students in Indiana, Pennsylvania, talking about
women in the military. Regardless of the issue at hand, we
were always brought back to passionate conversations about
activism. People didn't dwell on "What do you think?" for
long; they were dying to know "What can I do?"

September 11 underscored that most people—not only self-identified "activists"—wanted to help when faced with injustice. Among the many poignant responses to that tragedy was the sheer number of people stepping forward to contribute. People lined up at blood banks and hospitals in droves. Hundreds of non-Arabs turned up at the Arab-American Center in Brooklyn to escort Muslim kids to school and women in hijabs to the grocery store. Schoolchildren painted murals. Thousands of people donated food and local chefs from Manhattan's best restaurants set up kitchens on boats to feed the rescue workers. New Yorkers were shocked by the support and sympathy they received in their time of need. Sadly, though, much of the millions of dollars the American Red Cross collected at groceries and schools across the country ended up in the hands of wealthy New Yorkers. Even when would-be activists were activated, the institutions they turned to often let them down.

The frustration we were witnessing at our lectures could be heard by anyone who was willing to listen. When Julianne Malveaux criss-crossed the country promoting *Unfinished Business: A Democrat and a Republican Take on the 10 Most Important Issues Women Face* (with co-author, Republican Deborah Perry), she heard the rumble. "Regardless of whether our listeners [were] mostly Democratic or mostly Republican, mostly black or mostly white, one of the first questions [would] always come from a young woman who want[ed] to know how she [could] get involved in social change," Malveaux stated. Barbara Ehrenreich had a similar experience as she promoted *Nickel and Dimed: On (Not) Getting By in America*, her best-selling book detailing the plight of the country's working poor. As she told the *Democratic Left*, the newsletter of the Democratic Socialists of America, the top question she got after the publication of the book was "What can I do about it?" Social justice organizations, too, were haunted by this question. At Planned Parenthood New York City alone, they field one hundred calls every week from citizens outraged enough by that week's news to pick up the phone and become part of pro-choice forces.

Given the vast number of pleas to get involved, why don't we have a totally activist, voting, engaged citizenry? Why do so many issues remain unsolved? Why do shelters have to turn homeless people away and why don't more women hold political office? Where is the disconnect between these would-be revolutionaries and the pressing issues? We believe that the problem lies in how the question "What can I do?" is answered. Too often the response is what we've labeled The Generic Three: "call your politician," "donate money," and "volunteer." *Grassroots* is our attempt to move beyond these knee-jerk, minimally effective answers. We believe that in order to maximize this passion, we must have better, more specific, and *active* answers to the question "What can I do?"

Good answers might come from revisiting John F. Kennedy's famous inaugural quote: "Ask not what your country can do for you, ask what you can do for your country." Many older folks say that the last time they felt hope was during the Kennedy era. Perhaps it was Kennedy's message—citizens don't need to wait for their country to save them; they have the power to save themselves and their country—that gave them such hope.

Don't get us wrong: participation via contacting politicians, making donations, and doing volunteer work is all very crucial to the life of social justice organizations. These types of contributions give organizations the power to influence others. But it is also a one-sided relationship that encourages passivity in the would-be activists. The act is isolated from the larger world of direct action and solutions, which makes the individual often doubt whether his or her check or letter was effective. You know you gave $20 to Stop Hunger Now, but there are still people who don't have enough to eat.

MOVING BEYOND THE GENERIC THREE

The questions are basic and general, but the answers—the activism—*can't* be. Two stellar organizations, Dress for Success and Women on Waves, each began with one person identifying a problem—women on welfare don't have clothes to wear to job interviews and women in many countries don't have access to abortion. The people asking those questions—Nancy Lublin and Rebecca Gomperts, respectively—were reasonably average citizens whose sphere of influence was no greater than yours or ours. Nancy created a way to get suits to women, and Rebecca, a doctor, bought a boat to perform abortions in international waters.

Although the two of us are both longtime organizers and supporters of progressive nonprofits, we didn't really notice this lack of good answers until around 2000. We had just published our first book, *Manifesta*, to acknowledge the feminism and the activism that we saw among our peers every day. *Manifesta* was a response to the assumption that our generation was slack and had a dangerous sense of entitlement when it came to feminism—that we were too self-involved to care. We presented numerous real-life examples of young people acting on behalf of themselves and their community. We were surprised and heartened that the most popular sections were "What Is Activism?" and the resource guide that made up the last eighty pages, including contact information for every organization mentioned in the book. Even the feminists and academics who criticized us for our lack of Marxist analysis or relative naïveté about transgenderism had to keep our book around because their students wanted the resources. It was our goal that people use *Manifesta*, to encourage the reader to make feminism his or her own, rather than simply complain that feminism didn't sufficiently address sweatshop laborers, for example. Usefulness is not the usual mode of political writing, but we took this extra step because we noticed that even a very accurate book with activist theories could drop the ball on providing solutions—to the detriment of social justice. For instance, Naomi Klein's insightful and well-reported book *No Logo* takes readers through a cornucopia of obscene corporate misdeeds. At the end of the book the reader is left outraged but still thinking "*Now* what can I do?" with no direction in sight. (Klein *does* have a resource-rich Web site at nologo.org.)

Although *Manifesta* was a call to action, we were nonetheless surprised at the number of people who turned to us for guidance in that endeavor. "What can I do?" became the big question of the years we spent touring with *Manifesta*. Sometimes the question was born of privilege: "How can I use my college education or my trust fund, or the fact that I've never gone hungry to help others who are?" Just as often, it was an urgent personal need: "I work at Sammy's Clam Shack and I'm five months pregnant. My boss says he'll fire me if I try to take maternity leave. What can I do?" At first we tried to arm ourselves with possible suggestions. Before arriving in a new town, we made sure to contact the local Planned Parenthood or independent bookstore to learn what they had going on so we would have something to offer when the question inevitably arose. Soon, however, it became apparent that the groups we referred people to didn't *really* have an answer. They still relied on The Generic Three. What people needed were tangible and specific steps, not boilerplate platitudes to "do something." Clearly, the organizations needed better answers, too.

Initially, Amy started toying with the idea of forming an activist idea bank housed at the Third Wave Foundation: a "place" where people could deposit their good ideas for others to borrow. Then, as we began to offer more detailed solutions to people's problems, Jennifer realized that some of our presumed-brilliant activist ideas hadn't exactly been tested. We didn't know where the snags might lie or what to do about them when they arose. For instance, is it legal to do voter registration in an abortion clinic in Iowa (one of our suggestions for using clinics as organizing spaces)? What happens if you call Loews Theater and ask them to donate twenty tickets a month to a local battered women's shelter? (*Whom* do you even call at Loews?) We decided to work one-on-one with the people we met in our travels. We found out what issues they cared about—for some it was getting studio art classes in their high school, for others it was getting dioxins out of the rivers, and for others it was protesting a sexist ad. We helped them figure out what resources they already had—a full Rolodex, or money, or an office with a new photocopying machine, or a big conference room. If they were seasoned organizers, we asked what worked for them in the past. We listened to their organizing problems and brainstormed different approaches. *Grassroots* was born. Persistence paid off: these activists stuck with their idea, and now each has contributed to changing the lives of many others.

Looking at the people who have contacted us, it is clear

that individuals, just like Lublin and Gomperts, are spurred to action because they have confronted injustice in their own lives. It begins by taking seriously what otherwise could be passed off as a personal frustration: the teenager, for instance, who is outraged when she hears that one can enter a secret code on Play Station's Tomb Raider and watch Lara Croft get gang-raped and doesn't know how to find out if it's true and what to do if it is. Or the woman in Texas who gets married and changes her name for $31 (the cost of a marriage license) but must pay $450 to petition the court and hire legal counsel to undertake her case when she decides to change her name back. Or the historian from Southern Oregon University who, while doing research using census data, learns that the census doesn't allow women to be traced by their maiden names, thus preventing him from documenting women over the course of their lives.

There is probably no more impassioned an activist than a victim who has healed from a trauma such as rape or incest and now, several years after the incident, has the perspective and insight to act on the issue. The actress Anne Heche, for instance, was sexually abused as a child, but it wasn't until she was already a well-known actress that she dealt with her past, raised her consciousness about the prevalence of incest, and committed to join the movement to end childhood sexual abuse. (As a public figure, one of the most influential things she can do is to speak out about her own experience.)

Sometimes a step toward activism is, in fact, to reveal what makes us insecure. It could be your transgendered father, your alcoholism, the fact that you have acne, or that you are or were once poor. A woman we met at a Planned Parenthood conference in Philadelphia admitted that she

didn't have any sense of urgency for the rights of disabled
people before she had her legs cut off in a car accident several years ago. Until recently, she had the privilege of being
ignorant about accessibility. She is now a fierce activist for
the rights of people with disabilities and a great bridge between the disabled and able-bodied communities. Acknowledging vulnerability not only gives you a reason to be an
activist; it releases you to join a community of people who
may have issues to resolve as well. You can fight together.

Taking action can be a brief moment in your day: Jennifer Locke wrote to us from Milwaukee, Wisconsin, wanting to raise public awareness about the two rock radio
stations in her city that were marketed entirely to a male demographic. "I love rock music," she wrote. "Radio should
not be so degrading for a woman that she has to only listen
to CDs." She e-mailed both station managers and asked if
there was any way she could convince them that their female listeners are just as important as their male listeners.

Or it can be a years-long endeavor: Brenda Gillming,
from Owasso, Oklahoma, used to be a poultry factory
worker. She had the lowest position in her department—
"floor person"—which consisted of picking up chickens that
have fallen off the conveyor, washing them, and placing
them back on the belt for packaging. Brenda brought a
sexual harassment suit against Simmons Industries in the
early 1990s after years of being called "floor dog" and
pelted with meat by her male co-workers. She sought two
things with her suit: for a sexual harassment policy to be
formed and for it to be enforced. "It took so much from me
and lasted about three years till all [was] said and done,"
Brenda wrote, "but I'm glad I stood up for my rights and
also for all women in the future."

Often "What can I do?" means taking a good look at what resources you already have and committing to using them. After September 11, Julia Pershan noticed a sign on one of the businesses on her block in TriBeCa, a neighborhood just north of Ground Zero. Directed at local business owners, the sign simply stated: "Should we get together?" Though Julia was not a business owner, but a recent business school graduate, she attended the meeting. At Julia's suggestion, they decided to form a coalition—the Tribeca Organization—with the express purpose of preserving area business during this catastrophic time. They raised money to take out an ad in *The New York Times* that made the connection between patronizing TriBeCa and rebuilding New York. They offered incentives, such as a weekend where everything was 10 percent off in the neighborhood, and agreed to defy typical capitalist rules of competition and cooperate. What made the difference between Julia and others in TriBeCa who felt helpless and worried is that she turned the question on herself and asked, "What can I do?" What she could do was use her business degree, use the fact that she had just graduated and didn't yet have a full-time job, and use her neighborhood connections to strengthen the economic foundation shaken by the terrorist attacks.

WHAT'S SO SPECIAL ABOUT FEMINIST ACTIVISM?

We didn't always think that we were qualified to help those who wanted to get more involved. With *Manifesta*, though, we came into our own—and got the confidence to answer questions about feminism. Our qualification was that we took the initiative. We were as entitled as the next person to do our homework and present a perspective. And a necessary part of that perspective involves an understanding of women's struggle for equality. Now, we lecture frequently on the topics of feminism and activism. We begin our talks with a thumbnail sketch of the last 160 years of feminism in America. Knowing that this activist history exists and that others have turned their idea or thought into a piece of legislation, an organization, or a changed attitude had proved to be inspiring, thus we've included that history lesson here.

To begin with, a definition: feminism is the movement toward full political, economic, and social equality for men and women. We add to that simple definition that feminism implies having enough access to information to make informed choices about one's life. Therefore, it's not so much the choice you make that reflects feminism, but your power to make a choice. For example, you can be pro-life and a feminist, but you couldn't actively undermine another woman's ability to have an abortion and call yourself a feminist.

The first formal women's rights conference occurred in 1848 at Seneca Falls, New York. Many of the 240 attendees were part of the flourishing antislavery movement of the time and also were inspired by the example of equality by local Iroquois. Within those native communities, each woman controlled her own personal property, violence against women rarely occurred and was treated seriously when it did, and women could vote. The abolitionists applied their raised consciousness to their own lives and realized that they didn't have the rights they were fighting for others to have. So they called for women to be able to own and inherit property, to divorce, to be educated, and, most controversially, to vote. In the seventy-two years it took to get the vote, those other rights were earned. In 1923, suffragist Alice Paul realized that the right to cast a vote was meaningless if society itself remained unequal. That year Paul wrote the Equal Rights Amendment to the Constitution.

We don't yet have the ERA, but many strides have been made. Beginning in the sixties and continuing into the seventies, laws were passed guaranteeing equal access to education (Title IX), outlawing gender discrimination (Title VII of the Civil Rights Act), and coining phrases for date rape, domestic violence, and sexism—serious problems that used to just be called life. In hindsight, these two movements for women's rights have been organized into waves—the First Wave dedicated to the rights of citizenship and the Second Wave dedicated to equality under the law and in opportunity. We are still working on those goals, but younger people have begun acknowledging a Third Wave of feminism, that continues to work with and toward the same goals as the Second Wave, but as a generation raised with the privileges of feminism.* If the waves can be reduced to their central goals, the First Wave was about women's rights to citizenship, the Second Wave concerned women's equality, and the Third Wave stresses the power and the responsibility of the individual.

The concepts of "giving back," public service, and activism are not feminist preserves. However, we believe that feminists are positioned particularly well to become power-

---

*The Second Wave was instrumental in creating access for women but mostly benefited those who were white and middle-class. Third Wavers grew up not only with feminism, but with a critique of feminism from within by women of color, poor women, gay women, and women with disabilities. In that integration, the Third Wave is an evolution of feminism.

ful change-makers. After all, the whole politics of feminism
is based on going to the root of the problem, providing
prevention rather than a cure. Meanwhile, like punk rock,
feminism is also based on the idea that you, an average
schmo, have the right and the power to take matters into
your own hands. You don't have to rely on someone like
Ralph Nader, Oprah Winfrey, or Senator Hillary Rodham
Clinton to save you. Sometimes using Dr. King or Gloria
Steinem as a role model has a paralyzing effect, like "Oh,
someone legit is taking care of it" or "I could never do that."
In fact, that is why *Grassroots* will mostly focus on what non-
famous activists did.

Making tangible change is often the way women and
men come to feminism and it is always the way the movement transforms the world. Activism was behind abortion
rights, girls' sports teams, the right to vote, and fighting
sterilization abuse. Because both of us are feminists, we see
our activism through that lens. When people express confusion about feminism or discomfort with the label, it is because feminism is presented as a concept or a theory (what
books we have read or classes we have taken) and not action
or experience (what we have done that affects the status of
women or changed our own lives). Activism and feminism-
in-action aren't different concepts.

While activism shouldn't just be about sacrifice, mani-
festing our values in the world can be hard work. It's like
building a new house rather than just living in the old di-
lapidated one you inherited. It requires faith, because you
are imagining something that doesn't exist and you have
to believe not only that it should exist but that it *could* exist. We might all use different words to describe ourselves
as activists—volunteer, environmentalist, good friend—but

what unites people is that we have a commitment to translate our politics into action, getting from the point of asking "What can I do?" to establishing a group, a petition, a line of organic tampons, or anything. We hope that *Grassroots*, our activist advice book, unveils the process of becoming active.

chapter 2 | Of Minor Importance

"I mean to resist the hatred of these times any way that I can."

—June Jordan, great American poet who died of breast cancer in 2002

AMY

Until age thirteen, I attended public school in a small, predominantly working-class town in central Pennsylvania. By the next year, my mother had relocated to Marblehead, Massachusetts, a super-preppy suburb of Boston. After only two years in Marblehead's public schools, I went to a boarding school in Marion, Massachusetts, which somehow managed to be less ritzy. My school, Tabor, had begun admitting girls just four years prior to my arrival. The ratio of boys to girls was 4:1 and I therefore got to be a pioneer in a lot of my endeavors, such as being part of the first girls' soccer team that the campus had ever had. Having absorbed Title IX's "equal access to education" message without knowing it, girls wearing the boys' old uniforms and supplying their own soccer balls when the boys got new equipment donated every year simply seemed wrong to me. I bristled at the fact that my team always had to play on the cruddy practice field several blocks from campus. During away games, we were expected to watch the boys play whereas the boys showered and got lunch while the girls sweated it out on the field. I complained to the athletic director and the coach, request-ing that the guys occasionally watch the girls' games, that we should have equal access to the nice field, and suggested that both teams get new uniforms and balls every *other* year.

In response, our team was encouraged to fund-raise to buy new uniforms. This is a typical response to feminist de-mands, and we caved and did just that. Taking on the re-sponsibility of providing our own new uniforms and balls only reinforced our marginal status. At first the idea of be-ing a minority amidst all of the boys was appealing (more dating opportunities and personal attention). But through my soccer experience, I quickly learned that being a mi-nority meant being marginalized.

In my junior year, after I was done fighting my battles on the soccer field, I ran for head of school, the first time a girl had done so. I competed against four boys and I still cringe when I think of my campaign slogan: "It's Time for a Change." I learned what to me is the essential feminist lesson: you don't promote women because they are women; feminism is acknowledging people's individual gifts and talents regardless of gender. The only change I promised as a reason to vote for me was my gender. I provided no other vision or plan, and not undeservedly, I lost. Still, I like to think that I broke new ground simply by running. Several years later, while I was visiting the campus, I noted with some satisfaction that the 1996 Tabor head of school was named Kara Burbank. No woman has won since then, though, so equality is yet to come.

JENNIFER

I attended high school at super-average Fargo South High, where I often wished I were at a preppy New England boarding school. My favorite activity was theater, where everyone, both male and female, is marginalized.

Along with being a drama geek, I was an intense abortion rights supporter, especially engrossed in the politics of my town, the site of the state's only clinic. My mother had made a point of leaving the Lutheran church we'd attended for years based on the antichoice sentiments of the head pastor and I was always the one (and usually the only one) to take the pro-choice side during the "persuasive speeches" module in English class.

In my senior year of high school, I went head to head against the Lambs of Christ, a radical antiabortion group that invaded my town. Their mission was to disrupt the business of the clinic by barring patients from getting to their appointments and to clog up the city jails with antichoice protesters. The local news was swarming with stories about these radical activists who liked to bike-lock their heads to the clinic's medical equipment, and the besieged clinic director who put out a call for pro-choice volunteers to come protect the clinic's patients. It didn't seem odd to be escorting patients or confronting angry activists publicly—I saw other (usually adult) Fargoans doing it and it appealed to my theatrical side (there were occasionally TV cameras) as well as my radical side. The one summer that the Lambs were particularly active, I learned how to escort, was trained in nonviolent resistance in case there was a fight, and began writing letters to the editor of my local paper, one of which was published. Looking back, that was my first experience of protests and the heady power of mass resistance. I still choke up when I first get a glimpse of the crowd at a rally or a march. I love coming together with so many other people, who under other circumstances I might not get along with, and being transformed into a community with a common goal.

*   *   *

Hi! I am an eighteen-year-old feminist in Birmingham, Alabama. As you can imagine, my environment in the heart of the Bible Belt doesn't lend me a lot of space as a feminist. But I digress . . . I am a senior at a quirky little private school called Indian Springs School. A group of guys at my school started the "Man Club." To counteract this group, my friend Kate and I have started a Women's Alliance. So far we've done various activities, like volunteering at a local women's shelter. For Women's History Month, we have planned a silent auction. We are trying to collect donated products to auction off. The proceeds would all go to the National Organization for Women (NOW). I would very much appreciate it if you would drop me a line (can you say that with e-mails? Just kidding).

> Thank you so much,
> Lauren Brannon
> Birmingham Alabama

Lauren is one of dozens of high-school students who
have written to Ask Amy over the years wanting support
and information in order to start (or sustain) a feminist
group. Ask Amy is a fairly small venture, so we have to assume that many more feminist groups are cropping up
among adolescents in burgs throughout the country beyond the 150 that have reached out to Amy. For *Grassroots*,
we decided to follow up with many of these girls. We even
set out to meet a few of these young women and see what
they had accomplished, including Lauren who is now a
student at Hampshire College. In general, about half of the
girls were successful in achieving their goals; even those
who weren't successful helped to shed light on what's
needed besides an interest in feminism or the observation
of sexism to effectively start a group.

As for Lauren, her Women's Alliance auction was held
in the spring of 2001 and was a huge success. (We did what
we could to help: we sent signed copies of *Manifesta*, Third
Wave's I SPY SEXISM T-shirts, CDs from Daemon Records,
and autographed copies of Gloria Steinem's books.) Her
success speaks to the fact that there is a need to direct resources to those high-school activists who, like Lauren, have
energy and chutzpah, but need a little confirmation that
starting a group is a worthwhile venture. And that it's quite
doable by almost anyone.

Affirmation is necessary when you consider that any kid
who wants to form such a group will be asked "Why?" by
teachers, parents, and peers. *Why* start a feminist group in
high school in this day and age? Why? Because while girls
are learning math right along with the boys, they are less
likely to continue on to higher math. Because while girls
play sports, the girls' sports teams still receive less money

and aren't given the same concerted effort to bring audiences to their games, which affects how women's sports are valued in high school, college, and ultimately in the professional arena. Because dress codes are directed almost solely at girls—the number-one banned item is the tank top—and they are cautioned against wearing clothes that may "distract the boys." (Why not lecture boys about maintaining control of themselves, regardless of whether the girl next to him has exposed shoulders or even a bra strap revealed?) Because the "slut" label is still being used to keep girls in their place. Because in our informal polling, many high schools celebrate—or at least acknowledge—Black History Month and Martin Luther King Day, but it's rare for Women's History Month to be noted. In fact, most students still leave high school with only the most superficial understanding of what women have contributed to culture, and usually nothing of the struggles women have gone through to get closer to equality.

Lucretia Mott, Alice Paul, and Sojourner Truth were orators and philosophers responsible for getting women the vote, but we rarely learn about them in high school. Students graduate with the impression that Betsy Ross is one of the most pivotal women in history. In truth, scholars of the Revolutionary War agree that Ross didn't sew or even design the first American flag, the action that guaranteed her place in history. Instead, this role was most likely played by a popular patriot and congressman from New Jersey, Francis Hopkinson, who was the Donna Karan of the Stars and Stripes. And, while this might be the one moment in history where a woman is given credit for something a man actually did, students can't enjoy that irony because so few schools have any women's history curriculum. If they did, high-school students could learn about the vision of egalitarian society that white feminists saw in the Haudenosaunee (Iroquois) people of upstate New York during the early 1800s, a story that has the benefit of being not only positive but, in contrast to Betsy Ross and the flag, also true.

Adding women's history to high-school curricula is one of the primary reasons girls are motivated to found groups. But many girls want to start groups for the same reason Lauren did: to protest an incident of regressiveness and sexism—in her case, the jokey sexism of *The Man Show* (Comedy Central's ode to beavers and testosterone) and her male peers' interest in perpetuating it.

Others aren't protesting so much, but want to celebrate feminism, girl power, and female accomplishment. That was the case with Shauna Shames, who started the Tam High Equality NOW! Club after her principal suggested that someone start a feminist group. Shauna's group created skits and poems about sexual harassment, a carnival booth where you could play Pin the Tail on the Newt (as in Newt Gingrich, who previously had issued a "Contract with America"), and later organized a "young feminist sleepover" before the huge 1996 NOW March to Fight the Radical Right in San Francisco. Still others are motivated to affect political change, from revamping dress codes to lobbying for tax increases in order to get teachers better pay. In 2003, for instance, a budget crisis in the Oregon public schools prompted students to hold a mock bake sale–protest to address the fact that school was ending a record seventeen days early and teachers were losing nearly a month's salary. (They priced the brownies at $1 million apiece, since they needed to raise millions to make up for funding gaps.) Their work succeeded in pushing through a temporary income tax increase that made up for the budget shortfall. (You know young people are passionate when they lobby for *more* school days.)

PUBERTY POWER: WHAT HIGH SCHOOL STUDENTS HAVE TO OFFER

Superficially, high-school students are often seen as powerless. As minors, they can't vote and thus don't have the presumed value that comes with being a constituent. They don't have the right to organize their life the way they'd like: they often have curfews, mandatory attendance in school until at least age sixteen, and what they learn at school is dictated to them by conservative national norms and requirements, such as abstinence-only sex education or science classes that teach creationism along with evolution.

A more positive and accurate assessment of high-school students is that they are unique as social change-makers. Their power is under the radar and those restrictions can also be interpreted as freedom from mundane responsibility. High-school students have time to spare and are not yet jaded. They typically aren't Democrat or Republican yet: they are unlabeled and free to create their political identity. Meanwhile, they have to convene with hundreds or more of their peers 250 days a year for four years, which is ideal for organizing and building networks. High-school students often believe they have no influence, but if a student like Lauren was able to do something to alter the general curriculum—such as getting a book by Haitian writer Edwidge Danticat added to her state's standard reading lists— she has affected her peers' education in a revolutionary way.

Sometimes the most vulnerable position holds the most

power, because change is needed so desperately and there is little left to lose. Fargo native Wendy Brovold, for instance, was driven to start a support group for gay students when the harassment at South High (Jennifer's alma mater) reached such a fever pitch that jocks "literally tried to run over the queer kids" in the parking lot. "Not only was the harassment ignored when we reported it," says Wendy, "but there wasn't anything accurate in the library about homosexuality, just a couple of books—and one was about the 'cure.' Being gay wasn't even talked about in health class, which I found really disturbing."

So in 1992, when Wendy was a freshman, she founded South High's first Lesbian Gay Bisexual Transgendered support group. There was plenty of resistance, even from presumed allies such as guidance counselors who didn't take the harassment seriously enough to think it justified starting a group. But Wendy had weapons of her own: her mother worked in the school system as a secretary, and through Mrs. Brovold, Wendy was able to build faculty support. While Wendy was at South, the group met every week and created a gay community. Ironically, Wendy discovered years after graduation that some of the biggest harassers turned out to be gay. "I'll run into them with their boyfriend or girlfriend," says Wendy, laughing. It's much more common today than it was in 1992 for schools around the country to have gay-straight alliances (GLSEN, the Gay, Lesbian and Straight Education Network, notes sixty-five chapters), but if your school doesn't have a group and needs one, perhaps Wendy's story can provide a template. (See the Resource Guide for step-by-step details.)

Like Wendy Brovold, Allison Sparkuhl wanted to fight stereotypes and increase visibility for a maligned group, but her cause was feminism and women rather than the rights of queer people. Allison attends the Cate School, a boarding school near Santa Barbara, California. Six months after she wrote to Amy seeking tips on starting her feminist club, she had already organized a group, which they named Keep on Living, after a song about homophobia and child sexual abuse by the band Le Tigre. The impetus for the club arose from a discussion in her history class that covered women in America. When the teacher introduced the "We Can Do It" poster from World War II featuring Rosie the Riveter, it sparked a debate about women's rights. According to Allison, some of the guys believed that feminism was all about women "who hate men and want to cut [their] penises off." (Note: given that dismemberment has only happened once to public knowledge—and Lorena Bobbitt was no feminist revolutionary—it's remarkable how this myth persists.) Allison concluded there was a lot of misunderstanding about the term and thought it would be a good idea to found a club devoted to exploring its many meanings.

Whether Allison knew it or not, her approach mirrored that used by the consciousness-raising groups of the Second Wave of feminism. She decided to shed some light on what she regarded as a very positive word and movement. When she returned to school for her sophomore year, she met with her guidance counselor to discuss starting a group. The first thing her counselor suggested she do was locate a space in which to meet. Allison called the librarian and secured a room in the library. She called a few friends to tell them about the meeting, e-mailed the whole school, and made an announcement at a general assembly. Twenty people (around 10 percent of her school) came to the initial gathering, including some faculty.

Allison and her feminist group read *The Women's Room*, the early-seventies consciousness-raising novel by Marilyn

French, thus making a connection between Second and Third Wave experiences. (Both of *our* mothers read *The Women's Room* as one of their first feminist acts in their women's groups many years *after* high school. As Gloria Steinem always says, each succeeding generation has better "shit detectors" and is ready for feminism at a much younger age.) Keep on Living then lobbied the school to change the signs stenciled on all of the girls' bathrooms from LADIES' ROOM to WOMEN'S ROOM, as is depicted on the cover of French's book. They wanted to make the girls' bathrooms equivalent to the boys' bathrooms, which, after all, weren't stenciled with GENTLEMEN'S ROOM, or LORDS' ROOM. To change the bathroom signs, Allison approached the headmaster. "He seemed cool with it," she reports, "but that may be because our request doesn't affect that many bathrooms."

Keep on Living has kept on trucking. For her junior year, Allison planned a fund-raiser to coincide with parents' weekend at the Cate School. The cause? To raise money for the Revolutionary Association of the Women of Afghanistan and for women in India who didn't have access to birth control. Keep on Living also brought in a representative from Men Against Rape and, in response to how "outraged" they were about "Bush's recent discrimination against abortion," organized Cate students to attend the April 2004 National March for Women's Lives in Washington, D.C. "There are a few guys who come to the group and some of the sweetest girls who have the strongest opinions in the school," she wrote to us. "I think that through the group we have shown the community that feminists (1) can be men, and (2) aren't *always* lesbians, and (3) aren't *always* scary people."

We asked Allison if her classmates now use the word

"feminism," given that clarifying the term had been one of her goals. "Definitely not," she replied. It's disconcerting that Allison and her peers feel the need to justify themselves. The question of whether or not you call yourself a feminist is often unfairly directed at young women, yet the few public opinion polls that have addressed this reveal that younger women are consistently *more* likely than older women to embrace the label. If you want to check, see the summer 2003 issue of *Ms.* and the 1994 September/October issue of *Marie Claire*. From *Ms.*'s Harris Poll findings: "Among women in the 18 to 24 age group, a sky-high 92 percent rate the women's movement favorably," a higher percentage than any other age group. We asked why—after all, she had been so successful. "We probably don't use the term because of guys' reactions. But also because we want to be humble," she said, commenting that she felt she wanted to do good things without the grandiosity of being called "a feminist." This was actually a new and different answer to a complaint that we hear often: Why do girls eschew the feminist label? The traditional feminist take is that the media has brainwashed them to fear the label or, worse, that girls today simply don't have enough consciousness or self-respect to identify with feminism. Allison and her friends believe that they embody feminism without feeling that what they call themselves is more important than what they do.

CAN YOU SPELL S-U-C-C-E-S-S?

Some factors in Allison's success have to do with her own copious initiative, enthusiasm, and smarts. Others have to do with the kind of fantastic private school she goes to,

which tends to have hands-on teachers, a low level of bureaucracy, and parents paying significant tuition. That last
point means that the students are seen as economically in-
trinsic to the school—customers, of sorts—just as college
students are, thus they may have more power to influence
campus life and the curriculum. Not only that, but students
at elite schools are often given messages that suggest they
have rights and importance in the world. This sense of entitlement can be parlayed into the cause of social change.
Kids at boarding schools or private schools usually have another resource that comes in handy: access to wealth. Even
if their parents are poor and they are at the school on scholarship, they have entered a milieu of money. Amy went to
boarding school for her final three years of high school.
When she graduated from college and found herself fund-
raising for a voter registration drive, she recalled friends
from boarding school who had second homes or went to
Africa on safari for spring break. From this, she realized for
the first time that she—a middle-class kid from small-town
Pennsylvania—had access to an actual funding circle.

Allison, Lauren, and Wendy were able to achieve concrete goals. What made their achievements possible was
their specific visions replete with tasks—such as reading
The Women's Room or having an auction. Allison, Lauren,
and Wendy made it up as they went along, but at other
high schools, there is an existing infrastructure that helps
students start a club or initiate social change. While this is
more bureaucratic for the activist, it also forces her to imagine in a detailed way what she will be responsible for and
what she believes her community needs. For instance, Rochelle Terman decided to start a women's rights group as a
sophomore at her Ohio public high school. She talked to
her co-curricular adviser, who gave her a list of several steps

required to start a registered club. She didn't have to be registered—Rochelle could have started her group informally and met off campus. But being a registered club had advantages. Rochelle could have access to school facilities and potential funds. So with three friends, Rochelle tackled the steps. They were required to write a constitution clearly stating the purpose of the group, appoint officers, and figure out how membership would be determined. Most challenging, they had to get at least twenty-five people who were willing to sign a petition saying that they wanted the group to be recognized and those same people had to agree to attend their first meeting in order for it to be official. (This is a moment when a petition served a valid and specific purpose. Petitions that are to show general support or opposition are only as effective as their final resting place. E-mail petitions in particular often don't get to their intended recipient and can create chaos—overwhelming servers and making all of that e-mail forwarding for naught. Because of how rapidly e-mail petitions disseminate, they are notorious for spreading inaccurate information. Some online forums for gathering signatures are effective—such as those created by MoveOn.org—but they usually must have people maintaining the site, making sure to gather addresses along with virtual signatures, since politicians are only required to listen to their own constituents.)

Although the steps were time-consuming, completing them proved to the adviser (and to Rochelle) that she was serious. It also gave Rochelle experience that could be translated into starting a club at college or even a foundation later in life. In particular, gathering constituents is perhaps the most critical facet of starting a group. It requires that you know you have an audience and that you are able to articulate your purpose to others. If only one person shows up at the first meeting, it might not be the right moment to start your group—or it might just mean that you need to change your message or your outreach strategy. For example, "Feminist Meeting at 4 p.m." might not have as much allure as "Is Ani DiFranco Your Hero? If so, meet in room 432 at 4 p.m."

As it turns out, Rochelle's idea for a women's issues organization had legs. She and her three friends surpassed the twenty-five-member quota through a creative campaign, reaching out to the local alternative high school, making posters that quoted the male president of the school saying "Feminism is not just for girls," and publicizing their meetings in every venue they could, from e-mailing friends to having it announced on the school public-address system.

At the first meeting, Rochelle and other members laid out the group's proposed structure. They decided it would be a discussion forum, initially, but would potentially grow into sponsoring events. Soon they programmed events to prompt debate about feminism in the community, such as screening a film about women in the media and hosting a talk by a local feminist art history professor. Rochelle reached out to two other area high schools suggesting that they pool resources and have one larger feminist group rather than two (or more) small ones. The next year her Women's Rights Coalition took the lead in organizing her high school's participation in the Race for the Cure, using that event to connect to national women's organizations.

Right from the beginning, Rochelle was aware of how important fund-raising was and asked the principal for ideas about how to get money for her group. He recommended that they talk to the parent-teacher organization. In the meantime, the principal authorized the school to pay for the speakers that her feminist group solicited. In general, Rochelle tackled the bureaucracy with aplomb and earned the respect and support of her administration in the process. Since Rochelle told us that she wants this group be a permanent part of her school, her next task is to recruit younger students who will take over the reins when she graduates. (Sustaining a group often requires that you nurture new leaders, making sure that your idea lives on long after you have moved on. This is especially crucial for high-school and college groups, which recycle students every four years.)

Casey Yannella also started a "women's issues" group after reaching out to Ask Amy. When we checked in with her, though, she was disheartened. "I didn't have so much luck," she reported. "Feminism didn't go over too well with my school." It turns out that Casey ran up against a brick wall when it came to finding an adviser and gaining support from her principal, who thought the endeavor was too controversial. "Strangely enough," she said, "I attend an all-girls school." But all-women settings often don't have a designated feminist component, since it's generally (and falsely) assumed that places like these are less burdened by gender politics. The absence of boys, though, doesn't guarantee that feminism is present, as evidenced by the male principal's reaction to Casey's idea. In the end, Casey felt she gave in to the lack of administrative support too quickly. "A single-sex school with no gender studies curriculum could have benefited greatly from a women's issues group," Casey told us. "I somehow lost the courage of my convictions, but I didn't lose interest in feminism!"

Casey shouldn't be too dismayed with herself. She raised the idea of having a gender studies curriculum at her school, which is a critical first step, and perhaps she has inspired another student to take it further next year. Most valuable, she revealed that all-girl settings aren't devoid of sexism—a radical thought.

Another student, Melody Woodward, reported to us that she was able to start an official feminist club at her high school in San Diego, with ten or fifteen people attending pretty regularly. The issue that she felt her peers would connect with was linking animal rights to women's rights. To that end, the group hosted a one-time vegan buffet (donating the proceeds to a local women's center) and they created a feminist-vegan zine. While her group had staying power and was still in existence a year later, Melody didn't feel like it was particularly successful. Why? "We were really stumped on ideas of educating people about feminism. We couldn't think of interesting new ways to tell a high school community how sexism in the world [affects] their lives—or ways we can change it."

Perhaps Melody could have taken the one-time vegan buffet and turned it into a way of connecting to the larger community—holding it one month at the battered women's shelter, the next month at a homeless shelter, and so on until they got to know the many social services in their town. Or perhaps they could convince their school to have the cafeteria go vegan once a month and they could do table tents that talked about the resources saved when animals aren't used for food and quote Frances Moore Lappe's *Diet for a Small Planet*, a pioneering book that encouraged people to eat in balance with the environment. Melody and her gang could also align themselves with national groups such as Feminists for Animal Rights (whose mission is dedicated to ending all forms of abuse against women, animals, and the earth) and in doing so gain access to their newsletters and resources. They could use the work of Antonia Demas, an activist in Ithaca, New York, who has piloted a vegan curriculum called Food Is Elementary in more than fifteen states. Demas challenges the myth that kids' palates aren't sophisticated enough to be satisfied with anything beyond fast food. She teaches students about nutrition and has them prepare the food. "If they are actually educated about nutrition and presented with a choice," she told us in an interview, "many young people will choose vegan or vegetarian diets." Changing school lunch programs can have enormous ramifications. "Think of the significance," says Demas, "of 53 million kids essentially captive in the schools, and our government is feeding them food that isn't nutritious—food that will actually harm them."

Though we think Melody was off to a good start with her club, her sense that there was no momentum points to the importance of creating a group that matches the profile of one's student body. For instance, if your school hosts a "freestyle Friday" every week, featuring student rappers, perhaps your group could be about hip-hop and activism and focus on the revolutionary roots and potential of that style of music. Melody wanted the group to offer a more consistent series of events, but the one-time event and one-off zine are valuable in and of themselves. Sometimes it is best to organize informally—like a once-a-week lunch chat about women's issues or producing a large-scale one-time event like bringing in a speaker for Women's History Month or Earth Day. There is no point in forming a whole organization when all you really need is a lunch date.

WHAT ARE THE ISSUES?

People mobilize around issues that directly impact their lives. So what is relevant to a high-school student? As we mentioned earlier, dress codes directly affect many girls and have an obvious feminist component. In fact, when we addressed a class of forty high-school junior girls who had gathered at Barnard College for a leadership institute, 90 percent of them had dress code sexism horror stories. As Mary Varner, one of the girls, told us, "Last spring, my [all female] gym class was lectured on appropriate clothing. I sat there, pulling on the hem of my skirt, as a teacher commented that while our clothing was fine for going out, it was inappropriate for school as it would distract the boys. Several of us were infuriated. Why should our clothing decisions be based on what others may find distracting?" You'd be hard-pressed to find a teenage girl who hasn't dealt with eating disorders, either personally or with a close friend. Title IX certainly affects high-school students. Sex and sexually transmitted diseases are central to teenagers' lives, though they are not always subjects they want to discuss in public or a group setting.

The above list may sound negative—and some of the resistance to women's groups is, of course, due to their perceived focus on doom and gloom. ("A woman is raped every five seconds!" "Title IX is being eviscerated!"). But while you don't need to sugarcoat reality, you may need to ease people into the issues. Don't be afraid to convene your group around good news. In other words, gather around a vision of what you want rather than the problems you want to change. For instance, one of the most useful acts one can do if worried about Title IX is not to forward a scary, vague, probably out-of-date e-mail petition but to organize twenty people to attend women's sporting events or create a roving cheering squad. Think up a funny or powerful name for your booster group and change the conventional wisdom about the audience-garnering potential of women's athlet-

ics while you have a great time. If you go the route of cheerleading, you could take a page from the Radical Cheerleaders and expand your revolutionary school spirit beyond
sports. With at least fourteen "squads" across the country
(and one in Poland), the Radical Cheerleaders have queer-
positive cheers, girl-power cheers, environmental cheers—
you name it. They show up at protests, state capitols, activist
events, or on random street corners to cheer, undermining the negative girlie-airhead stereotype that commonly
surrounds cheerleaders.

Rather than creating something outside of school, perhaps you could convince your school to add to its curriculum. That is what two industrious teenagers in suburban
Ohio did. Jackie Arcy and Jessica Hatem, both sixteen
when we met them, are longtime best friends. (They met at
age ten.) Superficially, they are opposites—Jackie is blond
and tall, Jessica is shorter with dark curly hair streaked with
purplish dye—but when it comes to their interest in feminism, they could be twins. Like many girls their age, they
were raised being told that they could be whatever they
want. "My mother expects me to be President," notes Jackie.

We met Jackie and Jessica when they wrote to Ask Amy
requesting a reading list for the feminist theory class they
were in the process of devising at their public high school,
Linworth Alternative (they called it "Chick Lit"—no rela-
tion to the Bridget Jones fiction genre). A few weeks after
that virtual meeting, we were speaking at Ohio Wesleyan, a
college near them, and Jackie and Jessica asked us if we'd
visit the class they had created. We did and were inspired
by the high-intensity feminist course they designed and
team taught. It's easy to imagine that the students at this
small alternative high school would have been the outcasts
at a larger mainstream school. Many were punkish or hip-

pies; they wore lots of black and dyed their hair crazy colors, and many of them were openly gay. But to go to this school you had to demonstrate not weirdness but maturity and the ability to think independently. So much so that when Linworth students are seniors, they are expected to spend at least one term on a walkabout, named after the Aboriginal Australian rite of passage. (Jackie and Jessica decided to spend their walkabouts with us in New York for two months.) At Linworth outsiders were respected rather than maligned. The mutual trust between teachers and students was striking. In fact, when Jackie and Jessica started reading whatever feminist books they could get their hands on, their English teacher, Chris (no Mr., Ms., or Mrs. at Linworth), suggested that they were expert enough to teach their peers.

To prepare for their class, they looked at a variety of feminist works and asked people from Amy to Jackie's mother for suggestions on important readings. They ultimately decided to focus on Third Wave feminism because they wanted to demonstrate that feminism is relevant *now*, not just as part of the past. "We wanted to use younger writers," Jackie told us, "because they'd be easier to relate to."

When the course came to fruition, Jackie and Jessica taught twenty students (half of whom were boys) in an eighty-minute class every other day for a full semester. The major books were *Yell-Oh Girls*, by Vicki Nam; *Cunt*, by Inga Muscio; *Slut!*, by Leora Tanenbaum (they needed permission slips for the last two because of the racy titles); *Transforming a Rape Culture*, edited by Emilie Buchwald, Pamela R. Fletcher, and Martha Roth; and *Manifesta*. Jackie even found an old booklet of her mother's that talked about raising children in a nonsexist way. "We gave extra credit for going out into the community and seeing feminist things, such as V-Day at Ohio State University, or participating in national feminist campaigns such as the I Spy Sexism campaign," says Jessica. They analyzed media, looking at TV programs such as *The Man Show* and *Fifth Wheel*. "We talked a lot about how plain old music by women differs from feminist music—like Britney versus Ani, or Sleater Kinney and Hole," says Jackie. Mainly, the class facilitated discussion, and they were continually surprised by how enthusiastic the guys were. "We had a class where we discussed our periods," recalls Jackie, thinking that there wasn't going to be a lot of participation from the male half of the class. "But then the guys talked about their first experience seeing pads under the sink and we realized that they had a [relationship] with periods, too."

The two friends also had to figure out how to grade their classmates. Each of them independently provided a grade for an assignment and then they averaged the two. They felt like they had to be stern in evaluating their peers. Being the same age as their students made them feel as if they were being harsh. One of the hardest things was when their friends wouldn't do their assignments and they had to discipline them.

"I found out that I don't want to be a teacher," says Jackie, despite all of the valuable lessons she learned. For her, the biggest challenge was the responsibility of being an expert. "It seemed like I had to know everything about feminism in order to teach it. Students would ask questions and if we didn't know the answers we'd have to go home and research them. Basically I matured. We were taking hard classes at the time and then had to teach."

"I really enjoyed it, despite some of the problems," says Jessica. "I think we had a big influence on the school and the way the kids think. Even kids who weren't taking the class would borrow the books from other kids and people's parents would come to some of the events."

EXTRACURRICULAR ACTIVISM

You don't have to be in a formal school setting to rock the teenage status quo. In the informal realm, writing zines and magazines is a platform for political change that doesn't require meeting space—and if you can get the photocopying donated, you don't even have to include your school's administration in your plans. Plus, you can be a publishing house of one and still make a splash. Christine Doza, now a writer, dancer, and musician in New York City, wrote the zine *Upslut* when she was sixteen and miserably alienated at her suburban high school. She didn't realize that there might be similarly disaffected kids who would appreciate her talent and what she had to say—that is, until she created her zine and distributed it in her school. She sounded off about her angry stepfather, her alienation at school, and her cresting understanding of feminism. "I expected to get punched, but instead I got kissed," she wrote of the reaction from peers the first time she published her zine.

Kenya Jordana James, a home-schooled thirteen-year-old who lives in Atlanta, took self-publishing one step further. In 2002, she decided to address the lack of healthy images for black female teens by creating *Blackgirl Magazine*. The first issue featured an interview with Atlanta recording artists Outkast, and it sold out—all two thousand copies. The magazine is now bimonthly and runs between twenty and thirty pages, with ads, and has a print run of nearly four times the size of the first.

When Christi Steiffer was fourteen, she wrote to us after being harassed on a routine walk to the library. Her response was not to start another group—by her own count, Christi was already a part of the ACLU, GLSEN, Human Rights Campaign, and NOW—but to write a response to the harassment and circulate it on the Internet. It begins: "I have heard some people say that the 'feminist movement' is over. That it's all just a joke; a way for lesbians to 'hook up.' So now I ask myself . . . why are we feminists?" She continues, "Walking down the street in some of my badass gear (i.e., flannel zip capris, Doc Martens, Bob Marley shirt, and black bandana) I just assumed that when people looked at me, they would be scared off like they usually are." After three guys honked and ogled her, she realized that dressing the part didn't ensure freedom from unwanted male attention. "Why do I ask for so much?" She answers her own question: "I don't think that I should be scared walking down my own neighborhood streets in the middle of the day. I don't think that I should have to put up with the stereotype that I am just a piece of meat just because I have tits. And I don't think that at fourteen years old that I should have forty-year-old men hitting on me from strange vans. Is that really too much for a feminist like me to ask for?"

Christi's writing was activist on at least two levels: she was able to deflect the bad feelings of being harassed by talking back to the harassers—and she even had the last word. By circulating her statements, she both raised awareness of the issue and let other girls harassed by random guys in trucks know they weren't alone.

In other informal arenas, area high-school students in Waukesha, Wisconsin, created a zine based on interviews they conducted with the elderly members of a local gay organization called SAGE (Senior Action in a Gay Environment). They did another zine, called *Pam I Am*, that dissected body image and sex education. It was distributed to middle-school girls. Another project consisted of posters they designed with statistics—such as the percentage of women who are raped and that 10 percent of students are gay, lesbian, bisexual, or transgendered—that they hung up on International Women's Day all over the school. "We upset a lot of kids and the administration," says Carissa Trenholm, who was seventeen when she initiated the Waukesha art project, "but we did it." The posters provoked conversations in the classrooms and "made a difference just by disrupting the flow of a regular day."

One of the potentially limiting characteristics of zine publishing is that it's disposable. Lisa Holt, age eighteen in 2002 and a self-described feminist dyke rabble-rouser from Excelsior, Minnesota, used a $3,000 writing prize she had won to collaborate on an anthology of youth writing called *Litkids*. Lisa's distribution system is out of the trunk of her car, like Ani DiFranco's record distribution in the early days. Fearless, she shows up at indie bookstores around the country and asks them to carry the book. Often she'll set up a milk crate and a pile of books to make her own little store. "This is only workable in good weather and white-collar cities," she adds. Some people might think that Lisa's ambition to self-publish a book demonstrates how extraordinary she is. True, but it also demonstrates how accessible writing and publishing a book can be.

The two of us are genuinely amazed at the level of activism and engagement we have witnessed in presumably slacker teenagers. We have had five high-school–aged interns in the last few years, each of whom sought out feminist activist work. All of the energy and initiative we see flies in the face of the cultural anxiety about this age group. Authority figures from Democratic Senator Joe Lieberman to conservative pundit Bill O'Reilly are horrified by the music that young people like, the video games they play, and their abject consumerism. If adults—politicians, parents, preachers, and teachers—spent the same amount of time talking *to* teenagers as they do talking *about* them, they'd learn that every town has at least one Jackie and Jessica, Rochelle, Lauren, Wendy, or Lisa. And they'd also learn that the pop culture that the kids are consuming isn't always as threatening as they believe. The messages that teens are taking out of music, magazines, and games are often translated into action, not just consumption.

To wit, Jackie and Jessica's entry to feminism, like that of many young people, came out of music. When Courtney Love said in an interview that she read *Backlash*, Jessica decided to read it, too—and what Jessica did, Jackie also did. "I was fourteen," said Jessica, "and I had to read it with a dictionary." (So did we and we were in our senior year of college when we got hold of the book.) Jessica was also mentored by a fellow teen—her older cousin Angela, who broke Jessica of the high-school parlance "That's so gay" (meaning "that's uncool"), by saying: "I know you don't actually dislike gay people but you sound *so* ignorant when you say that."

Starting a group, a zine, or a class, or simply calling someone on their witless homophobic language are just a few of the ways people are entering activism while in high school. Teenagers are acutely aware of what is wrong with the system and they have no investment in reinforcing empty authority figures, because they are rarely granted respect or authority themselves. More than that, high school is a period in life during which even the most perfect rock-band guy or most athletic girl can still feel like an outsider whom no one understands. This sense of alienation can often help promote empathy for others and can inspire high-school students to be interested in social justice because they are developing a political and moral spine, one that isn't bowed yet by compromise.

If you are looking to make change at any stage of life, high-school students are important allies—and they are often overlooked, for the same reasons that they overlook themselves. They don't have conventional power, but they are the future and will soon be a voting bloc. Not only that, but they have time and idealism to spare. A word of caution, though: this isn't a call to get high-school students to do political "chores," such as picking up trash on the side of the highway or enforcing volunteerism. Including young people is important because they bring a different perspective and life experience that only they are capable of, one that is born of their own unique experiences and politics. We're arguing that teenagers have something to offer morally and politically—and we don't get far by ignoring them or their perspective.

High-school activism means that you learn when you are young that you have the ability to make a difference. The world doesn't have to remain the way you found it. Activism funnels the angst and rebellion of that time into something bigger—and whatever change you create is something that no one can take from you.

chapter 3 | Rebels with Causes

"We know what we stand against (sort of), but what do we stand for?"

—Van Jones, founder and national executive director
of the Ella Baker Center for Human Rights

JENNIFER

I went to a small Midwestern college called Lawrence University where students were more likely to hang a yellow ribbon on their door than protest the first Gulf War. We did have something called the Anti-Apathy House, but its members' main contribution was providing alternative keg parties to the ones the frats were hosting. I was a big radical fish in a very small pond, which gave me confidence, organizing experience, and perhaps a reputation for being self-righteous. My boyfriend was a buff frat boy and, while I was very enamored of him, he was separate from my radical feminist life. Many of the things I did as a fledgling and earnest activist back then strike me as ill-informed now. I was so over-the-top adamant that pornography was bad, for instance, but I never stopped to consider that I had almost no experience with it—had never asked guys why they watched it or women whether they did. I relied on received wisdom that, while it was from feminist sources, wasn't always accurate. Another misstep was my knee-jerk contempt for the book *Lolita*—before I had read it. (Once I actually opened the book, I was quickly seduced by the incredible wordplay, and the subtlety of the story itself.) Still, gaffes aside, college was the first time that I was identified as a political leader. I incorporated my interest in theater and writing into a political agenda—co-founding a guerrilla theater collective to protest the war (we invaded the commons at dinner the night before the first Gulf War began—I tell the story on pp. 157–159) and co-creating an alternative zine, called *The Other*, to get diverse voices into the campus media.

Whether it was writing about the list of date rapists posted anonymously in the women's bathroom or running tearfully out of class when my English professor cast aspersions on Madonna's talent, I was passionate. In my mind, I was Lawrence University's antidote to its apathy and conservatism. I felt empowered, but I hadn't yet figured out what *I* believed as a feminist. I was consumed with finding out what "the feminists" thought. I think I was so overwhelmed by this sudden profusion of feminist philosophy and power—I had just been exposed to Andrea Dworkin and *Thelma and Louise* came out the year I graduated—that I had a hard time seeing how I could be myself (someone who liked *Lolita* and dated a Sig Ep) and be a feminist.

AMY

I went to Barnard—a women's college in the biggest city in the United States—where the feminism was as common as the yellow taxicabs that whizzed by outside the school gates. For me, feminism wasn't limited to Take Back the Night marches and women's theory classes—it was everywhere and I was one of many true believers on campus. This doesn't mean that I was taking every opportunity to express my feminism. In fact, I was more like a passive recipient, happily absorbing a women-oriented atmosphere. I remember an economics class where the professor's examples were all automatically female (for instance, "a farmer needs to increase her output"), and a Renaissance art class where the majority of the artists I studied were women. Prior to that time I didn't even know there were women artists in that era.

I did get involved in two overtly activist campaigns— one was for the secretaries' union, which was striking for better benefits; the other, a protest opposing the destruction of the Audobon Ballroom in Harlem, the theater where Malcolm X was assassinated. Columbia University (of which Barnard is a college) owned this historical venue and was proposing to turn it into a medical-waste facility. These issues grabbed my attention, but only to the extent that I showed up at a few meetings, signed some petitions, and generally grumbled about how insensitive this rich elite college was to working-class secretaries and black history. Beyond the campus, I attended a few marches—a 1991 protest to oppose the war in Iraq and the 1992 reproductive freedom march, both in D.C., with homemade posters in hand. A few days after that second march, I grad-

uated. My friends and I decorated our graduation caps
with a slogan we learned in D.C.: "We're Fierce, We're Feminist, We're in Your Face." (When an older friend proudly
reminds me that I did this, I hate to tell her that this mortar-
board statement now strikes me as simplistic.)

This was perhaps the easiest I have had it as an activist:
I thought that all that was required was that I show up and
express outrage. I learned to be an activist on behalf of others in college, but I hadn't yet realized how my values regarding civil rights and class issues related to my *own* life.
Soon after college, I made the connections between these
interests and activism on behalf of myself. Once I started
organizing with diverse groups of people, I realized that
being white and middle class was suddenly something I felt
insecure about (odd, since I spent the first twenty-two years
wanting only to be middle class). Denying this privilege got
me nowhere, so I quickly regrouped and began assessing
what it meant to use the unique resources I had and in
what ways being privileged had its limitations. The summer
after graduation I co-organized a cross-country voter registration drive. By that time I knew I was doing it not to
"help" poor, disenfranchised black people in the South, but
because *I* wasn't served if I didn't live in a participatory
democracy.

*   *   *

I'm a college freshman. I was really looking forward
to the Women's Caucus at my school (University of
Rochester). Unfortunately, I was really disappointed.
At the first meeting, a bunch of people came, but
now, only about four come to meetings and they
seem mad that they are there. I know the Women's

Caucus is a member of the Feminist Majority,* but
we don't have many activities and are not a big
presence on campus. Do you have any ideas about
how I could improve the situation?

> Emily Feldman
> Rochester, New York

Although campuses are actually magnets of activism, often more so than workplaces or churches or homes, most college students believe that their campuses are apolitical. In the three years that we have been traveling to colleges, the students at nearly every single school we've visited (close to two hundred in all) worry that their campus is "totally conservative" and "extremely apathetic."

Inability to answer the question "What can I do?" haunts college students in particular. Perhaps they are measuring themselves against the sixties, when sit-ins were as popular as instant messaging is today and protests were so intense that lives sometimes were lost. The sixties, that tale goes, was the era when the kids all wanted to give peace a chance and integrate schools and have sit-ins to effect change. The kids of the twenty-first century (and the eighties and nineties that led up to it) are presumed to play violent video games and gaze at their navel piercings rather than organize for the common good.

The truth is that no era—neither the Greatest Generation nor Generation X—owns the desire to make their world a better and more just place. Political activism wasn't invented in the sixties and it didn't die with Watergate. We

---

*Emily is referring to the Feminist Majority Leadership Alliance, a network of campus chapters of the Feminist Majority Foundation.

have to stop believing that hype and perhaps even acknowledge that there is power in *not* being a wide-eyed ide-
alist. As conservative writer David Brooks put it in *The
Atlantic Monthly*: "Boomers grew up drunk on idealism and
have always spent an inordinate amount of time congrat-
ulating themselves for this quality." We might be more
cynical, but we are also realistic—perhaps less likely to
be resentful or fail to understand strategic compromise.

The movements against exploitative globalization and
sweatshop labor are evidence that the generation that is currently young has no shortage of passion and energy to commit to social justice. What is lacking, however, is what every
generation has had to invent for itself: the means of change.
In the early sixties, civil rights activists adapted Gandhi's
techniques for nonviolent resistance to their own situations.
By simply sitting at a lunch counter where they weren't allowed, they enacted profound change. But we can't simply
copy techniques to address a specific time. Someone sitting at
a lunch counter today would have no effect, nor would it be
life threatening (do we even have lunch counters anymore?).

Experts often measure young people's so-called political disengagement by the fact that very few young people
run for office or join NOW. This mind-set frames politics in
the narrowest of ways and judges engagement by a person's
willingness to pay $20 and add his or her name to an e-mail
petition. It's hard to distinguish this contribution from paying our cell phone bill. When you actually ask young
people if they are political, the majority say "yes." In fact,
only 1 percent of seventeen- to twenty-four-year-olds actually call themselves "apolitical."

We have always believed in our generation's political
will, but these past few years we witnessed it as a fact. In our
observation, no college is as conservative or apathetic as the

students at the school fear. Ironically, it's often at the more liberal-leaning campuses where students find it harder to see the activism in their midst. At super-PC schools, the feminist groups can be as intimidating, cliquey, and dismissive as the popular girls are in high school. "At Macalester College," says Andrea Baumgardner, Jennifer's sister, "there was this feeling that if you weren't already well versed in feminist history and culture, then you just couldn't be a part of feminism. I remember saying I was a humanist, rather than a feminist, because I was so terrified of the womyn's collective." By contrast, students at Ohio State University tend to resign themselves to the campus identity of Big Ten sports and frat parties, but those who don't fall into that category have carved out an active, inspired feminist community.

All schools—whether small two-year community colleges or big jock universities—have outlets and an infrastructure for activism in the form of meeting spaces, funding from student activity fees, and already formed entities such as gay, lesbian, bisexual, transgender groups or the Black Students' Organization. The snag in their activism tends to be a shortage of fresh and relevant ideas—something that will grab students' attention when they have a million things vying for their time. At college, it isn't *whether* you are going to do something political; it's *what* you are going to do. Students are riled up, but often don't have ways to funnel the energy usefully. Whereas the high-school student might need advice on how to build an infrastructure, college students are more likely to need strategies for effective activism, ways to take them beyond their outrage and move them toward solutions.

Feminists began organizing on college campuses in the sixties and seventies. Their first task was establishing women's studies programs and women's centers and addressing glaring omissions such as having just one female tenured faculty

member or the complete lack of women's sports teams. Today the need has moved from gaining access toward the
quality and longstanding impact of the activism. It's not
simply about having a women's team anymore; now we have
to build the audience for women's sports so that women's
athletics are as valued as men's. One great thing about having grown up with the Second Wave already in full flower is
that most colleges and universities have women's studies,
women professors, and some sort of feminist club. Some
schools have a dozen feminist organizations: Iowa State
University—as of winter 2003—boasted a Feminist Majority group (known as FMLA), a women's leadership organization, and a women of color feminist group, to name just
a few. The downside of having feminism so integrated and
structurally sound is what Emily describes above about her
experience at Rochester. What is left for these groups to
do? Rightly or wrongly, people assume all the necessary
goals have been achieved. If there is one drawback to the
proliferation of Feminist Majority campus groups, it is that
their top-down structure—activist priorities are provided
from the home office—isn't flexible enough to allow local
campus issues, which might be more timely and inspiring,
to dominate the agenda.

Besides a shortage of ideas, we diagnosed Emily's problem as "meeting fatigue." This assessment won't come as a
surprise to anyone who has dabbled in organizing, feminist
or otherwise. We have all attended the never-ending meeting that keeps splintering into break-out groups to process
slights and never gets anything accomplished because everything must be done by consensus. When Amy responded to
Emily, she pointed out that four members doesn't have to
be a discouraging number—sometimes it's more effective
when you have fewer people to build consensus with. (As a

two-person organization, we can attest to its efficiency.) With smaller numbers you are more able to hold one another accountable. In bigger groups, some people can become invisible and their contribution—or lack thereof—isn't noticed.

FINDING YOUR GOAL

If we assume Emily's gang of four is adequate, then the issue is not diminished rosters and student apathy but the lack of a goal. We suggested that Emily's caucus take on a specific campaign or assign tangible tasks. She could approach her endeavor as episodic events or a range of actions by taking on anything from recycling her dorm's glossy magazines to providing quarters for laundry to a local shelter. The point is simply taking initiative.

When we followed up with Emily after her freshman year, it turned out that she was able to make the Women's Caucus thrive. She had the following good advice drawn from her experience. First, build on what already exists, rather than assuming you always have to create things from scratch. "Look for other feminist things happening on campus," she told us. "I was in a production of the *The Vagina Monologues* that was not run through the Women's Caucus. Through it, I was able to meet lots of like-minded people which made me feel better and which may also help in recruiting people next year." Second, she recommended working with other activist groups, like Amnesty International or Greenpeace. "This will help in networking and will gain strength and support for your group," says Emily. True, part of building a movement is tapping into the stream of already activist people who have had to attract an

audience to their events. (It's the quid pro quo effect.)
Emily's approach was to take the current group and reener-
gize it. She gave it some vitality by bringing in a few new
members and building alliances with complementary groups
on campus.

All it takes is one individual like Emily or one visible
success to transform last year's impassive campus into this
year's activist powerhouse. Every year *Mother Jones* does
a "10 Most Activist Campuses" issue. In 2002, Harvard
University—notably conservative even among the already
reserved Ivy League colleges—was one of the honorees.
Harvard is hardly radical, however—Professor Derrick Bell
relinquished his law school tenure in 1992 to protest the
lack of women of color on the faculty, and women are still
rarely on the masthead of the university's humor paper,
The Harvard Lampoon. But, in 2002, the students staged a
sit-in and took over an administration building to protest
the lack of a living wage (as opposed to a minimum wage,
which is often not enough to live on even if one works full-
time) for staff on the campus. Thirty days later, students left
to take much-needed showers after the university agreed
to negotiate with their demands.

We have observed other instances of creative activism
on the campuses we've visited, each piercing through the
same kind of group apathy Emily experienced. For instance, a group called Students for Justice in Palestine at
Yale University re-created the humiliation and harassment
Palestinians must go through every day to get to work in
the occupied territories. They set up mock checkpoints and
stationed "defensive forces" with cardboard rifles. In 1998,
Duke University students staged a sit-in and successfully
pressured the school to adopt the first Code of Conduct for

University Trademark Licensees in order to ensure that their sweatshirts, boxers, and baseball caps were subject to labor and human rights standards. Other schools quickly followed their lead. What made each of these a success is that they were unique ideas, and that they were tangible. Students had a clear goal—such as getting their university to sign on to a code of conduct—that was realistic enough to be achieved. This is satisfying and thus spurs on more activism.

Determining what makes an issue feminist is a central dilemma for budding women's groups like Emily's. If Emily's Women's Caucus took on sweatshop labor or a living wage campaign, in the process they would make the point that both are women's issues. When people insist on "purely" feminist issues, they usually get down to just two topics to focus on: rape or abortion. (Or in the parlance of the women's movement, violence against women and choice.) Some students feel almost obligated to take on these issues. If they don't make abortion rights central to their activism, they play into a fear that young feminists are backing off from the most important of "controversial" issues. Students feel this pressure automatically, but the groups working with them don't help. The Feminist Majority Foundation has successfully placed its campus branch, the Feminist Majority Leadership Alliance (FMLA), on more than 130 college campuses, including Emily's school. Although the Feminist Majority Foundation is a multi-issue pro–women's equality organization, the FMLA has primarily pushed reproductive freedom for their campus activists—implying either that young people need to have the pro-choice message reinforced or that there is only one priority issue. Further, it could be construed that the FMLA is more concerned with "their" issue than finding out what younger feminists think the current issues are.

Reproductive choice does affect young women personally because many college students are having sex, but the issues around sex don't boil down to something as generic as "choice." The problems that resonate for students are the cost of contraception, getting one's partner to get tested for sexually transmitted diseases, exploring attraction to other women, having condoms available in their health centers, how to have an orgasm, where to buy vibrators, figuring out what one likes sexually—none of which are what people think of when they hear the word "choice"—or even "reproductive freedom." In order to get young women motivated about reproductive freedom issues, choice groups could sponsor "Take Your Boyfriend to the Clinic Night," or dialogues between pro-life and pro-choice people, or simply make sure that there is adequate gynecological care available on campuses. Providing a space for students to discuss their discomfort with the historical slogan "abortion on demand without apology" or to contribute to the evolving language of choice could be more productive than printing up more "No more wire hangers" buttons. Emergency contraception campaigns are important, but so are campaigns for sexual pleasure. *The Vagina Monologues*, with its emphasis on labia-shaped chocolates and mimicking epic orgasms, achieves this spotlight on pleasure, as do ads for vibrators in the magazines *Bitch* or *Bust* (not to mention the magazines themselves). Men learn about sexual pleasure through pop culture, porn movies, and magazines like *Playboy* (with sexual responsibility low on the ladder). As feminists, we can't discuss sexual responsibility with women and leave pleasure as the man's domain.

MOVING BEYOND 1 IN 4: THE SEXUAL ASSAULT POLICY

Of course, it's difficult to talk about bliss when so many women have had experiences of rape, sexual violence, and bad or unwanted sex. Sexual assault is a central theme for college students, both because many young people have firsthand experience with rape and because of a long legacy of feminist students organizing around the issue. We are fortunate to have vocabulary for things like date rape and a body of feminist legal theory about consent. Most colleges have a Take Back the Night march—which, incidentally, began as a protest against pornography in 1978, but has morphed into a day to protest women's lack of safety after dark and to provide people with an opportunity to break the silence about their own experiences of rape and molestation. Most campuses also have some sort of sexual assault policy and a rape crisis hotline, if not on their campus then in the town in which their school is located. The language, hotlines, and support for victims are all the legacy of a successful Second Wave of feminism that transformed campuses from places where girls were actively preyed upon, limited, and discriminated against to places where equality might reign. Much has changed to increase awareness, but nowhere are students entirely satisfied with how this issue is treated on their campus—nor should they be. Only 37 percent of universities are in full compliance with federal law in reporting crime statistics, according to a congressional report cited in the spring 2003 issue of *Ms.* magazine.

While the complaints regarding sexual assault issues are several, the two most common are that the university doesn't report the number of sexual assaults accurately in its materials to prospective students and that rapists aren't adequately punished. "There were dozens of rapes!" exclaimed a female student at Manhattanville College, in Purchase, New York—a school that claimed no sexual assaults in their 2003 brochure. "It galls me that they lie," she continued, "but then how women are treated when they do report is much worse. And the guy gets off with a slap on the wrist." Sasha's take on the way sexual assault is handled on her campus is the usual complaint we hear.

Campus sexual assault is a severe problem all over the country. One large part of the problem is disinformation between students and the administration. It is actually in the university's best interest to report rapes since they in fact have a direct investment in student safety. Students are usually operating with very little knowledge of how the current system works, while colleges are subtly discouraging students from pursuing rape charges through either the school or the criminal justice system.

The two of us have some regrets about how we, during our own college experiences, perpetuated myths like these and treated the issue of date rape. Although both of us were very vocal about rape and what we saw as administrative apathy, neither of us ever requested the campus sexual assault policy in order to read it and assess whether it was appropriate. We were more likely to make snippy generalizations about how "more rapes happened at frat houses" than to figure out how to truly reduce sexual assaults, and, not surprisingly, we didn't foment any lasting productive change at either Lawrence or Barnard. As Sasha's complaint points out, it's typical for colleges to list the number of rapes in the preceding year as zero, which outrages female students who have usually heard of several date rapes after just a short time at school. Universities justify these statistics because a federal law, the Clery Act, requires that they count only rapes that were adjudicated. That is, only rapes that were reported using formal structures and that went to a hearing. As for the treatment of perpetrators, universities can censure or expel a student but not send him or her to prison. While they sometimes feel like worlds unto themselves, colleges are part of a larger town or community, one with a formal police station with procedures for treating criminals. A common reason that a perpetrator is still at school or even in class with a victim is that there was no criminal procedure—a school-based inquiry is not a formal criminal investigation. A school cannot remove a student who has been accused but hasn't been formally charged and found guilty.*

Another example of received wisdom run amok (an urban legend of college injustice, if you will) is the assertion that many schools with Greek systems will sanction fraternity houses but not sorority houses because, according to old blue laws, more than half a dozen women living together in a house is considered a brothel. When we first began hearing this, we challenged it to the degree that we'd ask where students got the information, and suggest that it was in violation of Title IX if true. Amy Coombs—a law student in Utah—wrote to Ask Amy offering her research services, Amy asked if she could verify whether there was a law on the books in that Mormon state or any other about women living together constituting a brothel. Coombs found nothing at all to support that fact, but she did find an old law that decreed that every resident of a small town in Utah must own a gun. (By the way, snopes.com, a Web site that confirms or debunks urban myths, is always a good place to start before spread-

---

*Much of this information about date rape on campus was gleaned from Professor Diane Rosenfeld at Harvard University.

ing the latest outrage. Indeed, the sorority house as brothel myth is disproved on the site.)

Outrage is only valuable when it leads to reform. Students like Sasha from Manhattanville College are reacting to a system that doesn't yet work. So we'll ask the question we failed to ask when we were in college and that all student activists need to be asking: What needs to change to make sexual assault policies more effective? If we could do it over, we'd request and review the current policy and we'd try to understand the roots of underreporting. If the goal of a campus is to get accurate reporting of rapes that occur within the campus community, then something has to change to get women to come forward by notifying the police *and* the administration. Some of the reluctance is obviously stigma—and some of it is confusion. Perhaps it is unclear who to tell and what the repercussions will be. It might also be a police department's reputation for being discriminatory with racial profiling or not believing gay or transgendered people when they say they've been raped.

When Ashley Burczak was a senior at Barnard College in 1999, she tried to make rape less common. Her inquiry led her to reform Columbia University's ineffective sexual misconduct policy and to compel the university to report accurate sexual assault statistics. Besides this policy transformation, her accomplishments included expanding the hours that crisis services were open to students and persuading Columbia to include sexual assault prevention training in their new student orientation. "Before that, the prevention training had been the old 'Give out whistles and scare the women' routine," says Ashley. She concretized her strategies by founding Students Active for Ending Rape (SAFER) on her campus in 2000. Then, in 2001, SAFER became a national advocacy group that trains campus activists in revising their school's sexual assault policies.* SAFER is an accessible and evolving model. Trainings include teach-ins with student organizers to raise consciousness about sexual assault, and getting the students to understand the difference between an actual written policy and a general "philosophy" of not tolerating rape.

We also spoke with Harvard law professor Diane Rosen-feld, an innovator in the study and prevention of rape on campuses, who believes there are three essential elements to any solid sexual assault policy:

> The first is *Mandatory Preventative Education*: This means teaching students about affirmative consent, making them understand and abide by rules of conduct that respect their fellow students. Second, Survivor Resources: There needs to be a hotline or someone well trained to call 24/7 if a student is raped. If a victim's first call is to someone who is not trained or discourages her or him from reporting, or gives out incorrect information, that can ruin the victim's case and opportunity to address the crime later. Lastly, a Disciplinary System that takes rape cases seri-ously: Schools should have a separate board, specially trained in cases of sexual violence, to hear and adju-dicate these cases. Since schools operate under fear of being sued by defendants—the perpetrators always seem to have money—there is a lack of pressure from the prosecution. It's critical to build up that pressure.

We would add four more elements to Professor Rosen-feld's comments:

*As of fall 2004, SAFER is active on eleven campuses.

1. *Sniff out and rat on the actual illegality.* Colleges use various illegal ways to discourage people from reporting
   rapes. Boston attorney Wendy Murphy offers some examples of this behavior such as "insisting victims turn
   over all information on psychological counseling and
   medical exams prior to the assault and waiving any con-
   fidentiality to those files, instituting a strict statute of
   limitations, [and] erroneously warning victims that if
   they get a rape evidence kit done, they will have to press
   charges, even if they later change their minds." Universities are required by federal law to report any actual
   rape charges to the police—but they frequently do not.

2. *Work with, not against, your administration (at least until they
   prove unworthy).* Once there is a system in place for easy
   and thorough reports, work with the university to pub-
   lish a breakdown of assaults. The information should
   include how many rapes were reported to the university, how many to a counseling center, how many to
   police; how many were prosecuted; and how many pros-
   ecutions resulted in a conviction or other resolution. To
   achieve accurate counts in college brochures, the victim
   should be encouraged to report to the campus authority. Theoretically, no college supports rape or protects
   rapists, but the decisive issue is whether they have a
   clear strategic policy. (We say "theoretically" because,
   in fact, schools have historically protected the accused
   student more so than the accusing student.)

3. *Commit to developing communication skills between students
   having sex, regardless of gender or sexual orientation.* Coercion
   is just as possible among same-sex partners as among heterosexual couples. It is not "blaming the victim" to acknowledge that college students (who are often away
   from home for the first time and trying to fit in) do not

know how to talk about consent or even know what they are comfortable doing sexually. Antioch College in Yellow Springs, Ohio, developed a Sexual Offense Prevention Policy in 1996 that is based on conversation. While it's not perfect, it *is* a step toward real communication and overtly consensual sex.* Students engaging in sexual behavior must articulate their desire and get consent before making a move. During orientation, students are required to read the policy, which includes assertions like this: "The person who initiates sexual conduct is responsible for verbally asking for the consent of the individual(s) involved. Consent must be obtained with each new level of sexual conduct. The person with whom sexual conduct is initiated must verbally express consent or lack of consent. Silence conveys a lack of consent. If at any time consent is withdrawn, the conduct must stop immediately."†

4. *Acknowledge that these inadequate and vague sexual assault policies are as harmful for men's sexuality as they are for women's.* For example, at Appalachian State in Boone, North Carolina, the sexual assault policy is interpreted as such: if a woman has consumed any amount of alcohol, *any* sex she has is not consensual and she could report it as a rape. This presumes that men consuming alcohol are automatically in control of themselves and

---

*And it certainly isn't perfect. A current student wrote to Ask Amy in the summer of 2004 detailing her own experience of being date-raped. When she went to campus security, they neither offered a rape kit nor documented the bruises on her neck. In her own informal poll, this student learned that in the fall of 2003 twenty to thirty women on campus had been drugged and date-raped. "Despite rape kits that provided evidence," she told Amy, "the student committing the rapes was only expelled after the administration found out that he was selling drugs."

†To read the whole code, go to http://antioch-college.edu/community/survival_guide/policies_procedures/sopp.htm.

the situation. Make it clear in your policy and educational materials that men are capable of being coerced into sex and sexually exploited, and that coercive sex often happens between people of the same gender. "It's crucial to have male sexual assault prevention counselors," says Ashley of SAFER, which works with the national organization Men Against Rape, too. "Especially since we advocate connecting violence against women issues with violence against lesbian, gay, bisexual, and transgendered communities."

Another element of the problem is that there is no national network of campus rape crisis programs or Take Back the Night events. Ashley's SAFER organization is trying to change that (and has a grant to do so), while Diane Rosenfeld is working to "advise schools on how to draft good policies that don't run afoul of Title IX" and on organizing students and informing them of their rights. Professor Rosenfeld is linking a key concern of women students with sports in a way that isn't typical. Although the famous law is synonymous with sports, the act is intended to guarantee equal access to resources in education generally—not just in athletics. Funding a national campus sexual assault project would both address unequal resource allocation and have a beneficial impact on reporting violence on campus, which would be one step toward eradication.

MONEY TALKS: SPEAKING A LANGUAGE ADMINISTRATIONS UNDERSTAND

When it comes to changing campus policies (sexual assault and beyond), most students overlook their own power, seeing themselves only in opposition to the administration, which has a clear decision-making capacity while students do not. However, the power students have is twofold: sheer numbers (at least 10:1 in favor of students), combined with the fact that their tuition sustains the university. But do students have a say in how their money is spent? In short, yes—but you have to know how to follow the money. Following the money reveals the true values of any system—be it a school, a political campaign, or the U.S. budget. It states our priorities, exposes the gap between rhetoric ("No Child Left Behind") and reality (no money for schools), and identifies whose voice will be heard. Sometimes the activist instinct is to avoid contributions under the premise that there is no such thing as clean funds. This is short-sighted, since understanding how the money is made and spent provides evidence for a social justice argument and is an important tool for organizers.

Here is just one example. Federal law requires colleges and universities (whether public or private) to submit their wage reports and they are regulated to provide equal pay for equal work due to the 1963 Equal Pay Act. Even with protective laws in place, there is pay inequality. Female college professors are no longer saddled with the Second Wave problem of being completely overlooked for these jobs. They have access, but they are still likely to be concentrated at the lower levels, to remain untenured, and to make less money than their male counterparts in all ranks. *Academe*, the publication of the American Association of University Professors, publishes an annual report that lists average salaries by rank and gender. Looking at all ranks together from all universities, in 2002–2003 women made $62,000 per year to men's $80,000. At private secular universities, women made $74,000 to men's $96,000.

Barnard College, which as a women's school has supporting women inherent in its philosophy, also falls into this pattern. We asked two of our interns, Anna Davies and Liz Masuhr, to track down current salary statistics. They went to the Office of Planning and Research and asked an institutional research analyst for salary information. She directed them to a Web site that listed salaries by gender and rank. They learned that there are more female faculty members than male—as of the 2002–2003 school year, it was 111 women to 74 men. But as you go up the career ladder from freelance "lecturer" to full professor, the ratios swap; there are 31 male full professors and just 24 females. Salaries are even more revealing of the enduring gender gap. The average salary for men who teach at Barnard is $79,713—25 percent more than the women, who make an average of $63,913.

Amy undertook a similar study when she was at Barnard in the early 1990s—and got similar results. (Sad that the situation didn't change in a decade.) It's not difficult to do this kind of survey since university salaries are public information. Furthermore, it's an effective tool, arming oneself with knowledge that could lead to a gender equity campaign.

Imagine you are going to build such a campaign. What do you do? There are six basic steps:

- gather evidence
- garner allies
- approach the administration
- suggest a solution
- follow up
- repeat as necessary

After acquiring proof of sexist pay scales (as Anna and Liz did by simply looking up the information), you begin having casual conversations with your fellow students and garnering support for your point of view that female professors are not adequately compensated. In your future campaign, it helps if there is broad support—current students, alumni, trustees, etc.—and evidence that others are equally surprised and disappointed by the professorial wage gap on your campus. After you establish that there is support, go to your administration such as the dean of faculty or the teachers' union at your school to set up a meeting about your findings and concerns. Have a solution or range of solutions sketched out in advance.

Simply asking questions and gathering evidence goes much further than a slogan or incensed rhetoric ever could. There is still rampant sexism in hiring and wage discrimination, but sometimes it persists because people don't ask or act in order for it to be changed. In 1994, three tenured female professors at MIT were out for a collegial dinner. One of them wondered aloud how many tenured female faculty there were at MIT. They learned that out of 209 tenured professors in all, only 15 were women; and the percentage of women in tenured positions had not changed much in fifteen years. They called the heads of every department—mathematics, physics, astronomy, etc.—and asked two questions: "What are your requirements for tenure?" and "Why don't you have more women?"

When given the opportunity to assess both hiring practices and department composition, many of the male professors were equally dismayed. It was more a case of inertia and the assumption that the problem was solved than active resistance to women's careers. At the same time, MIT was attempting to recruit and retain more female students. The upshot is that the three female professors took all of this evidence to the provost of the college with several recommendations: improve the status of and ensure equity for senior female faculty; improve the professional lives of junior female faculty; and increase the number of female faculty. They made the policy on maternity leave uniform throughout MIT and challenged the assumption that having children meant women faculty couldn't achieve equally with women who didn't have kids. Within five years, the number of women on the School of Science faculty increased by 40 percent. The MIT women did their research, which in turn got people to listen to them (rather than be defensive); and they used that research to make realistic goals.

In our experience, it is always better to assume that the administration will see things your way until proven otherwise. It is a more powerful and self-confident position to assume that the administration will support you than it is to assume that you are a thorn in the side of some generic system. If they do support you, they are your most powerful allies.

If you're not that lucky and the administration doesn't show interest, you can take your case to the student press, and send letters to the board of trustees directly. The board is listed on any annual report and is most likely on the university's Web site. The board is also the body responsible for making gender balance the "law" of the university. Public outcry is often very effective in prompting changes that will cost the university money. One precedent: up until the early 1990s, most universities were heavily invested in companies working in South Africa and thus supporting the highly racist, colonial system of apartheid. Students at many schools formed antiapartheid groups and compelled their universities to pull out any money they had invested in South Africa. The bad publicity that universities experienced due to these investments spread beyond campus walls, putting direct pressure on corporations to divest from South Africa. Perhaps corporations would follow universities' lead on hiring and salary parity, too.

REACHING OUTSIDE THE COLLEGE "BUBBLE"

It's important to transform the campus itself, but students also have power beyond their ivory towers and fraternity quads. Take spring break, for example. When we were in college, spring break meant Cancun or Fort Lauderdale. At least it did for those who had the money and the desire for underage drinking and wet T-shirt competitions. (Neither of us went that route. Amy usually went back to Marblehead to catch up on school reading and Jennifer went home to Fargo to vegetate in front of the TV and eat at the Olive Garden.) For others, an alternative spring break of helping others—increasingly popular on campuses since our college days—has become a great bridge between what students learn in political theory classes and "real world" problems.

In the last few years we have heard about not just longstanding classics like building houses with Habitat for Humanity International (founded in 1976 by Millard and Linda Fuller) but the University of Washington's Pipeline Project where undergrads help rural grammar-school students write their own books. Some of these spring breaks are pegged to a specific social justice campaign—such as the 2002 Taco Bell Truth Tour, which took several dozen activists and tomato pickers across the country to Taco Bell's headquarters in Irvine, California, where they agitated for a one-penny-per-pound raise for the farmworkers who provide tomatoes for the chain. Students and activists joined the laborers on two buses, traveling for two weeks until they reached Taco Bell's headquarters. Students gained insight into how their food is produced, workers' rights, and some of the struggles of Mexican nationals who work on farms in the United States. Ultimately, Taco Bell wouldn't negotiate, but the tour was momentous for the students and workers involved. They learned about each other's lives by being on a bus for several days, when they were able to confront whatever assumptions they had about the other group. Beyond that, just the guts and initiative it took to see a campaign like this through is inherently empowering and transforming for all the people involved. Even when a specific political goal is not met, the alternative spring break provides skills and ongoing activist opportunities for students.

This was the case with Kate Palmer's spring break in 2003. Kate is a super-activist at Ohio Wesleyan University in Delaware, Ohio. She has organized everything from a senior trip to South Africa to alliances between pro-life and pro-choice organizations to, of course, OWU's alternative spring break.

We met Kate as a freshman in 2001, after she was picked from among many applicants to go on Third Wave's Reaching Out Across Movements (ROAMs) trip. In a nutshell, ROAMs takes twelve young women (chosen from many applicants) from town to town in a given region where they meet with every social justice group they can locate and in the process bring together groups in the same small locale that previously didn't know each other. The twelve activists come away with a deeper sense of how organizing plays out depending on locale. Third Wave produced ROAMs three times: once in the Southeast (where they visited pickle farmers and the Highlander Folk School, famed for training such activists as Rosa Parks), once in the Pacific Northwest (where they observed the isolation of rural communities), and once in the Southwest (where they connected mainly with immigrants). Their conversations were both practical and philosophical, exchanging information about the region's political landscape with strategies to support the work. The ROAMers went to the South, for example, assuming that Southerners were more racist and left realizing that no region is more or less morally evolved than another; each has its own relationship to racism and civil rights. Kate in particular used her ROAMs experience to devise a well-planned alternative spring break.

Kate has the the personal style of Cyndi Lauper and the chutzpah of Bella Abzug. She was about to leave for her alternative spring break in Washington, D.C., when we met up with her in February of 2003. A few weeks later, we checked in to see how the trip went. Five fellow Ohio-Wesleyans participated on Kate's trip, which was designed in conjunction with the National Coalition for the Homeless's Urban Plunge. Arriving in Washington, D.C., on a Saturday the students immediately immersed themselves in the homeless population. As Kate explained: "We were homeless for exactly forty-eight hours from 8 a.m. on Sunday to 8 a.m. on Tuesday," Kate said. "During the plunge we were partnered up with two people, David and Ely, who are currently homeless. We experienced various activities such as sleeping on cold concrete, panhandling, going into businesses and asking to use the bathroom, and eating at soup kitchens. A lot of the time was also spent getting to know David and Ely and learning about their lives." The value of Kate's experience isn't that she underwent true homelessness—an integral component of homelessness is the lack of choice in that matter—but that she put herself in a situation to experience discrimination, fear, and hunger, some of the things the indigent confront daily.

In the end, Kate and her group achieved the mission of the Urban Plunge spring break, which as she told us was "to confront and acknowledge our own stereotypes and perceptions of poverty and the homeless, and to put a more personal or human face on those issues." Kate wanted to have as authentic an experience as possible. So prior to the plunge, she e-mailed us for contacts of any activists we knew in the capital. We put her in touch with Choice USA, which organizes college campuses around reproductive rights, and Mark Andersen, who runs the community outreach program for the Emmaus Services for the Aging and has organized benefit concerts from within the D.C. punk community for almost two decades. On her own, Kate secured meetings for the group with Bread for the City, Community for Creative Non-Violence, and Christ House, a clinic that serves homeless people.

By the end of the break, Kate and her teammates had made connections between various persistent social ills, especially racism, and also homelessness and poverty. For Kate, the week was "full of contrasting emotions." The "forty-eight hours I spent living as if I were homeless were incredibly challenging," she told us, "emotionally, mentally, and physically. I would also find myself looking at their problems from my own perspective and then wanting to try and 'fix' the people I would meet."

WHEN WORKING FOR FREE IS A GOOD DEAL

Besides spring break and direct organizing experience, Kate has interned with Erin McKeown, the folk singer and songwriter; Third Wave; and the nonagenarian labor organizer Millie Jeffries.* Interning is a great way to expose yourself to vast possibilities. We are often asked how we started our careers and the truth is, we were both unpaid interns: Jennifer at *Ms.* magazine right after college and Amy for Senator Ted Kennedy when she was seventeen. We both learned essentially all of the office skills we would ever need and made ourselves indispensable by creating crucial filing systems and being the only ones who could photocopy accurately. Not only were we both skilled secretaries, having to file or answer phones made us the gatekeepers of information. Amy knew where the senator was at all times and the ins and outs of the legislation he was about to propose. Jennifer saw every story that came in to *Ms.* and spoke to Alice Walker and Andrea Dworkin during receptionist duty. Interning—or volunteering—can also be a form of activism, especially if you are interning at a social justice organization. As an intern, your role is less formal—which is both bad and good. The bad: you aren't getting paid. The good: there is much less bureaucracy around you so you can imagine a project and your bosses are happy to let you see it through. You are under the radar.

We have had ten interns in the last three years. They have fact-checked *Manifesta*; helped to develop a prochoice project that encouraged women to be "out" about abortion; organized mailings for our company, Soapbox, Inc.; and assisted with research for this book and two others (Amy's shopping guide and Jennifer's book on bisexuality). From our perspective, we have exposed them to as many elements of the women's movement as we possibly can, from a meeting at the UN to a day spent in the editorial offices of *Bust*, so that they have a better understanding

*Sadly, Millie Jeffries died in 2004.

of what careers might await them. (We also try to do fun things like go to the Public Theater or have lunch at a great cafe during New York's restaurant week. We hope this makes up for the hours they spend in the dysfunctional East Village post office helping us with mailings.) We get something out of it too, obviously. Besides the extra brainpower, we get the perspective of women who on average are ten years our junior, which is increasingly crucial since as even we get older we are still considered generational spokeswomen and frequently asked what's on the minds of young women.

You already heard about two of our interns, Anna and Liz, who tracked down Barnard's salary statistics. They also undertook another task we'd been kicking around: getting movie tickets donated to a battered women's shelter. We knew that basic needs are taken care of in shelters and that safety is the most crucial element, but women in shelters still need to have a break, just as we all do. These nonessential pleasures, which they are also deprived of when they flee from their homes, are almost never addressed. (We go into "Grace Activism" more in another chapter.)

Anna and Liz were ultimately successful—and in the process learned the value of flexibility and serendipity. After no luck for weeks trying to make contact with a domestic violence shelter, Amy suggested they call Karen Austrian, a Columbia alum she had just met for coffee, who worked for the Coalition for the Homeless. The meeting with Karen was random and lucky, but being adaptable enough to alter their original goal from a battered women's shelter to a homeless shelter enabled their project to work. Their first task was simply to call the shelter and make sure that they were on board with Liz and Anna's plan. "We asked Karen, the contact at the shelter, if providing free movie tickets was a service that would be useful to their clients and whether or not anyone else had ever done that—in case there was a group we should already be hooking up with," says Anna.

As it turned out, Karen was ecstatic about it—people almost never reach out to the coalition to help, or if they do it is only with food or donated clothing. "Both of those things are really important," says Liz, but Karen told them that what her clients needed most were things that helped make them a part of everyday society. Liz reported: "These women [homeless or recently homeless] usually don't have a chance to enjoy the good things in New York City; they just have to work all of the time at hard jobs like street cleaning." Most nonprofits would agree that Anna and Liz were ideal volunteers, because they approached the shelter with a specific idea of what they wanted to offer. More common are those who call in with the age-old "What can I do?" Sometimes figuring out how to manage a volunteer is more than the already stretched nonprofit can take on—thus, the ongoing proffering of The Generic Three.

Having established that the movie tickets were both wanted and needed, Anna and Liz set to getting them. "Convincing theaters to donate the tickets was actually more complex than we could have even imagined," says Liz. "There was so much bureaucracy—especially in the larger chains," added Anna. They started by looking in the local paper to see what movie theaters and companies were in the shelter's neighborhood. The first calls were to random, local theaters in Brooklyn. They figured that the theaters would be familiar with the Coalition for the Homeless and would want to do something for their community. This sadly proved wrong. Liz and Anna rarely got anyone on the phone—and when they did, they were referred to the corporate owners. The managers and employees at the actual theaters didn't have any discretion over their venue—and what's worse, they didn't see themselves as part of the neighborhood that made up their customer base. (This is one bad thing about corporate-chain America. Businesses aren't truly local, which affords them an excuse to have no stake in the community or sense of responsibility about local needs.)

Soon after being rebuffed by the local affiliates, Anna and Liz turned their attention to the theaters' corporate headquarters. They called Loews (which owns 153 cinemas across the United States) and Clearview (which owns 56). "With both there was a huge voice-mail directory with tons of official titles," says Anna. "We learned *never* to leave a message in a general voice-mail box." "Right," says Liz, "It's better to follow a huge maze of getting forwarded everywhere and dialing people's extensions randomly until you get a real person." The first human they connected with happened to be the community outreach person for Clearview Cinemas—whose sole job, it seemed to Anna and Liz, was to tell callers to go away.

Loews, for its part, has a national fax number dedicated to ticket requests. So Liz and Anna faxed Loews with a request for ten tickets per month. They called to follow up, then faxed again.

Loews responded within two weeks—and they said yes. They were quite helpful, too, even calling Anna and Liz to confirm that the shelter got the tickets. There was, however, one snafu: Loews will only donate tickets once per year per organization, which Anna and Liz didn't know when they made their original request. Thus, if they were to do it again, they would ask for fifty tickets up front.

When Anna spoke to Clearview Cinemas, they didn't come close to matching the Loews performance. The Clearview Cinemas community outreach specialist said that there was no way that they, a subsidiary of the multibillion-dollar company Cablevision, could donate tickets to a shelter. "She said, in fact, that if she donated to 'my' homeless shelter, she'd have to donate to 'everybody's' homeless shelter," reported Anna, rolling her eyes.

Since Clearview's slogan is "We Bring Neighbors to the Movies," Anna argued her case by pointing out that these women *were* the movie theaters' neighbors. Clearview apologized, saying it was "company policy." Anna told her they should change their slogan, and hung up angry. This experiment gave Anna and Liz some valuable information about the differences among corporate policies: Clearview has no community-oriented company policies while Loews has established a way to provide a sliver of its resources to people who can't afford them. "I felt personally offended by the fact that Clearview—which is based in my hometown in New Jersey—didn't care about community," says Anna, shaking her head in disbelief. "I went to that theater all of the time." While they haven't launched an official boycott, Anna and Liz haven't gone back to Clearview Cinemas. One activist step led to many more.

Liz and Anna learned how to turn an idea into action. "Initially, I was totally discouraged because we first heard only 'no,'" says Liz. "But eventually we prevailed by being persistent, calling again and again until we got someone on the phone." Anna adds: "I think that the trick is to be confident but flexible. Don't assume that the person you are calling has authority over you and your project. If they say 'no,' be polite, but keep in mind that they may not know any more than you about what their company can do and ask if there is anyone else you should talk to."

They also gained enough confidence to make requests of companies and individuals. "When I first started to call I felt as if I was inconveniencing everybody," says Liz. "But after a while, I really got used to it and I feel so much better at it now." What keeps more people from taking initiative like Anna and Liz did is the fear of being a nuisance. However, the best time to be a nuisance is when you are in college. After all, what are people going to do? Fire you?

USEFUL WAYS OF LOOKING AT ACTIVISM

There are various approaches to organizing, none of which is better or more important than any other. In fact, while radicalism (which can include tearing down and reinventing) might seem to conflict with reform (which fixes up existing institutions), they work as complements. In August of 1967, just months before his death, Martin Luther King Jr. was quoted in *Harper's* magazine saying: "For years I labored with the idea of reforming the existing institutions of the society, a little change here, a little change there. Now I feel quite differently. I think you've got to have a reconstruction of the entire society, a revolution of values." Well into his career, Dr. King had exhausted reform methods for civil rights. His radical peer Malcolm X was having a similar evolution, but he hadn't availed himself of the benefits of coalition building and working from within the system yet. The radical approach addresses a problem at its root. Negotiating and compromising are not part of radical politics. The benefit of radicalism is clarity of goals and the momentum that a bold stand can engender. Radicals imagine a world that does not exist. The power of radicalism lies partly in that it is *not* realistic.

Take sweatshop labor. The radical approach is abolishing sweatshops. While sweatshop abolitionists are incredibly successful in raising consciousness, an unintended result is that they are putting the people they "help" out of work against their will—which is unjust in its own way whether or not it's for a larger good. Meanwhile, the reform approach tries to make sweatshop conditions better—by raising the minimum wage, implementing restrictions on how many hours a laborer can work, and making sure that people get bathroom breaks and that the machinery is safe. The reform approach enables this first wave of workers not to simply be sacrificed for the sake of larger principles and a better, but distant, future.

As the examples of Dr. King and Malcolm X show, most long-term activists find that each approach has its season. In the sixties, before women had the right to legal abortion, the Jane Collective in Chicago took matters into their own hands and learned how to do abortions themselves. None of them were medical professionals, but they managed to provide thirteen thousand safe early procedures before they were busted (and for about $100 per patient at a time when abortions could cost $5,000). These women used radical means to confront the illegality of abortion. The radical feminists of the seventies broke ground and created hope with their clarity and their generalizations—they said things like "All men oppress all women" and were able to lob the idea of sexism and patriarchy into the country's consciousness. They had a clear goal, in that they wanted to take down patriarchy, not work within it successfully.

While a few radicals were challenging all assumptions about gender roles, millions of reformers changed society in more subtle ways. Most American females who tuned in to feminism did not want to leave their husbands or to revolutionize their marriages or, often, didn't want to take on a full-time job. They did want parity and access to anything that men had access to. Maybe they wanted men to help with the housework or for their work in the home to be visible and valued. Even the women who provided abortions through Jane were happy when *Roe v. Wade* meant that they no longer had to take matters into their own hands.

As for the two of us, we usually err toward reform tactics with a radical goal. We believe in integrating the system and not being afraid of power. Our friend Farai Chideya, author and television journalist, has been instructive on this point. Chideya tells high-school students who want to know how they could get a cool job like hers—she's worked at places from ABC to MTV—that often bosses expect you to assume white values, such as wearing a suit or broadcasting about people of color as "they" rather than "we." After all, those are the values of the institution. When there are only five black people out of 150 that work at your company, racial integration is not just a matter of numbers but of culture. Once a company has more than a token black or of-color staff, Chideya argued, the stories they produce could begin to reflect the diversity of America.

Whether you are undertaking action as an individual (like Anna and Liz) or as a group (like Emily at the beginning of this chapter), the key is to set specific goals rather than thinking that a vague restatement of your values is your mission. Thus, rather than aiming to "end homelessness," you can aim to raise your consciousness about why people are homeless and what homeless people need in terms of social services. You can make alliances with the many organizations and churches working with the homeless and provide the resources that the organization can't prioritize, as Anna and Liz did. By being meticulous and specific in your plan, you can avoid meeting fatigue and all of the other travails that get in the way of actualizing your ideals.

College usually brings with it a social paradigm shift—you no longer have to conform the way high school demands. (In fact, in college, being different becomes the new norm.) The traditional college student is an activist in transition—most students are not yet regular adults with major responsibilities, but neither are they kids to be ignored. It's the perfect place to hone one's righteousness before heading out to the big bad real world. The more nontraditional students (older, immigrants, working full-time parents) enter college, the more institutions are bound to be radicalized. Moreover, if you're in college and are reading this book, your school has at least one person who isn't conservative or apathetic—and probably many more. Find each other.

|||||||||chapter 4 The Real World

"I don't know what your destiny will be, but one thing I know: the only ones among you who will be really happy are those who will have sought and found how to serve."

—Albert Schweitzer, humanitarian, theologian, missionary, medical doctor, and winner of the 1952 Nobel Peace Prize

JENNIFER

I have now been out of school for more than a decade. Because I work from home, I have an unstructured life and a job that in a way I have to make up every day. I love it for the freedom and hate it for the instability. As an activist, I have had to learn to work without formal affiliations and I've grown to be effective even without the label "editor at *Ms.*"

And regardless of whether I'm working in an office or on my own, there have always been three scenarios where inspiration simply descends on me, fully formed: in the shower, walking the streets of New York, or reading a good book or article. This all makes sense to me. The heat from the shower increases my blood flow, the rhythm of my feet hitting the pavement and all there is to take in tramping through New York unsticks my mind, and reading wonderful writing is always stimulating.

I happened to be taking a shower in the spring of 2003 when the idea to start a campaign to encourage women to "come out" about their abortions hit me. Things had been percolating along those lines for a while. My feminist Listserv had grumbled about how women weren't really allowed to say that they were relieved after an abortion anymore— we wondered, did we need a documentary? A holiday? At the same time, a thirty-seven-year-old customer service rep in Richmond, Virginia, named Pat Beninato was annoyed. Every time she turned on the news, antichoicers were yelling about babies being slaughtered or erroneously claiming that women who have abortions are destined for clinical depression. "I had an abortion," thought Pat, "and I'm glad I did. Someone should put up a Web site for women who had abortions and don't regret it." She happened to be between jobs and had always wanted to do something concrete about abortion rights, so she founded imnotsorry.net—and has since gathered more than one hundred stories. I knew about Pat from Katha Pollitt's column in *The Nation* and had corresponded with her a bit. Meanwhile, years ago my friend Sandy Fernandez had mused that she wanted to make T-shirts that had the thing that made each of her friends vulnerable spelled out right across the chest. (At the time, mine would have said, I HAVE HERPES. Now I think it would say I HAVE CREDIT CARD DEBT.) Sandy's idea—a contemporary Scarlet A, but self-chosen—stuck with me. In the shower, it all came together. I thought: I want to do a campaign that makes the millions of

women who have had abortions visible. I'll ask my friend
Gillian (a filmmaker who had worked for years with Michael
Moore but was now doing more corporate, boring work) to
shoot the documentary, get my friend Erin to design everything, and I'll raise money from friends to fund it.

I began working with various friends and colleagues to
create a campaign recasting the *Roe* anniversary, January
22, as I'm Not Sorry Day. The campaign itself consists of
three elements: a film directed by Gillian Aldrich documenting women's experiences with abortion, T-shirts that
read I HAD AN ABORTION, and a postcard that lists resources
such as unbiased after-abortion counseling and the National Network of Abortion Funds. During the process, the
intent of the campaign evolved from the original "I'm Not
Sorry" message. Now it asserts that women might have
complex, or even painful, experiences with abortion, but
they are still very grateful to have had access to the procedure. For most, abortion did not end a life—it prevented a
disaster. The "regret" is often for getting pregnant, not for
choosing an abortion. In other words, the point of the day
isn't to get people to "celebrate" their abortions—though
many people have written to me saying that they would
love to do just that—but rather the point is to "come out"
and link the decisive issue of abortion with those of us who
have had them. These women are our mothers, grandmas,
friends, sisters, and selves—we all know and love women
who have terminated a pregnancy.

With the help of Katha Pollitt and activist-academic Rosalind Baxandall in getting the word out, I was able to raise
$1,500 almost immediately. The Third Wave Foundation
agreed to underwrite the T-shirts with a minimum of bureaucracy, and carefully written (I hope) letters to my mother's
pro-choice friends in Fargo brought in another $1,000-plus.

So far the gaggle of friends working on this campaign have distributed T-shirts (to be worn whenever, but I'm assuming most people will only wear them to a pro-choice event), staged an event in New York for the *Roe* anniversary in 2004, and filmed more than twenty women's stories—from seventy-year-old Gloria Steinem who had an abortion nearly fifty years ago, to A'yen Tran, a twenty-one-year-old Barnard student who had an abortion when she was sixteen. I have personally distributed thousands of the resource cards to abortion clinics that were really eager to have them for after-abortion care. The film is due to be completed in early 2005 and, I hope, will have distribution beyond my two hubs of New York and Fargo.

Most important, though, this project has deepened my understanding of the abortion issue. I was surprised at how hungry women were to tell their stories and more surprised by the range of stories there were. Some women really did want to pray for the "baby that died," others felt adamantly that until a baby can exist outside of the womb, an abortion is not killing. A surprising number of women said that they had been terrified to tell their mothers, only to do so and learn that their mothers and grandmothers had also had abortions! The only unifying theme among the women in the film and the hundreds who have written to me with their stories was that everyone was grateful to have had access to a safe and legal procedure. To me, it only strengthens the pro-choice, public health advocates' side of the debate to embrace the honest details of women's individual stories and not be threatened by the sadness or pain some women had over the decision. By mid-2004, I was several months pregnant and finding shirt distribution onerous. Planned Parenthood helped me distribute the remaining 250 shirts, in an alliance that came in very handy. Even though Amy and I are individuals, our web of friends and organizations has made many ambitious projects possible.

AMY

In the early days of the Internet, circa 1995, before anyone worked for a dot-com or knew you would need a Web presence, an intrepid explorer named Marianne Schnall registered the name feminist.com and envisioned approaching major women's groups like the National Organization for Women and the Ms. Foundation for Women to provide them with Web sites. I didn't know Marianne, but I knew the actress and comedienne Kathy Najimy. Kathy was an early supporter of the Third Wave Foundation and Marianne had just interviewed Kathy for *InStyle* magazine. During the interview Marianne mentioned her plan to start the site. Kathy suggested getting Third Wave on board and that I might be a great networking resource in the feminist nonprofit community.

Marianne called me. I happily provided the contact information to many women's organizations but I repeatedly assured her that I was *not* the person to help her. I barely used e-mail and did not understand the point of the Internet. Soon her site hosted organizations from Equality Now to Girls Inc., along with the National Committee on Pay Equity and the Ms. Foundation for Women. Within months, Marianne began receiving random queries about feminism from the large network of people online at the time, mainly college students. "I'm looking for a quote from a famous feminist. Help!" was a typical request, or "How many women are killed each year as the result of domestic violence?" or even "How will I know when I have my period?" Marianne didn't feel equipped to answer this broad and odd range of questions, so she called me again.

I agreed to answer a few queries. I looked up feminist quotes in a reference book, called the Family Violence Prevention Fund for domestic violence statistics, and passed on the ordering information for *Our Bodies, Ourselves* along with a personal anecdote about my own first period. It's odd to think that there was a moment when these resources didn't already exist on the World Wide Web. After six months of answering these forwards, Marianne suggested formalizing the relationship and Ask Amy, my online activist advice column, was born.

For nearly a decade, Ask Amy has been my most consistent form of activism. I take my laptop with me on the road to answer queries from wherever I am—Turkey, Oregon, or my apartment in New York. My portable activism has its own structure and rituals. Once a week, I devote most of the evening to "powering through" the Ask Amys. I didn't realize until several years into this process that providing resources to people and networking individuals was a skill and, moreover, that it actually helped people. It was so second nature to me that I overlooked it as my main activist contribution.

When burgeoning activists ask me how to begin, I now point to my Ask Amy column. I learned through becoming an activist advice columnist that I couldn't solve everyone's problems, but I *could* direct people to a resource or two that might help them solve their problem. I could also just listen—innocent enough—but for many a sympathetic ear is something to which they don't have ready access. I have my share of crazies and cranks, of course, like the sixteen-year-old who sends me e-mails about how abortion is never necessary and how feminism's goal is to make men subservient to women. When I reply to my e-mails, I am shocked by how many people write back and say, "You were the only one to respond." During these ten years, I have corresponded with thousands of men and women of all ages from all corners of the world. It's common that I will be in some small town in Iowa or North Carolina delivering a lecture with Jennifer and someone in the audience will have already met me via my column.

Ask Amy isn't entirely about me helping others. Because I am identified as a representative of young feminists, the relationships and information gleaned from working through people's problems provide me legitimacy when I make statements about feminism today. This experience enables me to stay ahead of the curve of public opinion polls, just based on the ten Ask Amy questions from across the globe that I received that day. For instance, a few years ago I was getting dozens of e-mails about the need for men to take responsibility for their "reproductive" health. Today there are dozens of programs sprouting up to address male accountability. This is useful for my career as a consultant to progressive organizations and as a resource for various funds and projects.

To enter my East Village apartment, you wouldn't know it was the epicenter of my most passionate activism. But it has everything I need to be Ask Amy right there in my home: all-purpose resources like *Our Bodies, Ourselves* and *The Reader's Companion to U.S. Women's History*, orderly files stuffed with clippings I have torn out of magazines and pamphlets, my phone to call organizations and friends for referrals, and my Internet connection (recently cable, making life easier). All of which goes to show that anyone with some compassion, curiosity, and a few reference materials could be an Ask Amy.

*   *   *

> Hello. I am very interested in becoming a feminist.
> I am an action person, not really a talker, so I was
> wondering what I could do in my neighborhood . . .
> what I could protest and how can I get a group
> together to do so. Could you help me by giving me
> information on how I can start a movement here?
> Morgan Shumate
> Concord, North Carolina

As Morgan's rather desperate e-mail hints, without the infrastructure of high school or college, lone individuals often find it difficult to figure out how to contribute to activism or make change. After all, you aren't surrounded by hundreds or thousands of peers every day, there isn't the instant community that you have at a school, and you don't have access to free photocopying, meeting spaces, or student activity fees to help subsidize your women's group. Then there are the other commitments that fill up your day. You might be trapped in a workplace where either you don't think there is anyone else there who shares your beliefs or you may have been conditioned not to interject politics into the office. If it's "just a dumb job" or it "just pays the bills," you probably feel all the more urgency to have something meaningful in your life—something that will give you an identity, purpose, and a sense that you are more than a cog.

On the social front, you and your friends are starting to partner off or have families. It's harder to get people to meet often enough to maintain friendships, let alone try to jump-start a recycling project together. This may also be the time you organize (and let lapse) a book club or knitting circle. Friends, and you as well, start to get very protective of personal time. Dinner plans are made weeks in advance and suddenly require confirmation the day of. It can be a very isolating juncture, especially if you aren't going the route of having a baby or living with a boyfriend or girlfriend. Identities are in flux: your girlie-girl sister has started dating a woman; your vegan housemate who wouldn't let you flush the toilet in order to save water just bought an SUV, and your anti-marriage friend got hitched *and* decided taking her husband's name was "just simpler." Hard partiers are joining AA; oddly, everyone is doing yoga. The people whom you took for granted as understanding you and your politics are changing rapidly, and so are you.

Despite the personal upheaval, you want to get involved. You call your congresspeople, send in your $30 to public television, or contact Planned Parenthood to volunteer and are enlisted to stuff goody bags. In fact this cohort is more likely to participate in the system as a volunteer than by voting, according to research by Meredith Bagby in her book *We've Got Issues*. You *are* donating your time and your money, but if you are like most people who we have encountered in this situation, you aren't feeling satisfied. Perhaps you don't want to prop up an existing system—which a volunteer does—but actually want to be part of reforming these structures. You want more than a superficial once-a-month fling with an organization or don't want to be reduced to a checkbook alone. You have expertise—being a designer, accountant, or chef, for instance—that could be parlayed into activism. You just don't know exactly *how*.

It was when many of our peers in this age group started asking the two of us how they could be more involved that

we began to realize the need for a book like this. Some of
our friends were lucky to work for companies that "cared"—
and their activist needs were being met. Time Warner, for
instance, honors people within the company who are community activists by making fairly substantial donations to
a cause they support in their name. After September 11,
Time Warner also set up facilities in their building so that
employees could assist the relatives of victims—sending
family members to counselors or helping them acquire death
certificates and other paperwork. This filled a need both
for the survivors and for New Yorkers who were desperate
to help.

POWER IN NUMBERS

Don't worry: it's not all isolation and dissatisfaction. You
have power. It was this same age group that was instrumental in propelling the feminist movement in the late sixties and early seventies. The just-out-of-school types were
the women who sued *Newsweek* for sex discrimination (and
won), protested the 1968 Miss America pageant as humiliating, and organized the Jane Collective in Chicago to provide abortions pre-*Roe*. Why is this age group so primed to
make change? Perhaps because it's the first time that young
people begin to get angry on behalf of themselves, instead
of on behalf of others. The same person who campaigned
for a living wage for secretaries in college, all of a sudden
realizes that she earns less at the bookstore than the man
who was hired at the same time. In addition to the emotional perspective, you probably have more material resources than you ever did before. You are most likely a
nonstudent with a job (hopefully) and likely to have some

cash flow to direct toward good causes. If you work for a corporation, you have access to photocopy machines, conference rooms, and perhaps even unlimited phone calls. Even without a fancy job you have your nonmaterial resources: friends and family, work experience, old school friends. People power, creativity, and energy are just as much of an asset.

Meredith O'Neill Hassett was twenty-eight when she began to ask herself, "What can I do?" As a schoolteacher in Harlem, she was no stranger to New York families in need. Her students couldn't count on having clean clothes because they couldn't buy laundry detergent and cleaning supplies with food stamps. She often heard of kids whose families didn't have blankets or even beds. As we see in so many great moments in activism, Meredith shared her observations with two friends, casually, over dinner one night. The three—Meredith, Louise Rexer, and Kristy Irvine Ryan*—decided to start a fund to give away anonymous donations of household necessities to the families Meredith knew needed them. Thus, in December of 1998, the organization Secret Smiles was born when they assisted the first family. Soon after, Meredith formalized the resource and met with several caseworkers and other teachers to let them know that Secret Smiles existed.

Families they assist are usually fleeing domestic abuse, transitioning from welfare to work, getting out of homeless shelters, or have lost their homes because of a fire or other disaster. When a request comes in, Meredith personally purchases everything from dishes, sheets, and silverware, to bunk beds and tables, re-creating domestic space for people

*Tragically, Kristy Irvine Ryan died in the World Trade Center on September 11, 2001.

forced to leave their homes. "We usually get couches, dinette sets, pots and pans, dishes, towels, bedding, beds, gift cards to Old Navy, or anything else that will help the family get settled," says Meredith. As of 2004, they had helped nearly three hundred families. "Kristy, Louise, and I started this organization to let people know that we care," says Meredith. "Our main goal is to empower these families to help themselves, but in order to do that, they need sheets on their beds, dishes to eat off of, and a general sense of grounding. We try to provide a foundation from which they can rise."

This organization has two important characteristics. To begin with, families don't have to jump through hoops to get funded—they simply have to have a social worker contact Secret Smiles on their behalf*—and the organization doesn't specify a set amount to spend per family. In other words, they are flexible and allow space for serendipity. For instance, one grant they made was to a low-income girl who earned a scholarship to a ritzy private school; Secret Smiles provided her with an allowance. While it's great to send low-income kids to fancy academies, it impedes their ability to thrive—or fit in—if they can't afford to do any of the things their peers are doing, from having pocket cash for a cappuccino after school to owning an outfit appropriate for attending the ballet. The second characteristic is that much of Secret Smiles' fund-raising and giving is done informally and is highly replicable in any community. It might be as simple as initiating a toy drive at Christmas among your

---

*Secret Smiles goes through agencies such as the Family Service League, Greyston Foundation, St. Luke's-Roosevelt Hospital Child and Adolescent Psychiatry Services, and various homeless shelters.

friends or colleagues at work. Or it can be as structured as organizing ten friends to each give $50 directly to a family, rather than donating to the United Way's multimillion dollar budget and not knowing where your money goes or how it's used. All one needs to form a Secret Smiles is access to families in need and to a circle of friends who have any amount of money to give. You could do it easily as a teacher, as Meredith did, but also as a church secretary, or a doctor, or simply by cultivating a good relationship with a local shelter.

WHEN LESS IS MORE

Secret Smiles' mission is rooted in a deep belief that a fulfilling life requires more than the necessities. A person in need should be able to have pleasure and joy and beauty in his or her life. This is grace—an activist quality we highly endorse. Grace means beauty and goodwill—a favor. In the last chapter, we discussed the difference between radical and reform modes of activism. Grace is a third—an equally important though perhaps overlooked style. Because it is positive and often small, grace activism can be misunderstood as trivial or nonessential. Does the prisoner on death row need the improvisational sounds of Miles Davis to listen to while she's encased in a ten-by-ten-foot prison cell or does she need a pardon from the governor? Both, actually—anyone in a dire situation needs not just the basics but also that which makes life worth living, not to mention quality of life. Often, though, people in more privileged lifestyles don't always discern that beauty, art, and fun are part of maintaining one's sanity. Azar Nafisi, the author of *Reading Lolita in Tehran*, understood this when she started a secret

book group for young women during the most repressive
years under the Ayatollah in Iran. The students read
Nabokov's *Lolita*, F. Scott Fitzgerald's *The Great Gatsby*, and
other American and British novels, taking great risks to do
so for the simple reason that art inspires you to imagine
dignity and freedom, love and honor. "I don't know why
people who are better off always think that those less fortunate than themselves don't want to have the good things,"
one student told Nafisi. "That they don't want to listen to
good music, eat good food, or read Henry James."

Dress for Success, the aforementioned nonprofit founded
by our friend Nancy Lublin that provides business suits to
women who were essentially forced off of welfare, exhibits
this quality of grace. As a student, Nancy hated the way law
school was making her feel: stressed, capitalistic, and out of
touch with the people who most needed help. While she
was taking constitutional law classes, poor women were being commanded by welfare reform policy to "get to work."
As Nancy was cautioned by law professors about the need
to dress the part for law firm job interviews—and informed
that "ladies must wear skirts"—she realized that no one was
there to apprise poor women of this expectation or help
them with the material needs to make that transition. She
believed that this was one reason that these women weren't
getting hired. They didn't look like the women who were
already working. Nancy's approach is, in a way, quite radical: most people give away their old cast-off tacky clothes to
the generic "poor," but Nancy insisted that people donate
clothes they would wear to a job interview not what they
wouldn't be caught dead in. Dress for Success gives women
access to the very things that might actually get welfare-to-
work to work.

MAKING CHANGE FROM SCRATCH

We are not trying to push creating a new organization or foundation every time you have a frustration, an instinct to do something nice for someone, or a bright idea. Our overall goal for this book is simply pointing out that activism is something anyone can and should do, whether attached to another organization or not. In fact, social justice organizations often bring their own baggage. Most are designed to operate as alternatives to the government or to make up for service gaps in our system. The paradox is, though, that these institutions for change can become themselves promoters of the status quo—because they have to sustain their own reasons for being. When institutions meant to represent or protect people fail—as we see with the American government as well as with progressive foundations—all that is left is for the individual to break out of the status quo and create revolution. By revolution, we mean stopping violence, for instance, rather than building a bigger, better shelter system—which is, after all, a prison of another kind.

Sometimes doing a project for an existing organization is the best framework, like collecting nice suits from your friends for Dress for Success or agreeing to buy one new suit a year for a Dress for Success client. This way, you can also avoid the hassles of incorporation, payroll taxes, and other headaches. You don't have to reinvent the wheel and compete for limited resources, especially in tough economic times. Some organizations welcome this kind of freelance activism and most could benefit from it. V-Day, the global movement to end violence against women and girls inspired by *The Vagina Monologues*, is one such organization. For instance, in 2000, V-Day issued a worldwide call for innovative strategies to stop

violence: the International V-Day Stop Rape Contest. They received hundreds of applications gathered by their regional coordinators, all of which creatively tackled V-Day's mandate to
end violence against women by 2005. The Stop Rape Contest
ended up funding dozens of "freelance" activists, those with
no institutional affiliation, around the world in grants ranging from $3,000 to $21,000 for projects like a red "women's
taxi" in Slovenia that distributes information about rape and
picks up women who need rides. One of their most successful
grantees was Karin Heisecke (whom we met in London at the
2001 New Girl Order conference, which brought together
Third Wave academics from around the world). Karin first
heard about V-Day when she saw a flyer in New York during
the UN Beijing Conference on Women follow-up events and
then saw a flyer for the V-Day Stop Rape Contest in October
of 2000 at the World Women's March in Brussels, and at the
last minute submitted a proposal with her friend, Silke Pil-
linger, whom she had worked with that year to organize a
UN workshop on Women and the Media.

Karin, a young brunette from Germany who speaks
four languages, recalls, "Silke and I wanted to come up
with an idea that would be easily implemented in all parts
of Germany—not only in big cities but also in the often ne-
glected rural areas," Karin told us. "We wanted to reach the
whole population, not just those who are already sensitized
to social issues, such as violence against women."

With that in mind they thought: *Bakeries*! In Germany,
bakeries are like Starbucks—they're everywhere. Moreover,
everyone goes to the bakery, making them an ideal place to
reach a large cross-section of the population. "We knew this
because we are both the daughters of bakers," Karin told
us, "and grew up in family businesses in small towns." Since
bakeries are not usually associated with social activism,

Karin and Silke would be forging an original partnership in the fight to end violence against women.

In Germany, bread and pastries are sold in individual paper bags. Karin and Silke's idea was to use these bags as miniature billboards printed with rape statistics, hotline numbers, antirape slogans, and a calendar of antiviolence events specifically honing in on acquaintance rape. The slogan which Silke had spontaneously come up with—"*Verge-waltigung kommt nicht in die Tüte*"—meant literally "Rape doesn't go in the bag." While the phrase doesn't totally translate to English, in German it's an expression that conveys "rape is totally unacceptable," according to Karin. They envisioned the bags being put in circulation a month before the events advertised on the calendar to ensure that there was enough advance notice. Two months after proposing their bread bag idea, they found out that they were one of the top three winners of the 2001 International V-Day Stop Rape Contest and their project was announced in February 2001 at Madison Square Garden during the largest benefit performance of *The Vagina Monologues* to date. Silke and Karin received a $10,000 grant to implement their project.

Now they had to get to work. Their first big challenge was finding a nonprofit that would host the project with no budget for staff costs and with very short notice. The Family Planning Association in Saarbrücken, part of a network devoted to sexual and reproductive rights and a group with whom Karin had worked in the past, agreed to take on the project. They were well positioned to do so because they already had a good network in place and the coalition could share the workload.

Karin and Silke were both in Belgium when they wrote their proposal, but in the first several months of putting together the project, Silke's work brought her back to

Germany, and Karin was in the process of moving from
Belgium to the U.K. Working on the initial steps for the
project was a challenge for both of them. By May 2001,
Silke dropped out. If the project was going to happen,
Karin realized that she was going to have to go it alone.
"This was difficult on a practical as well as an emotional
level," recalls Karin. "We started it together so I wanted to
continue it together as well. The workload was hardly man-
ageable for one person. Still, it was better that I do it alone
than sacrifice the whole project." This was a crucial moment,
because one thing that stops many people from following
through on a good activist idea is an unequal level of commitment from a friend or partner. Karin stuck with it.

Karin decided on Saarbrücken, which has a population
of 200,000, and is the home of her sponsor, as the site of the
pilot program. "I had three ideas on how to approach this:
going via the marketing departments of big chains, going
via the Professional Federation of Bakers, or going via the
wives of the bakers, who are often, in family-run businesses,
the sales managers." Approaching the wives of bakers proved
to be the most successful, as the chains were either bogged
down with bureaucratic decision-making processes or didn't
see how Karin's antirape campaign fit with marketing break-
fast rolls.

Karin made use of her personal contacts, both in choosing the nonprofit sponsor and in the site of her activism. To
some it might seem that it was easy for Karin, who came
from a family of bakers, to institute this project—that she
somehow had an advantage that other people do not. But
the project evolved because Karin targeted her own assets
and drew on her community to shape her campaign. Using
the personal contacts and resources you already have is a
powerful tool. People often assume that you have to be the

CEO of Citibank in order to have any power. Not true. You have resources that are yours alone to wield. And often those personal resources are exactly how bigwigs make their projects happen. Less powerful people are entitled to this same access. Maybe you have an art degree and can make the environment of a local battered women's shelter less punishing. Perhaps through your job at the local Dunkin' Donuts you can lobby the corporation to print their bags at a co-op or to use White Earth Land Recovery Project's organic Muskrat Coffee. If you work at a huge corporation, you tend to have high-powered computers and copious office supplies. Anyone can and should do a rigorous accounting of one's own community, Palm Pilot, or phone book. This last is so obvious, yet so easy to overlook. In fact, we often forget it ourselves. For instance, in a last-ditch effort to raise money for Freedom Summer '92, Amy decided to write letters to the parents of friends whom she suspected had extra cash. She made a quick list of friends with a summer home, a Volvo station wagon, or an in-ground pool and was shocked and heartened by how many people wrote back with contributions ranging from $100 to $500. Jennifer has heard Amy tell this story dozens of times. Still, Jennifer didn't apply it to her own life until she needed to raise $3,000 quickly to fund the initial stages of the documentary on women's experiences with abortion. During a phone conversation with her mother one day, she realized that she had a whole community of untapped pro-choice women in Fargo—friends of her mother's who had watched Jennifer grow up—who would want to support her. Like Amy, Jennifer was moved by the generous donations and surprised to learn that she had a "donor base."

Meanwhile, Karin had personal contacts in Saarbrücken that served to help her in the organizational aspects. Her sister, who not surprisingly also used to work in a bakery, hooked her up with her first meeting. "My sister's ex-boss was very open to the idea and called two of her colleagues to tell them that I was going to come and speak to them about the project," Karin said. Soon after Karin made her pitch, she got confirmation from those three owners of their involvement, one of whom was in charge of eight retail outlets. Rolling with the momentum, Karin contacted the office of the Professional Federation of Bakers, told them her idea, and asked if they could help her contact their members. Karin had uncovered her natural constituency—the women in these bakeries immediately saw the value of supporting this project. Since most of their sales staff is female, they were sensitive to how many women were affected by violence. After only a few weeks, Karin was able to secure confirmation from thirty bakeries. Together they would distribute a total of 330,000 Stop Rape bread bags.

Since her grant was only $10,000—and that was used for printing and distribution of the bags—Karin needed to get almost all of her materials and labor donated. She got someone to contribute the design and logo and she asked the Family Planning Association and their local networks, which included the city government's equal opportunities officer, to take care of most of the media work, which turned out to be extensive: coverage in the local papers and on television and radio; a story in *Emma*, the German version of *Ms.*; and even a documentary about the project by the Belgian feminist filmmaker—and a friend of Karin's— Marie Vermeiren, made at Marie's own expense to help get the word out. (Another example of exploiting personal resources rather than looking to the Barbara Walters of Germany or Oprah of Belgium to cover your work.) The media coverage led to unexpected support from all realms of

Karin's community, including women business owners and the mayor of her hometown, Idar-Oberstein.

The following year, 2002, Karin worked with the rape crisis center of Idar-Oberstein, a town of 40,000, to run a paper bag campaign. This time, however, the town produced the project itself, and the bakeries paid for the bags. This was a sign of Karin's success and of the commitment the community had for the campaign. Sixteen bakeries, some health food shops, schools, and a gas station distributed 75,000 bags—all without Karin lifting a finger. Later that year, a rape crisis center in Trier, Germany, replicated the campaign, distributing 87,000 bags in twenty-seven bakeries, again without any involvement from Karin. Rape crisis centers in two cities in southern Germany produced the campaign in the fall of 2003. The idea has been picked up by a number of large German cities, including Cologne and Berlin, who are using it in conjunction with the International Day for Elimination of All Forms of Violence Against Women. A big supermarket chain has committed to distribute one million bread bags with an antiviolence message. The idea has been taken across the border to Luxembourg, where the paper bag campaign will be replicated. All of the work Karin had to do up front by herself paid off in the end. Though Karin's project didn't end violence against women and girls, the local rape crisis hotlines in the cities where the campaigns happened did notice an uptick in calls about stranger rape, very likely a result of their numbers being widely distributed on the bakery bags. The media coverage the campaign received also helped raise the profile of local organizations like the rape crisis center.

Eradicating a huge, entrenched problem such as rape requires work on many fronts, and Karin's project provided a valuable element. After naming the problem and creating the resources, providing rape victims with information about antiviolence shelters and hotlines is crucial.

Karin might seem like an über-activist—and she is—but she is also a rather normal person who simply, as she puts it, spends her "free time on feminist stuff." Her success is due to a basic formula: she accessed her unique resources (in this case, bakeries) and, in her spare time (when not working as an advocate and UN liaison at the Brussels International Planned Parenthood Federation or studying at the London School of Economics), was able to slowly cobble together an antiviolence campaign that others could copy. She also kept with the project even when she was frustrated. Many times she felt like she didn't have enough money or time, or even a partner to help her with all of the details and decisions, but she persevered. Ultimately, the only difference between Karin and someone who couldn't accomplish this feat is a few less hours of sleep each night.

NO TIME LIKE THE PRESENT

This is not to say that activism is simply time. It's also timing—and good ideas put into action in an attempt to change the status quo. But what ultimately makes the difference between a project happening or not is someone willing to commit to the task. In our own activist endeavors, what often frustrates us is when others drop the ball and, out of guilt for not having done the assigned job, are suddenly unreachable. We also know that about half of the gung-ho activists who reach out to us with a great idea have lost interest by the time we write back with advice and resources. Writing to us often proves a way to let off steam rather than a first step toward a solution.

Even though the two of us think of ourselves as doers, we don't see every idea through, either. About half of the projects that we tried to take on just for *Grassroots* fell apart, or we flaked after some initial work, or the time just wasn't right for that idea to take flight. For instance, we have yet to produce a performance of *Free to Be . . . You and Me* for International Women's Day (March 8), which we've been talking about since 1999, and we dropped the idea of turning clinics into organizing spaces for about two years until the 2004 March for Women's Lives reinvigorated our interest. (We elaborate on the clinic as organizing space in a few pages.) We approached Starbucks about copying Karin's bread bag project, and got as far as talking with the woman who handles music for the Starbucks label. During the one phone call we actually had with her, this woman expressed excitement about our plan—but she has not returned our phone calls since then and we have yet to learn who the appropriate Starbucks person is to actualize this project. In other words, for every great example in this book, there are dozens of ideas that never make it out of the lightbulb stage. We understand how easily one can lose sight of a project, and yet we can't help but think that if all of the flakers followed through on one project or activist inclination, the world would be a very different place.

Catherine Megill is among the few who do too much. The story of how her hosting network, Haven, came to be is a quintessential activist tale: a brainstorm in a young, idealistic person—who had no idea what she was beginning. Fresh out of college, this Ottawa native with waist-length strawberry-blond hair began working at the National Abortion Federation (NAF), a D.C.-based network of abortion providers. Catherine was drawn to this work for both political and personal reasons.

Years earlier, eight days after she turned fourteen, Catherine found out that she was pregnant. It was 1990 and she was able to get an abortion relatively easily since Canada doesn't have any legal restrictions in any trimester and abortions are paid for by the state. At fourteen, she thought she was far too young to have a child, and she has never regretted this decision. "I had to lie about my age," says Catherine, "because the age of consent for *all* medical procedures, according to hospital rules, is sixteen." Somehow the hospital managed to process her health card for payment without discovering that she was underage. The political component of the procedure didn't strike her until a few years later, when she learned that the abortion rights she accessed had only been in place since 1988, a mere two years before her pregnancy. (The Canadian version of *Roe v. Wade* is known as the Morgentaler decision, after the doctor who spent time in jail for openly doing abortions with the goal of changing the law. Before Morgentaler, abortions were technically legal but only when approved by a hospital panel of three doctors. Friendly panels were hard to find.) "If I had gotten pregnant two years earlier, what would have happened to me?" she wondered, chilled by the randomness of the timing. She then began making connections between her own story and the politics around abortion.

Perhaps she would have ended up working in the field of reproductive rights regardless of her own experience, but the personal lens made her see all of the weak spots in that medical right. At NAF, Catherine's primary job was managing their hotline, which received dozens of calls daily from women looking for the abortion clinic closest to them, or funding help, or advice to overcome state restrictions. A typical call might be like the story of S.J., who needed $1,300 for her abortion. She was twenty-one weeks pregnant and

twenty-three-years old with two children already and was
dealing with an abusive boyfriend. Or A.C., a fourteen-year-
old who was twenty-four weeks pregnant and afraid to tell
her mother.* Through the stories of hundreds of women
with desperate needs, Catherine learned of the big obstacles
to getting abortions in the United States: such as being
forced to wait twenty-four hours when you have already
driven for many hours to get to the clinic (making a one-day
procedure take two days); or being under eighteen in one of
the forty-four states that require written permission from
parents; or living in one of the thirty-three states in which
Medicaid doesn't reimburse for abortions. She also discovered the ways women were working around these barriers—
through services that hosted women traveling great distances,
judicial bypasses for minors, and financing networks (like
those gathered under the National Network of Abortion
Funds) for those who can't afford the $300 to $2,800 for the
procedure. "At the hotline, we did a lot of collaborative funding, clinic negotiating, and travel coordinating," says Catherine. "We also had a small abortion fund that I administered."

After more than a year of living inside the Beltway,
Catherine moved to New York City in 1999 to work at Westside Women's Clinic, one of the few clinics in the United
States that provides termination procedures through the
end of the second trimester, up to twenty-four weeks. Every
state has different laws regarding abortion, including how
late into a pregnancy they will perform them. Most clinics,
regardless of locale, only provide abortions up to fourteen
weeks. Westside served many women who were coming from
far away and often required later-term procedures. The later

*These were both real cases, subsidized by the Third Wave Foundation's
abortion fund.

the pregnancy, the longer it takes to dilate the cervix. Sometimes it's a few hours but it could take two to three days.
Dilation is spurred on by medication, metal dilators (for first-
trimester procedures only), and in the form of sticks of sterile seaweed that absorb moisture and gently expand the
cervix. After dilation, the doctor employs suction, forceps,
and/or curettage to remove the lining of the uterus. Many of
Westside's patients couldn't even book an appointment because they were without a place to stay for the two nights required for them to prepare for their procedure.

At the clinic, Catherine spoke with women who needed
funding and she redirected them to the member funds of
the National Network of Abortion Funds (NNAF). However, she wasn't prepared for the number of women looking for a place to stay, rides, or meals. She knew and had
worked with two informal, cash-free networks of volunteers
who provided this type of practical support—the Cleveland
Abortion Network and Northern California's Access. "I always knew that I could offer [this type of] support as an
individual, but I came to realize that there really was an impact on funds from not having this service available," says
Catherine. "And sometimes I couldn't raise the money, which
was the worst."

She decided to let the social worker at Eastern Women's
Clinic (one of the other abortion clinics in New York City)
know that her couch and a home-cooked meal in her Brooklyn apartment were waiting for any woman who needed it.
(Catherine couldn't make this same offer to the women she
counseled at Westside, because it was deemed a conflict of
interest.) There were already two women in the Brooklyn
Pro-Choice Network, Rachel Friend and Lee Pardee, on the
social worker's informal "can call" hosting list—but there
was no organized system. Soon Catherine was getting so

many requests to sleep on her couch that she was afraid she
might have to refuse someone eventually. A fund in Philadelphia sent someone her way on a weekly basis—and soon
Catherine realized that she needed to get help. She sent an
e-mail to the New York Abortion Access Fund, a recently
formed abortion fund in New York, and the Brooklyn Pro-
Choice Network, a longtime escorting (and occasional hosting) group, asking if other advocates would volunteer their
space and time. She decided to formalize the process and
name the group the Haven Coalition—or Haven, for short.
Soon there was a network of fifteen to twenty volunteers
whom she interviewed over coffee, going by her gut to determine who passed the screening process. Primarily, she
wanted to make sure that the hosts were stable, kind, open-
minded, and weren't looking for a captive audience to pros-
elytize about abortion (either for or against). Jennifer was
one of the first new hosts.

The network of volunteers now works like this: a call
comes in to one of the clinics with which Haven works. The
clinic counselor assesses what the patient needs. If it's a bed
or an escort, the counselor calls a central Haven number
(just a cell phone that one volunteer's sister donated) and
makes a request. The Haven coordinator calls either a volunteer who has signed up for that day or, if no one has,
starts going down the list of volunteers until she gets a
taker. If no one can host, then the coordinator herself will
take the request. When called on, a volunteer is given the patient's name, age, how many weeks pregnant, and whether
the woman is traveling with her mother, a partner, or a
friend or sister. The host is instructed to pick up the client
before 6:30 p.m., when the clinic closes, and to bring her
back at 7:30 a.m. for the next phase of the procedure.
Sometimes being a host is low-impact, like having a very in-

dependent houseguest. Other times, the woman getting the abortion needs a ton of attention and affirmation—because she is sad that her parents aren't supporting her, feels alone because she didn't tell anyone she was doing this, or is having awful cramps and can't sleep.

Catherine worked at a clinic, so she was familiar with the late-second-trimester abortion process and had access to medical information and guidelines for these procedures. In this organic and haphazard way, she built the guidelines that are given to the hosts (things like no eating after midnight as it interferes with getting general anesthesia the next morning, and Advil or Tylenol but not aspirin because it thins the blood and can cause uterine bleeding).

In the summer of 2002, there was an article in *The Village Voice* about Haven and suddenly it was no longer just Catherine and her couch. By that time, Catherine was getting ready to return to Canada to attend medical school and become an abortion provider. "It was wrenchingly hard for me to leave Haven," she says. "I left it in the hands of someone who was fabulous,* which helped." But it was hard for Catherine to leave supporters, community, and this cause—in two short years she had created a thriving network that attracted passionate volunteers and helped hundreds of women. "Still, if I stayed, I would be choosing an activist path which I knew others were doing and doing well," says Catherine, "and not a medical path, which not as

---

*Initially, Catherine left Haven in the hands of Shauna Shames, a dynamic young activist from San Francisco, whom we quote in Chapter 2. Shauna has since passed the reins herself in order to attend graduate school in public policy. We are confident that Shauna will eventually become a senator—if not president. Now that Shauna has moved on, the coordinator's job is shared by three volunteers. Haven has grown, and they can hardly keep up with patient need for a place to stay.

many abortion rights activists take although the need for abortion providers is dire."

While Catherine is finishing up premed in Montreal, she works at a homeless women's shelter. She still informally offers her couch to any patient who needs it—but without many takers. After all, as Catherine pointed out to us: "There are as many abortions in the city of New York every year as in the entire country of Canada—around 100,000. Besides, abortions are paid for here, so the few hundred in travel expenses isn't so prohibitive." True, it's their only expense.

Haven is an inspiring success story, but it started off as just Catherine's couch and a good—even simple—idea. In fact, if Catherine had started with grand ambitions, she might have been too daunted by the work ahead of her to take action. "As I was forming Haven, it never dawned on me that I was building this activist group. It was so small. I didn't even think of it as an organization." The most important thing Catherine learned, she now says, is that creating an organization "doesn't have to be fancy. With a cash-free organization, you don't need to have a board or insurance," says Catherine. "You don't have to start out by saying you want to become a group like Haven—if you work at a clinic, you could just say, I want to find a way to provide better or more complete services to the patients."

In her own life, Catherine is now quick to make the connections between personal choices like abortion and the larger political environment, which is why she plans to attend medical school. Haven began because, in effect, Catherine was shocked and upset by the realization that if she had gotten pregnant two years earlier, she would have had no choice about whether to have a baby (she suspects her minister father would have prevented any therapeutic abortion board from granting such a request). Yet, though Catherine is intensely political, Haven doesn't promote politics—it is dedicated to "supporting women as opposed to women's rights," says Catherine. "We don't only help the women who are having abortions for feminist reasons." Providing direct access and resources, as Haven's hosts and Catherine do, is certainly a part of women's rights and a larger political goal, even though political education is not what they prioritize with clients.

UNLIKELY ORGANIZING SPACES

Haven doesn't vet the beliefs of the patient, which we think is appropriately sensitive to how vulnerable the woman may be at that moment. It is also problematic if we take seriously the need to change the system. After all, the reason that a woman is in the position of needing hundreds or even thousands of dollars to pay for an abortion as well as someone to put her up for the night is due to a series of political decisions that are hostile to women, starting in 1976 with the Hyde Amendment banning federal funding for abortions. Haven's work, the work of the funds, and even the work of clinics benefit people who don't necessarily support abortion rights. If you talk to clinicians, you learn that most have a story of seeing someone who normally protests outside their clinic suddenly inside it needing an abortion. In practical terms, however, we must transform the clinic into an organizing space, so those who use the services have access to the political tools and education that will preserve these services. Patients should also be urged to recognize that very personal moments usually have political consequences.

This is the crisis of the so-called pro-choice majority. If we count everyone who uses pro-choice services (from birth control to prenatal care to abortions) along with everyone who votes specifically to support this issue, then, yes, it's a majority of Americans. The fact is, though, that many people who use the services that a clinic provides (far beyond abortion) don't vote—and some who do vote, don't vote specifically to support these rights.

The two of us were bothered by this problem when we first began visiting clinics around the country on our eclectic book tour. We started reaching out to clinics in order to understand the communities we were in and to augment our own sense of what issues were critical in different locales. The abortion clinics usually provided copious information to their patients, but rarely did the posters and pamphlets make the link between using the services and politics. (Some clinics do prioritize voting, such as the Aradia Women's Health Center in Seattle, which has a poster that reads DON'T ASK FOR EQUALITY . . . VOTE IT!)

Instead of just pointing out what these clinics weren't doing, we brainstormed some solutions. The first idea was using clinic volunteers to add a page onto the intake form that would, in effect, register the patient to vote (if she wasn't already registered) and ask if the clinic could contact the patient around election time to remind her to vote and make sure she had a way to get to the polls. Two wrinkles in that plan emerged right away. The first was that clinic advocates were resistant to bringing up politics and civic responsibility during a potentially emotional and certainly personal time. We countered that politics is already in that decision, whether or not they are building on that political presence to strengthen the pro-choice cause. In fact, perhaps it's pro-choice advocates' reluctance to make political facts a part of the experience that contributes to the ambivalence of many patients. After all, on any given day that a woman is sitting in a clinic, Congress is on Capitol Hill potentially debating stem cell research, the D&X procedure (also known as the "so-called partial-birth abortion"), or contraceptive coverage. The second issue is that while every clinic could do voter registration, only for-profit clinics can lobby for patients to vote for a certain candidate or issue (nonprofit, 501(c)(3) clinics, like Planned Parenthood's eight hundred affiliates, are barred from partisan lobbying).

When we ultimately gave a presentation on our findings for the NAF annual conference, our takeaway message was to have an in-house person (this could be a volunteer, intern, or a representative from a voting rights group who actually sat in the lobby doing voter education, voter registration, and consciousness-raising about the connection between this office visit and our government. For those clinics that didn't have ready access to a volunteer stream, it provided impetus to reach out to local college women's groups or even the League of Women Voters to collaborate.

A couple of years after our NAF talk, we decided to create a simple postcard for I'm Not Sorry Day that listed various ways a patient could contribute to the pro-choice cause. The card reads "You had an abortion, but you don't have to be sorry" and lists resources such as information about how to start a fund, how to host a fund- or consciousness-raiser for a group. It also simply urges you to tell your own abortion story. That last is actually the most radical—and perhaps the most daring—thing to do.*

---

*Shortly after we wrote this, Barbara Ehrenreich used her *New York Times* column to make a similar point in a July 22, 2004, editorial titled "Owning Up to Abortion."

EVERYDAY ACTIVISTS

Telling one's story as a radical act points to how activism can take place through a small detail rather than in a grand job. In other words, you don't have to be a women's studies major to work for reproductive rights. Moreover, if you are a women's studies major, you don't have to get a job at NOW or Planned Parenthood to prove your degree worthwhile. Many feminist and activist types have a hard time seeing their mainstream job prospects as anything other than a giant detour from their values. It's important to recognize that any location where an activist finds himself or herself has the potential to become an activist space.

Chelsea Hoffman, a Drew University graduate, used to worry that she was off track. After graduation, the then twenty-two-year-old, moved to Washington, D.C., and began working at a Borders bookstore. At first, she had difficulty recognizing her job at Borders as an effective use of her women's studies degree. Eventually she figured out that she was, in her words, a "feminist satellite." Outside of work, she was helping her fifteen-year-old half sister, Iris, who was struggling with an eating disorder. At work, when people would come in seeking books about eating disorders, Chelsea began drawing out these customers, acknowledging their interest in anorexia and, she hoped, making them feel less alone.

Over time, she decided her Borders job was not fulfilling and moved back home to Martha's Vineyard. Around then, her five-year high-school reunion came up. Chelsea soon found herself back at her alma mater, the all-girls boarding school Dana Hall in Wellesley, Massachusetts, and reminiscing with her former classmates. At first they simply recalled the good times, but then they began talking about the isolation some of them felt as a result of going away to school at such a young age as well as the preponderance of eating disorders. "One friend told me she was essentially on suicide watch for her roommate for all of junior year," says Chelsea. "[The suicidal girl] didn't think that there was any adult at Dana Hall that she could trust."

Chelsea surmised that the situation at Dana Hall probably hadn't changed in the five years since she left. She decided to write a letter to the twenty classmates who had attended the reunion, recapping what they had discussed and requesting their support when she contacted the head of the school to talk about eating disorders. "I maybe got six or eight responses," says Chelsea, but the activist ideas she got were exciting to her. One classmate, for instance, suggested a four-year women's health course; another proposed bringing in an eating disorders expert like Kate Dillon, the plus-sized model and recovered anorexic, to speak at the school's annual health day; a third suggested that since students don't always trust the administration to help, they should be empowered to support—in the form of a peer education network—other students who were going through a bad time. Chelsea sent these suggestions to the head of the school along with a homemade resource kit containing printouts from useful Web sites and a packet of fliers that she got from the Eating Disorders Coalition for Research, Policy and Action. The crown jewel of her efforts came when she received a response inviting her to address the administration if she was ever in Wellesley. "Unfortunately, I haven't been in the area yet," says Chelsea. "I forwarded the positive response to my classmates and then that was the end of it for me."

While Chelsea's participation is finished, she started a fertile process that could grow in many directions. First of all, she galvanized her peers' experiences and allowed them to see that this wasn't merely a case of a few of them suffering from depression or having eating disorders; it was a larger, more universal problem—one of the most intractable of feminist issues as a matter of fact. The media have long been the favored target of feminists concerned about body image as evidenced in films such as *Killing Us Softly* and *Beyond Killing Us Softly: The Strength to Resist*, or books such as *The Body Project* and *The Beauty Myth*, along with dozens of other books, articles, and videos that support this accusation. Beyond critiquing the media, though, even feminists haven't provided much in the way of solutions. Chelsea and her friends don't have it figured out either, but they are acknowledging that the root of the problem is not so much measuring ourselves against Gwyneth Paltrow as being afraid to talk honestly about where we are with body image. Chelsea was the match that lit the rest of the actions, and she left her friends and school administrator with the resource guide and many other ideas on which to build.

As an instigator, Chelsea already served an important role without providing the final steps, but it's never too late to revisit your project. In fact, having some distance between the initial spark of an idea and devising an action is good for clarity. We know from our own lives that when we first recognize an injustice, we are often distracted by the cynicism of others and compromised by our own righteous anger. We are so focused on ideals that we sometimes entirely lose sight of the goal. Yet urgent problems like eating disorders and access to reproductive freedom seem to have a long shelf life and there will never be a shortage of other issues to take on. The sheer enormity of all the world's problems can be paralyzing to contemplate tackling, which is why it's important to remember that getting involved even in seemingly small ways can have a far-reaching effect.

Sometimes, what comes out of this time in one's twenties is that you learn you don't want to be an "activist" in the traditional sense of the word. You sort of want to have a regular life. You like those extra hours of sleep. You don't want to have an opinion about the war or have to show up on a freezing cold Saturday to protest it. You need to earn a decent salary to pay your rent and you want a little extra to go shopping. Or, in fact, you want to be hard-core and live in a tree like environmental activist Julia Butterfly Hill did to protest the felling of old-growth redwoods by the Pacific Lumber Company. The point is you are figuring out what role activism will play in your life. But *not* tackling the issues that keep you awake at night, even in small ways, is even harder. The problems rarely cure themselves and you can only ignore them for so long. By your early twenties, you are coming out of a time in your life where you had both freedom and structure. Now the structure is up to you, and that comes with responsibilities. This is the time to take an accurate accounting of your life and figure out what you already do that contributes to the greater good. You don't have to take the world on your shoulders—you just need to take advantage of the opportunities your life provides for creating social justice.

|||||||| chapter 5 | The Activist at Work

"Activism should be directed at achieving immediate changes in daily life."

—Vaclav Havel, first president of the Czech Republic

AMY AND JENNIFER

The two of us make our living partly as writers, partly as lecturers, and partly as consultants for nonprofits such as the Ms. Foundation for Women and First Nations Development Institute. However, we mostly spend our time doing unpaid work: writing fund-raising letters, giving advice to organizations about how to get an audience for their events, and being research librarians for students and journalists. The hours we put in to get that work done while still paying the rent can be overwhelming.

While we had been making our living as writers and activists for years before publishing *Manifesta* in October 2000, the release of our first book was a pivotal moment for us. Superficially, authoring a book would make us more visible and successful as writers. More significantly, many of the theories and opinions we had developed over the years were going to be open to feminist scrutiny. We suddenly understood that sitting around with each other diagnosing problems within "the movement" was different from making a public critique. It behooved us to propose a solution or risk looking like ungrateful snots with nothing to offer in place of the feminist mode we were knocking. The stakes were much higher, in other words, and we were scared of the potential reaction to some of our arguments. Vulnerabilities aside, we were also excited to get out and start signing books.

Our publisher met with us months before *Manifesta* hit the shelves to discuss publicity. They promised us they would pursue radio interviews and print media, a Barnes and Noble reading in New York, and a trip to Boston or San Francisco. When Amy suggested they try to book us for City Arts and Lectures, a popular series in San Francisco that is broadcast live on NPR, the director of publicity let us know how competitive the booking was for City Arts and how unlikely it probably was that we would get on. It immediately became clear that our fantasy of a glitzy tour with an expense account was not in the future for this feminist book—or *most* first books, as they reminded us. The PR department would do what they could to ensure a healthy launch; the rest was up to us.

Our cluelessness about how the publishing industry worked helped us in our quest to get the word out about our book. Swinging between inferiority and superiority com-

plexes, we decided that nobody was too small or too big to
enlist for help. We didn't know that we couldn't get the
"important" gigs, so we didn't know not to try. We reached
out to long shots, people we hardly knew, anyone we had
ever met who had an affiliation with a university, worked at
a bookstore, or was an intern at a magazine. Amy, it turned
out, had a tangential connection to City Arts and Lectures—
years before, she had helped them create a Third Wave
feminism panel, so she contacted them. We were not un-
smug when they said yes.

We were quick studies in the core elements of publicity,
such as providing an angle, using contacts, making endless
phone calls, and being persistent. We developed our own
PR strategy: though book publicists primarily target book
reviewers, we believed that *Manifesta*'s themes were more
likely to resonate with editors of the political pages and
(paradoxically) the lifestyle sections. If we wanted coverage
in *Brill's Content*, we pointed out that *Manifesta* devoted an
entire chapter analyzing the media. For *Jane*, we underscored our defense of girlie culture. Our audience wasn't
necessarily the people who read *The New York Times Book
Review* but readers of *Bust* and campus publications. Our
reviews and coverage in those types of magazines probably
sold as many books as our tepid review in the *The Times*.

Two weeks after publication, we had been featured on
three different shows on NPR; spoken at City Arts; lectured
at Mills College, Sonoma State, and the University of Virginia; and had visited independent bookstores in Berkeley,
Portland, and New York. We slept on friends' couches
and ate at Taco Bell—or at Whole Foods when we wanted
to pay penance for our bad eating habits. People heard us
on the radio and then e-mailed to invite us to their universities. As we gained momentum, we got inspired and we

would cold-call a place where we knew no one and offer to visit their campus or organization. It was initially humiliating placing these calls—trying to make the case that they should have us speak *and* that they should pay us—but people said yes more often than not. Within the first year of the book's publication, we had spoken at some fifty universities, organizations, and bookstores. We were certifiably popular lecturers and the book was selling well. Most important, we had figured out how to book a tour ourselves.

We decided to treat our homemade tour more as an organizing trip than a book publicity junket. Rather than sit in our dank Holiday Inn drinking coffee, we decided to take advantage of cities and towns we weren't likely to visit again, like Milwaukee or Ann Arbor, and set up meetings with the local abortion clinic or YWCA. Our agenda was threefold: to get them to come to the university lecture, to gain knowledge of the community we were in so we didn't sound uninformed at the lecture, and to act as a bridge between myriad groups we contacted in each town.

By the summer of 2001, a lecture agency approached us offering representation. We were flattered, given that their roster included people like Susan Faludi and Howard Zinn (among many other public intellectuals whose work we admired), and we were eager to hand over the legwork of booking engagements. However, after a year of their arranging some twenty events for us—almost all of which came through our personal contacts—we realized that in effect we had already become lecture agents. It made no sense to hand over 30 percent of our fee to a third party, especially since they didn't have the contacts or interest in women's studies departments and women's centers that we did, and what's worse, they referred to us as the "Manifesta girls" when pitching events, which alienated many a women's studies professor. So we left and formed our own speaker's bureau: Soapbox, Inc.

Soapbox is our activism at the office. We took charge of resources that we had been handing over to someone else, and we created a business that can support our feminist peers and colleagues in getting the word out about their work and books.

Soapbox has been a business success—we booked fifty events for ourselves and others in the first year—but mainly it has been an activist success. Building a new business forced us to be the bureau we thought feminists needed rather than try to coerce an existing agency to meet our needs—and then complain when they didn't. (To be fair, we are now a bit more sympathetic to our feckless agency, having walked in their shoes—if only a bit.) Starting Soapbox forced the two of us to finally begin charging for work we used to do for free.

That last point—getting paid—is imperative to recognize as a form of activism. Feminist or activist work is rarely valued financially, either in the marketplace or by feminists and activists. A significant portion of the speaking we do is still for free or at reduced fees, but not being paid at all is a major reason people burn out. Free work not only keeps you poor, but can also send a message that your work is inferior in some way. To get over this fear of charging—we initially felt squeamish asking for $500 to $1,000 to speak to students—we had to justify the fee by comparing ourselves to other grass-roots activists. Tavis Smiley, for instance, gets $25,000 an appearance; Michael Moore commands at least $30,000. Political celebrities like Jon Stewart charge upward of $100,000!*

*We don't mention progressive female speakers because even the most popular feminists—Gloria Steinem, Naomi Wolf, and Rebecca Walker—charge no more than $15,000 each, and they often speak for less.

All of the unpaid spadework we did to give *Manifesta* a healthy life now meant that we could make (a little) money off of those resources, and we took the opportunity to financially value our hard work. In addition, we created a new resource that provides ongoing benefits for the women's movement as a whole. What we were doing has a symbiotic relationship with young feminists on campuses: we were figuring out how to create a speaker's bureau just as student program boards were figuring out how to turn their desire to bring Rebecca Walker or Inga Muscio to campus into a reality. It's been gratifying seeing students tell their administrations and student governments that while it's awesome to bring in a hypnotist who'll put students to sleep for $5,000, maybe that money could be better spent waking people up with the Guerrilla Girls. Selling *Manifesta* and creating Soapbox amount to more than personal validation for us; any feminist book or speaker that is popular shows that feminism is alive and kicking, despite the constant obituaries in the media.

*   *   *

I am an OBGYN physician, newly relocated to Cape Cod, Massachusetts. Since arriving, I have heard virtually nothing about violence against women. I would like to sponsor a campaign and a work session, if this is not being redundant. I work out of Cape Cod Hospital in Hyannis.

Thanks,
Steven Blumberg
Hyannis, Massachusetts

There is a reason why so many people fall in love with a co-worker or spouses get jealous of one's office mates. Most people spend more time at their jobs than anywhere else. Thus, as Steven Blumberg asserts, work is an obvious place to incorporate activism. The most universal quality of a job is that it takes up so much time, leaving so little energy for our personal pursuits. Being overscheduled and overwhelmed at work also gets in the way of one's ability to give back to the community or change the world. *Do I have time to join an organization, give an hour a week to be a literacy volunteer (plus the transportation time it takes to get there), rake leaves or shovel snow at the retirement home?* The problem is that activism is seen as another thing to add to one's never-ending to do list, rather than something organic to one's life.

Given the sheer hours dedicated to working, it greatly benefits activism to make it part of one's job, not an extracurricular activity pursued through NOW, the YWCA, or Amnesty International.

This wasn't always true. Within the feminist movement, many hoped that these alternative—and inherently progressive—spaces would be vital enough to become the new mainstream. Others tried to add egalitarian principles to the existing power structure. The title of bell hooks's famous book *From Margin to Center* encapsulates this same process. Unfortunately, the feminist margin—like any radical margin—has never grown to be as encompassing or long-lived as traditional jobs and lifestyles. Today, this leaves feminists with the challenge of taking our hard-won values back to the mainstream—and continuing to drain it of sexism or other injustices. Conventional jobs, institutions, and politics (that is, "the center") still need to be transformed, especially since these core structures of American society (banks, media, government, and schools) are where most people are employed and living their lives.

People just getting started in their careers seem particularly flummoxed by this. Perhaps this anxiety is due to the fact that, until now, they haven't experienced their lives as divided into work life and real life. In college, this isn't the case—you are the same person in class as you are in the dorms—but jobs bring work friends, work clothes, and ways of appearing that may not mesh with who you really are. Younger people tend to worry more about making a difference in the world and, if they chose a mainstream profession, often see their job as being in conflict with their ideals. We meet tons of students about to graduate who are incredibly anxious about making money and appearing to have compromised their values. It seems unimaginable to them that they could perform a job that paid adequately without somehow becoming corrupted or compromised.

We try to assure young people that they're not abandoning their values if they take a job that is outside of "the movement." Being in a secure or lucrative or for-profit workplace does not mean they have to sell out. In the case of the Indigo Girls, who were criticized for signing with a major record label, their contract with Epic afforded them a rare ability to produce and distribute records by other local musicians, to invest in lesbian-owned restaurants, and to help Honor the Earth fund an alternative wind-power initiative in the Midwest. The challenge for any idealistic worker is to find ways to be an activist from where you are, rather than trying to jam good deeds into the margins of one's life. If the point of activism is to be effective, consider this: you often have more influence as an employee or employer than you would as an agitator from outside. You know how decisions are made, who has veto power, and (we hope) you have the sympathetic ear of your fellow workers.

You'll never know what you can accomplish from a place of traditional power until and unless you try. In fact, it is frequently mainstream professions and companies that have the resources to meet our utopian idea of a workplace. (You know, one that pays a living wage, has great benefits, safe working conditions, reasonable hours, and a subsidized cafeteria.) Starbucks, for instance, is hated for squeezing out the mom-and-pop coffee shops, but it provides even its part-time employees with health insurance, prompting the two of us to consider working there for twenty hours each week. It impedes our larger goal of a fair and just society to ignore the value of huge corporate entities, pegging them as devoid of progressive attitudes and responsibilities.

There is no guarantee that a public service job will match your vision of the ideal workplace either. In our experience, young people working in the nonprofit sector are frequently disillusioned by "not having a voice" and the hidden hierarchies in a workplace that promotes egalitarianism. Workers tend to struggle with similar challenges no matter where they're employed—but the raised expectations of more pious jobs breeds resentment. Many of the nonprofit corporations—otherwise known as 501(c)(3)s—that were founded during the early days of the women's movement, for example, continue to be run by the founding members who are loathe to hand over authority to a new generation—yet still expect the investment and interest of young people. The women's movement has the same problem. There is growing consciousness of this conflict, but younger activists are more likely to start their own project or organization than fight for decision-making power in established organizations.

FROM CENTER TO MARGIN

Even if your job won't exactly mirror your beliefs, it can
certainly be influenced by your values. As we've discussed
before, activism is accessing the resources you already have
in the service of social justice. You have resources whether
you work at the feminist bookstore Bluestockings *or* at *The
Wall Street Journal*, but they're different resources.

Workplaces have long been sites for social good, whether
or not it's political—from being a prime place to get spon-
sors for the AIDS Walk to businesses adopting a highway
for litter patrol. If you start from that vantage point, you
enter into a long history of workers changing the workplace and their communities at large from within. In the
early years of industrialized capitalism, workers discovered
that their power lay in their numbers—if one quit, he or she
was replaceable, but if they all quit, the company couldn't
succeed. Trade unions were created to harness this collective power and ultimately to establish protective agreements
for the workers, such as overtime pay, safe conditions, and a
decent wage. Not only did unions improve working conditions, they became political forces unto themselves, determining the course of elections and lobbying the government.
Unions helped to define the worker as a citizen who should
be broadly politically engaged, not solely through elections
and special-interest groups.

Unions still offer organizing opportuinities for the worker.
Lauren Young, for instance, was a thirty-three-year-old
senior writer at *Smart Money* magazine in 2001 when she and
thousands of other Dow Jones employees got a provocative
e-mail from their union representative. The e-mail asked
if union members would prefer that their insurance plan
cover contraception. "Of course, I would," Lauren posted

back. "At $35 a pack, you'd have to be crazy not to want your birth control pills covered." She had been vaguely perturbed about the issue before, but this e-mail solidified her feelings that the insurance plan was sexist. It was patently unfair that the Dow Jones Corporation, an owner of *Smart Money* (it's a joint venture with Hearst), didn't cover contraception but did cover Viagra.

Lauren learned that the e-mail was part of an alliance between her union and Planned Parenthood Federation of America (PPFA). PPFA has had a Fair Access to Contraception campaign since 2000. Their first major victory came when a Tacoma, Washington, pharmacist named Jennifer Erickson discovered that her employer would not cover her pills. She called Planned Parenthood and was hooked up with their Fair Access to Contraception campaign as well as lawyers from the Western Washington Affiliate to represent her. *Erickson v. Bartell Drug Company*, decided in June 2001, established that excluding contraceptives from prescription drug coverage was a form of sex discrimination. Since that decision, twenty states have voluntarily mandated that employers who offer prescription drug benefits also cover birth control.

A key element to cases like this is understanding that employers, not insurance companies, determine employee benefits—something few people seem to know. If employees want to change their policy, their first step is to make a pitch to their bosses about contraceptive coverage. In addition to being egalitarian, the argument for coverage is actually very strong. It is cost effective to keep a woman from an unwanted pregnancy, as most abortions will cost more than a year of pills and a standard baby delivery (one day in the hospital and an epidural) costs twenty-five times as much. Planned Parenthood structured their campaign so that individuals like Jennifer Erickson could provoke change from within. This is strategic: employees have more power and more reason to change their own workplace than anyone ever could from the outside.

In Lauren's case, she wasn't alone in being peeved. Women in her office bombarded the union rep with e-mails requesting insurance plan reform, as did men—both those who helped pay for their female partners' pills and those who simply acknowledged the lack of coverage as wrong. Of course, expressing outrage is an earlier (and easier) step than doing something. Only two employees besides Lauren agreed to become plaintiffs. "I was initially shocked that more people who clearly wanted the insurance plan changed would not come forward and lend their name," said Lauren, noting that people were loathe to put themselves in a position to be deposed because they could be asked about their sex lives.

Lauren and her fellow plaintiffs made a request to Dow Jones to expand the insurance policy, which was denied. They then filed a claim with the Equal Employment Opportunity Commission (EEOC), the government office responsible for handling workplace discrimination cases. The lawyers got busy preparing their charge, while the co-plaintiffs filled out endless paperwork answering questions like "Why can't you be on your husband's insurance plan?" Over six months after they filed their EEOC charges, Dow Jones changed their insurance policy to cover contraception. In the end, Lauren's employer recognized that it was in their best interest to provide equal coverage, but it took the work of a smart union, a political campaign, and courageous individuals to help them see the light. (Lauren was actually planning on going off of the pill regardless of the outcome, but stayed on it long enough to get one pack covered, just for the satisfaction.)

What Lauren and her cohorts did is replicable and doesn't have to be limited to issues of birth control. If you want to take on a sex discrimination suit, follow her steps. First gather your evidence carefully and approach management to see if they will change company policy. If refused, you'll need a lawyer. Contact places such as Legal Momentum or Equal Rights Advocates—feminist organizations dedicated to taking on pro bono class action suits (and that can point you to a lawyer who can help, if they can't). Don't be dissuaded if they don't call you back right away. They are swamped with cases and prioritize situations with class action potential. Check their Web sites to see if your case fits the criteria for sex discrimination or sexual harassment (legal definitions are listed on the equalrights.org site) and to learn how best to gather evidence for your claim. When filing a sex discrimination suit, a charge is always filed first with the EEOC, which then determines if there are grounds for a suit. The claim must be filed within 180 days of the alleged discriminatory act and, ideally, there should be more than one plaintiff. To make this work, it helps to have colleagues on your side. It can take a lot of time and effort, but has major reverberations. As with Brenda Gillming, who sued the chicken manufacturer in Chapter One, taking on these cases has the benefit of changing the lives of thousands of others, even if you don't see the benefit personally.

CORPORATIONS CAN BE YOUR FRIEND

Although Lauren's company needed the threat of a lawsuit to nudge them, it's wrong to assume that corporations devote themselves solely to exploiting employees. It's true that corporate America is behind some of the most egregious extorting of the American people (Enron et al.), the most devastating pollution (General Electric, et al.), and the most exploitative labor practices (Nike, et al.). But America's major businesses are also in the position to enact the most potent change, if lobbied and advised well. Thus, it is a mistake for activists to write them off or slander them out of hand. For example: students at the University of Michigan, which contracts Nike to provide U of M apparel, asked the corporation to use their influence to reinstate recently fired striking workers from a plant in Mexico with whom Nike worked. Nike agreed and was successful—which is not surprising since they have more power than activists do to make changes in this situation. Cutting out Nike from the process undermines the goal of reinstating the workers. Whether we think Nike deserves to have that power or whether we like CEO Phil Knight is beside the point. Corporations can't stop themselves from being a global force. At this point it's the millions of people buying the products who constitute that force.* As a consumer, you aren't going to get to know Phil Knight the way you would the owner of your neighborhood ice cream shop, but intimacy doesn't mean that the organization is good, just small.

Lauren was actually lucky that she worked for a behemoth employer subjected to federal protection laws. Those laws, which encompass everything from the Americans with Disabilities Act to the Family and Medical Leave Act, affect only companies that employ more than twenty and fifty people, respectively, a little-known fact. Another lesser-known fact is that small businesses employ more Americans than

---

*Though we haven't prioritized consumer boycotts in *Grassroots*, they remain an incredibly effective tool to influence corporations.

do the businesses that comprise the Fortune 500. There-fore, it is critical to reform the businesses that are too small for unions or federal protection laws. As Lauren's example shows, having laws doesn't mean your work life is good—it just means that you can sue for redress. In addition to more and better laws, it helps to create models for moral employment practices. *Fortune Small Business* has a version of this. Each year they list the top ten best small companies to work for as rated by employees. The companies that make the list aren't those with fancy offices and huge bonuses, but the ones that incorporate respect for the workers' needs in addition to issuing a paycheck. Eileen Fisher's clothing company, on the list for 2003, provides employees with free yoga and spa visits, and the mission of the company includes a commitment to social consciousness, buttressed with a $1,000 annual stipend per employee for education and an-other $1,000 for wellness. Fisher's largesse pays off: employee turnover at her stores is less than 20 percent; the average in retail is more than 50 percent. *Fortune Small Business* reports that this equals a savings of $325,000 a year in recruitment and training costs. Moreover, Fisher's model suggests that all businesses would benefit from including a quality-of-life standard.

Despite how it might sound, we didn't get corporate underwriting for this chapter. It might also appear as if we think small or alternative businesses are destined to be hyp-ocritical, and are therefore advocating for working in big business because at least corporations pay. We emphasized working with corporations because the dominant activist mode has been only to protest them, which has its limita-tions. Many of our friends own or work at alternative busi-nesses or nonprofits, though, so we asked them how they create moral business practices. For instance, at Third Wave

Foundation, the highest-paid staffer cannot be earning more than twice what the lowest-paid worker makes, while at Daemon Records, employees have insurance, IRAs, and flextime.

Kathryn Welsh, the founder of New York City's Bluestockings feminist bookstore and now a student at Harvard Business School, gave us these insights on responsible capitalism: "To be a socially responsible business, in my opinion, is to keep in balance four important areas in all business decisions: your people, your environmental impact, your product/service quality, and your finances. Achieving this balance requires constant trade-offs and compromises, yet the 'greater good' should be a constant goal. Specific examples of ways that business people can be more 'socially responsible' include full health care for all employees, generous time off for both mothers and fathers with pregnancy/birth, providing on-site child care, choosing suppliers/distributors of products/services with less environmental impact (opting for organic/recycled wherever possible, finding alternative sources of energy—solar, wind, etc.)." In Kathryn's opinion, there are two companies that fit her image of a socially responsible company: Patagonia and American Apparel.

Johnny Temple owns independent publishing house Akashic Books, which he started with money he made as a bass player in the major-label band Girls Against Boys. He says: "Most Akashic book contracts with our authors are arranged as a 'profit split' rather than a per-unit royalty rate. This means that the publisher and author profit (or not) at the same level. This is an attempt to make a level playing field, to create more of a partnership, rather than the standard, more adversarial publisher/author relationship. The flip side is that since some of our books don't sell too well (especially the obscure literary fiction), then there isn't much profit to split . . . but even then, publisher and author are suffering the same plight. I adapted this model from profit-split deals I have experienced with my band and cool indie labels like Dischord Records in D.C. and Touch and Go Records in Chicago."

Finally, Lisa Jervis, the co-founder and editor of the independent feminist magazine *Bitch*, raises issues about what it means to be a "good" company: "We definitely use recycled paper (both around the office and for magazine printing, to the extent possible/affordable) and we're pretty flexible with people's schedules. Still, we don't offer benefits, which is a problem but we just can't afford it. Something we do that I feel really strongly about is that everyone makes the same amount of money. Since pay is not high it's important for us that we're all at the same level. This is less concrete, but I would never ask anyone else to do something I wouldn't do/haven't done at work."

Jane Lockett, a small-business owner in Dana Point, California, provides another progressive model: making community responsibility part of her business plan. A few years ago, Jane was on the verge of a career change. She had been working as vice president/CFO of Budget Rent A Car. She was impressed by how supportive Budget was of any time she took for mentoring a girl named Nina through Sisterfriends, an organization that matched pregnant teens with mentors who then kept them on track with their ambitions, such as graduating high school and pursuing college or a career. Sisterfriends had a particular resonance for Jane, who gave birth to her own daughter when she was seventeen. "I had Dina in the seventies, when the statistics for African American teen mothers was that [black women] will have two additional children by the age of twenty-two," says Jane. "After I gave birth, a nurse looked at me as I was getting into the taxi to leave the hospital and said, 'Okay, take care—see you next year!' She just assumed that I would be pregnant the next year." Jane was determined not to be a statistic and wanted to support other girls who had the desire for the same thing.

Jane eventually decided to open a UPS Store with her husband.* During the first four months of business, she had dinner with her three best friends and, as we've seen before, the conversation turned toward giving back to the community. All of the women agreed it was important. One friend mentioned that she knew the executive director of Laura's House, the local battered women's shelter. Jane knew she wanted to foster a supportive, community-aware environment in her new business and made arrangements to reach out to Laura's House. Her friend arranged a meeting with the executive director, Sandy Candello, who was immediately very receptive to helping them. The next step, according to Jane, was "to put a meet-date together to brainstorm this thing."

A few nights later, over a glass of wine and a fruit tray from the local deli, Jane and Sandy discussed the shelter and what the clients were going through—complete upheaval, loneliness, and fear for their lives. Jane explained the services UPS Stores provide customers—mailing services, stationery, photocopying, and office supplies—but she wasn't sure what she could provide that was of use to a shelter. "I bounced around possibly doing printing for them—invites for charity functions," says Jane. "Donations were always needed, too—so I thought of a gift drive." Then Sandy

---

*Jane Lockett actually opened a Mail Boxes Etc. but her store, along with 3,300 others, was acquired by UPS in 2003. To simplify matters, we opted to use the current brand name.

mentioned that Laura's House kept a post office box for the shelter's residents. "I asked, 'Why are you paying for that? We'll donate a mailbox to you. Besides, we can provide you with a street address so you can receive UPS and FedEx,'" says Jane. "Sandy was just elated with the possibility." (Jane didn't throw away the idea of the toy/gift drive. She collects a truck full of toys and gifts every Christmas and organizes an occasional Back-to-School drive during the fall season.)

Laura's House, like every shelter, becomes a woman's (and often her kids') temporary home—usually for just a few nights, but it can also stretch to weeks or months. Often these women have been forced to leave everything of their old life behind and the mailbox Jane set up is the only avenue for their families or friends to reach them. "The packages frequently contain food stamps or money that the women are desperately waiting for," says Jane, "and, of course, letters and care packages from family members who are worried about them." Because of the potential danger that these women face, the only way they can communicate with the outside world may be through that mailbox.

The mailbox and address are invaluable and providing such a service is decidedly low impact on Jane financially and in terms of staff. Jane estimates that the mailbox itself would otherwise cost around $300 per year with a $500 annual investment in staff hours to route the mail. The biggest commitment is that Jane has to educate her staff about Laura's House and train them to be on the lookout for abusers or other people who are trying to track down these women. Once, a man who identified himself as a law enforcement officer showed up at the store inquiring whether a particular woman was at Laura's House. "This guy said that there was a missing person report on this woman and he needed to know if she was receiving mail here," recalls Jane. "I told him that I couldn't confirm or deny it, but I immediately contacted the agency. Laura's House made some calls and found out that this guy *was* a policeman, as he had stated, but he was also a near-relative of the abuser." Presumably the officer was tracking down his relative's wife for the abuser—but whether or not that was the case, Jane didn't have to make that judgment call. The staff purposefully don't keep a list of names of the shelter's residents so as not to put themselves in the position of lying or inadvertently compromising someone's safety.

As the owner, Jane knows that she can set a tone or policy in her store, and while her staff are at work, Laura's House responsibilities go hand in hand with other employee duties like showing up on time and "providing world-class customer service." It's likely that if any of Jane's employees brought a new cause to her, she would find ways to support it, too. The lesson here is that you don't have to own your own UPS Store to provide this service. You could work at one of the 3,300 other stores and propose it to your boss, using Jane as a model.

"Ten years ago," says Jane, "I didn't realize that I had anything to share except empathy for the fact that life was difficult." While Jane has herself to credit for her success, she also believes that living an activist life is as simple as tapping into "the wealth of knowledge that pours out when women sit together over a glass of wine and a fruit tray."

Jane's commitment to service certainly has an influence on her employees. Besides learning about domestic violence and the shelter in their community, they learned that being an activist doesn't undermine Jane's business goals. Jane managed to bring her values to two large corporations, Budget and UPS. That alone can be a radical act. Lewis Platt, the former CEO of Hewlett-Packard, once could afford to be clueless about the time binds of working parents at HP— until his wife died and he was suddenly a single father. After that, Platt set an industry standard for family-friendly work policies.* Whether you are a single dad committed to flex-time or a transgendered person mid-transition, bringing your whole self to the workplace can have a profound impact on those around you. Transgendered people began provoking the creation of unisex, single-occupancy bathrooms. Before their efforts, fellow workers might not have realized that "women's" and "men's" rooms potentially leave people out.

In some ways sharing an office is as intimate as living with someone. You share a bathroom, know that your cubicle mate eats chicken salad every day and is off caffeine, and listen as your boss fights with her mother on the phone. Therefore, it's not just the benefits structure of the workplace that workers have in common; it's also the social fabric. Because employees often check their politics at the door, we lose sight of our shared political values and assume that the only thing we have in common is our work, not who we are or what we care about.

THE POWER OF ONE

Rani Chattergee† could easily be comfortable *and* political at the New York Civil Liberties Union. She used to run their teen health initiative where, among other things, she

---

*By the late nineties, nearly all employees determined their own workday schedule and 12 percent telecommute. *Source:* Reed Abelson, "A Push from the Top Shatters a Glass Ceiling," *The New York Times*, August 22, 1999.
†This name has been changed at the source's request.

distributed a pamphlet about minors' rights and took groups of teen peer educators to the New York state capitol to lobby legislators. When Rani left the nonprofit world to pursue a J.D., she had hopes of transforming law school culture with her progressive ideals, and specifically chose a school with a reputation for progressive teachers. By the end of the first month, however, she realized that rather than creating a whole community of like-minded students, the most courageous and revolutionary thing she could do was to resist the profession's culture of conformity.

After her second year of school, she worked for a summer at a high-powered law firm and experienced some of the benefits of having a lucrative and powerful job. Her employers encouraged her to take on pro bono cases such as representing a prisoner who had been denied necessary medical treatment and helping public housing tenants in the midst of eviction proceedings, and Rani saw that her law degree could be as valuable as her activist job, but with the bonus of extra cash. She was making enough money at this fancy job to pay off her student loans and give money to the Third Wave Foundation, Sakhi for South Asian Women (a domestic violence organization), and other groups that struck her passions. When it came time for graduation, she took an offer from the corporate firm from the previous summer. She assumed they would still be supportive of her commitment to law for the common good.

She soon found out that the life of an associate was vastly different from that of a summer hire. Once settled in her new job, Rani spent most of her time scrambling to surpass the minimum quota of billable hours required of all associates. Slammed by her caseload, Rani wasn't able to devote herself to any of the work she always imagined she would be doing. Her employer was no longer the support-

ive bleeding heart and she realized that the people she saw
in the high-tech elevator, gazing at the day's current events
on computer monitors, didn't share her worldview. "I saw
the daily news from an entirely different perspective once
I was at that place for real," says Rani. "The world had
changed since September 11 and people in that building
were for war, both in Afghanistan and in Iraq." Rani didn't
agree with them, and she decided that her point of view
desperately needed to be added to the conversation. She
embarked on a campaign to do just that, vowing not to remain silent in the face of rather conservative co-workers.

She became very creative in expressing her values. "After September 11, for instance, there was a lot of talk of
vengeance and bombing the Taliban," says Rani. "So one
day I intentionally left an article by Arundhati Roy called
'Why America Should Not Bomb Afghanistan' on the Xe-
rox machine. Some people were outraged. I watched the
senior associate whose office was right next to mine pick it
up and ask, 'What kind of lunatic would agree with this?
Does anyone know who this article belongs to?'" Rani took
a deep breath and then said, "It's mine." She respectfully
listened to the senior associate rant, assuming that he'd return the favor. He did and they ended up having a real exchange. It's very important to stick around for the other
point of view, if only to be knowledgeable about what you
are up against. "It turned out that he didn't know who Arundhati Roy was, and when he learned that she was a Booker
Prize–winning novelist and that I—another lawyer in the
firm—agreed with the article, he opened up a bit," she
reports. "He still didn't agree or anything, but he wasn't
dismissive."

Through this and other encounters, Rani earned a reputation as a good lunch date, one of the few who didn't rely

on small talk about the latest restaurants for conversation. After a year, though, Rani concluded that she wasn't cut out for the corporate law world. Despite the fact that women are attending law school at almost the same rate as men, the law-firm culture hadn't changed enough that it could be truly supportive of its female associates. Her firm demanded three hundred hours above and beyond the two thousand–hour quota of billable hours, thus ensuring that no one could have a personal life unless they also had a "wife" at home to take care of things. There was informal—but still potent—sex segregation when it came to mentoring. With only two female partners in her department, Rani and her colleagues found it challenging to forge productive relationships with the senior women and seek guidance from them. Meanwhile, there was no shortage of male partners for the young male hires to turn to as role models. There was no rule that men couldn't seek out female mentors or that women couldn't have male mentors, but pattern and tradition ensured that they didn't.

Women's marginalization played out in other dynamics of the office. For instance, Rani noticed that the male associates felt entitled to use secretaries for personal chores. When they started at the firm, all associates received instructions on the proper etiquette and work use of secretaries. Nonetheless, male associates had no compunction about asking the secretaries to order flowers for their wives, while Rani compensated by not feeling comfortable asking her assistant to photocopy or undertake any other task that she could just do herself.

The larger issue of entrenched sexism at high-powered law firms is one Rani could point to but didn't feel equipped to solve. Rani realized that no corporate law firm was going to meet her expectations. That's why she had to leave. As of

2003, she works for a legal services organization handling worker rights. This project is funded through foundations and doesn't charge for services. "It's a much better fit," says Rani. "I don't want my clients to be just people who can afford me—or for that matter, afford justice. The big law firms can only do pro bono because they are profitable in other ways. I understand that, but I don't want to contribute to it."

Even if most law firms aren't inherently progressive, the profession itself is meant to embody democratic values: justice, due process, and the right to an attorney. According to the American Bar Association's Web site, it "is the responsibility of the profession to insure access to justice for all by meeting not only the legal needs of those who can afford a lawyer but also the legal needs of those individuals and communities that cannot." People make fun of lawyers as ambulance chasers and crooks, but most disempowered people need a lawyer at some point, just like we need dentists, doctors, and accountants. Unlike other professions, though, lawyers subscribe to a built-in professional rule that requests and enables attorneys to do at least fifty hours of work per year without payment or expectation of payment.

Imagine if everyone realized the activist potential of a profession. Dentists could provide pro bono dental care once a week. Doctors could staff a people's clinic and organize in support of their colleagues that perform abortions. Club owners could donate their space once a month to host fund-raisers. Rock stars could give a percentage of each ticket to a local shelter. Grocery store clerks could organize deposits on bottles to be given to homeless people.* If we

---

*We realize that many people in these professions already do their own version of pro bono work.

followed lawyers' examples, a good fifty hours per year of one's work life could be devoted to making the world better. If all writers were required to do some pro bono writing, the two of us would be industry leaders, as it seems like half of what we enjoy writing is fund-raising letters or introductions in support of other feminist books. Placing one's activism in the context of a profession also lends it legitimacy and value.

Steven Blumberg's letter to Ask Amy earlier in this chapter points to this. He perceived a lack of resources in his community that pertained to his expertise and realized that it was up to him to help fill that gap. Perhaps others at the hospital were interested in domestic violence prevention, but he took initiative and that very fact could help provoke like-minded colleagues to come out of the woodwork. Although not part of his motivation, the fact that Steve is an MD lends legitimacy to the issue of violence against women, by taking it out of the context of feminism (where it is marginalized) and treating it as a public health issue. Some of the most creative activism comes from taking an issue perceived as personal and lending it the protection of a public entity.

Naomi Berman-Potash, a hotel executive, began a campaign to open up empty hotel rooms in Houston to the overflow from crowded domestic violence shelters. The undertaking (Project Debby, named after Berman-Potash's late sister) connects a network of domestic violence service providers to 125 hotels in cities, including Houston, Milwaukee, New York, and San Diego, and gives women a place of respite for up to three days while they figure out their next move.

You don't have to be in a powerful position to use the resources of your job as a tool to help others. Jennifer's friend Kristen Monahan works at a popular wine store in New York and has organized to get wine at cost for local fund-raisers. A girl who works at a Starbucks in New York City told Amy she felt defeated because she was "just" a counter person, but ended up convincing her manager to provide meeting space, a coveted and often costly resource, for a local youth group. In overconcentrated New York City, if you can provide space, you are powerful.

The activist worker is like the activist anywhere else, a person who asks not what can be done for him or her but what he or she can do. With independent contractors, free-lancers, consultants, and temporary workers growing as a segment of the workforce, it's all the more necessary to see your individual life as part of a larger whole. Not only is it now increasingly up to the lone worker to negotiate his or her own protections and social environment; the individuals have a responsibility to embody the change they want to see at their jobs. You are no longer just a cog; you might be the whole wheel.

|||||||||chapter **6** ||| Creating Activism

"[F]or me it's just very obvious that creating art is the same as being political."

—Sabrina Margarita Alcantara-Tan, founder and editor of *Bamboo Girl*

AMY

Before college, I traveled around Europe for four months by myself. The paintings and sculptures I saw in the majestic museums in Hamburg and Amsterdam told the stories of revolutions and revolts throughout history. Until then, I had found art inaccessible because I wasn't an artist. Learning history through famous paintings opened up art to me and inspired me to pursue it as a major in college. I planned to write my undergraduate thesis on the seventeenth-century French painter Nicholas Poussin, but the summer before

doing so, I became a self-identified activist with Freedom
Summer '92. After I spent the break registering voters in
low-income neighborhoods, my art history studies suddenly
seemed very frivolous. Fortunately, I had a thoughtful adviser who proposed that I combine my love of art history
with my newly inflamed activist values. My adviser suggested that I explore the Harlem Renaissance, Artemisia
Gentileschi, or perhaps a female patron of the arts.

As a result, I ended up researching and writing about
Maria de Medici, the seventeenth-century French queen,
comparing images of her to those of Queen Elizabeth I.
The comparison was politically revealing about the status of
women in both countries. Women could inherit the throne
in England—and thus the images of Elizabeth demonstrate
her "masculine" qualities of strength: holding a scepter, looking stern and androgynous, etc. France, on the other hand,
prohibited women from ruling. The images of Maria represent her role as mother, wife, or total vixen, reinforcing
the fact that her connection to power and the state was only
through her relationship to her husband and son. By ap-
plying critical feminist thinking to my decadent art degree,
I realized that beautiful art isn't devoid of politics.

JENNIFER

Until I was twenty, I was positive that acting *had* to be my
career. Auditions consumed my life, Bernadette Peters was
my idol, and I always had a cheesey head shot at the ready.
When I finally stepped out of my teens, I spent more of my
time passionately fighting with Tom Zoellner, the right-
leaning editor of the student newspaper, than memorizing
my lines for *Measure for Measure*. Gender studies had just

come to Lawrence and reading Andrea Dworkin, bell
hooks, and Hélène Cixous was having an intense intellectual ripple effect. As the country headed into the first Gulf
War in January of 1991, it looked as if I might jettison acting altogether, until my theater teacher (and adviser) told
me and a few fellow actors about the guerrilla theater he
had done in the sixties.

Fred Gaines, my adviser and the director of the theater
department, was a cool old hippie who wore long rainbow
knitted scarves in the winter. He told us about a performance of *King Lear* at Minneapolis's Guthrie Theater that
was interrupted in order to protest the Vietnam War. Fred
also helped our quickly formed collective get $100 from the
theater department and, having planted the guerrilla theater seed, left us to our own devices.

What we decided to do was a bit heavy-handed and not
exactly artistic in retrospect: we dressed as guerrillas and invaded our cafeteria (known as Downer) on the evening that
the United States was to begin bombing Baghdad. Two-thirds
of Lawrence students were on the meal plan, so Downer was
packed. Our theater troupe was divided into two sets: the
guerrilla soldiers who stretched nylon stockings over their
faces (a universally scary look), donned camouflage gear,
and carried big, realistic-looking rifles (we rented it all from
a costume store—the majority of our $100 budget went
there); and other troupe members who were going to por-
tray hostages and were planted in the cafeteria, to look as
if they were innocently enjoying turkey tetrazzini. I was a
soldier.

At exactly 6 p.m., we soldiers burst through the front
doors, yelling and swearing. We hadn't written dialogue nor
had we any idea what real guerrillas would say, so we just
yelled obscene nonsense. I hit the lights, another soldier bar-

ricaded the doors, and we ran through the cafeteria yanking out our "hostages" and victims, dragging them away violently. (We had originally planned to stage a fake sexual assault to make the point that women will be raped as part of war, but it all happened very quickly and we were too amped up to do anything choreographed.) Another actor (a teeny upperclassman who now makes her living doing children's theater) stood on a table with a bullhorn, yelling out statistics about how many people would die in the bombing of Iraq and distributing our leaflets, which said the same. The whole protest was chaotic and fast. By 6:03, the six of us soldiers fled through the back service entrance, hostages in tow, and sprinted to the Human Rights House (a community living house on campus) where we had already arranged "amnesty."

The impact of our protest? Mixed. It was a major growing experience for the protesters—I can't recall ever feeling the kind of adrenaline surge I did before charging through Downer with a stocking over my head. Apart from our excitement, we nascent activists learned how to translate our fears about war into a tangible action. The Lawrence student body wasn't as thrilled by the experience as we were, though. "I thought it was really scary and sort of sick the way they handled it," said one student interviewed by the local paper. Administrators allowed that protest was good, but lamented the fact that we dumped the sundae bar over on the floor during the melee and skidded through the hot fudge during our escape, leaving a huge mess and the students dessert-less.

Meanwhile a few students from Pakistan thought the attack was real and even chased after us with butter knives. At the time, their seriousness in the face of our invasion supported the points we wanted to make: that safe, comfortable Americans of 1991 didn't know what it was like to have their country invaded, bombed, or terrorized. This taste of terror was meant to breed empathy in the student body. After September 11, of course, I would never stage a fake terrorist attack, but looking back, I can't believe I had the guts—in a way—to stage that protest. These days, fund-raising, writing articles, and creating public education projects take up more of my time than guerrilla theater protests do.

*   *   *

I'm a dancer, actress, playwright, and director. I believe that one of the most effective ways to move people is through performance art. I would love to help my community make some sense of the emotions we have felt since September 11th. My idea is to stage an evening of monologues, scenes, and other dance/performance pieces showing war's devastating impact on women throughout history. I need money for the space, insurance, and royalty fees for using scenes from around five plays. I would appreciate any help you could offer to enable me to do my project.

Alexia Vernon
Las Vegas, Nevada

What happens when you, like Alexia, consider yourself both an artist and an activist? As a musician, must your lyrics contain rants about the spoils of industrialism? Or do you feel you have to time-share for each part of your identity— for every hour spent sculpting, you spend an hour volunteering at the rape crisis center—until you are in a frenzy? What if, like Oscar Wilde, you simply want to create art for the sake of art, making the world more gorgeous, witty, or harmonious through your creations—and keep your politics separate? Perhaps you don't make art but love it and appreciate its potential political uses. The two of us aren't artists, for instance, but we often engage with art politically—from using designers to make invitations and agit-prop posters to purchasing watercolors and sculpture by emerging women artists for our personal "collections." More than that, we connect the organizations that we support with the artists we know—from inviting Indigo Girl Amy Ray to perform at the Ms. Foundation Awards to asking Bill T. Jones to donate tickets to a dance performance to the Third Wave auction.

Alexia's project was gratifying to her as an artist but also enabled the viewer to tap into its activist potential. She wrote the above letter to Ask Amy in the autumn of 2001. She presented her project called *Women in War* on April 18, 2002. "It was a theatrical look at war's historical, cross-cultural impact on women," explained Alexia. "It culminated in a post-performance discussion of how to use theater as a springboard for action and pacifism." Her one-time event was well attended—a big success for Alexia and the community—and is an example of how artists can use their art as an activist tool that has political significance. Meanwhile, the audience learned of other ways to communicate and work for change. Combining art with activism not only feeds the artist, but also feeds art lovers, who pick up on the political reverberations.

"Art and activism have gone hand in hand for hundreds, if not thousands, of years," writes Daniel Sinker, editor of the independent magazine *Punk Planet*, in his book of interviews *We Owe You Nothing*. "To insist that they're opposite is really denying a lot of history." To wit, punk rock is a music form that has doubled as a movement in everything from its general anti-consumerism stance to more particular critiques ranging from machoism (thanks to early nineties feminist upsurge Riot Grrrl) to abstaining from drugs and alcohol (the straight edge movement). There is an obvious link in the creative process between making art and transforming culture.

THE CULTURAL IS POLITICAL

The filmmaker Nisha Ganatra knew that she had a perspective that was missing from the typical movie plot. She grew up in the United States, raised by parents from India. She had experienced the discrimination of being gay, the conflict of holding on to her family's traditions while embracing American culture, and the subtle sexism of being a woman at film school. Nisha knew that she wanted both to draw from and to reconcile her identities with her art. Her first film was a short called *Junky Punky Girlz*, which chronicled three friends (one South Asian, one black, one white) as they go to get their noses pierced. As Nisha describes it, "For the South Asian girl, getting her nose pierced was something she wanted to do in order to reclaim her Indian culture, which she had constantly rejected in her pre-college life. For her black friend, getting her nose pierced was a way of visibly identifying with the lesbian community, and for her white friend, piercing her nose was an act of fashion. Ultimately, the South Asian girl has to come to terms with why she is piercing her nose now—is it because it is fashionable and accepted, or because she truly wants to reclaim the Indian heritage that she had forsaken?"

Nisha's first full-length feature, *Chutney Popcorn*, continued that theme of culture and identity rubbing up against each other. It told the story of two sisters, one straight and one gay, and their traditional Indian mother (played by Madhur Jaffrey, the cookbook star). The married, heterosexual daughter is initially deemed the "good daughter," satisfying the mother's needs and imagination, while the lesbian daughter (played by Nisha) is a near constant affront. This all changes when they learn that the straight daughter is unable to conceive. At that point, the gay character becomes the ideal—a fertile woman who gets pregnant so she can act as the surrogate mother for her sister's child.

"It was a comedy—a popcorn movie," Nisha says, hence the name, "rather than a serious meditation on coming out and being gay and being sterile." By making an American comedy that doesn't star Adam Sandler, Nisha challenged the traditional notion of people of color in a movie by making Indian characters more than immigrants and showing that people of color and of all genders are funny.

Aside from being a filmmaker, Nisha also wanted to be an activist. Throughout the making of *Chutney Popcorn*, she was also busy as a board member for the Third Wave Foundation, organizing their first film festival and attending meetings and fund-raisers. At first, Nisha saw her art and her politics as separate tracks and was rapidly running into the burnout zone—exhausted by how much time art-making required and conflicted about her priorities that put filmmaking over her work with her community. "For years I had been struggling to remain a good activist and also do well in film," Nisha said. "And let's face it, film school was kicking my ass in ways I never predicted. For a long time I had this guilt about pursuing my passion, which is film, and working for the community. The first sense that there was a fissure was when I couldn't get to a Third Wave meeting because of a shoot, and the gap just kept getting bigger and bigger." It wasn't until a friend pointed out that Nisha's film work was political and changing the culture in ways that benefited her community that Nisha finally had her "aha!" moment and let herself off the hook. "I mean, it was so obvious—and yet it had never struck me until someone said it," recalled Nisha. "All of the reasons that I wanted to get into film and my agenda as a filmmaker—*of course* that was political! But I was so busy feeling guilty that I didn't register voters last weekend or protest some huge injustice in D.C., that I completely overlooked what I was doing and how I could contribute in another way."

This is a dilemma that many artists face. In fact, artists who are feminist—whether in their work or in their private lives—are often treated as if they have a responsibility to make deliberately political art. Your motivation shouldn't be indebtedness in becoming an activist but rather authentic commitment. Furthermore, being a female or minority artist in a culture that doesn't value women or minorities is activist in itself. Sherman Alexie, the Native American fiction and screenwriter addressed this in a *New Yorker* piece. "Do you feel you've snubbed your culture?" asked the reporter, likely referring to both Alexie's refusal to airbrush the Native Americans in his stories and in his film *Smoke Signals* and his popular appeal. Alexie responded, "You know, I believe the American culture is so infused and so assimilated and so combined that all of us contribute to it. Being a part of it confirms all of us. And my entrance into the mainstream has changed the mainstream—forgive the immodesty—but I think my career has totally altered many people's ideas of what an Indian can do and can be . . . Not the work itself. My success, my cultural power, my influence." The reporter's implication was that Alexie must only have a Native American audience or can only uplift Indians by portraying them as sober, wronged, or spiritual. Alexie pointed to himself—a successful, culturally influential individual who is Native American and writes the truth as he sees it—and concluded that was being an activist.

Similarly, Nisha's films make a political statement by adding more brown faces and a commentary on diversity to Hollywood, as well as by simply being made by someone who is female and queer in that industry, regardless of the message of the work. It took Kathleen Hanna of Le Tigre (and a mother of Riot Grrrl) *years* to recognize that being a female musician who was making electronic music when it was a male domain *was* activism. Kathleen realized that her power was in doing her art.

Artists can use their fame or talent to raise money or awareness about political issues, but they aren't required to do that, even if they are "liberal." As fans, we have to resist wanting activist artists to be everything and taking them out of the context of what makes them powerful. Asking Ani DiFranco to speak at a conference on body image might pale in comparison to watching her perform her overtly feminist song "Not a Pretty Girl." It was her songwriting that inspired us in the first place. Artists (and celebrities) have a responsibility to be part of their community and have political values and morals, but no more or less than any citizen has that obligation. Our best bet as activists is to start where we are and use the resources already present in our lives. An artist's fame attracts critical mass and media attention to issues and organizations. It's hard to imagine many people attending the Women's Campaign Fund panel about the "partial birth abortion" ban, but easy to imagine thousands at a Rock for Choice concert. Artists bring in new potential converts, and, therefore, more money for causes. The power of art is available to anyone, because it is in the work itself, while artists are under no obligation to make their work specifically political even if they are political people or from an "oppressed" community.

ART HISTORY 101

Feminists have a unique history in combining art and politics. In the seventies, feminist artists sought to change our culture by creating a separate woman-only space and by pioneering a genre of art that had female imagery and specifically feminist intent. Judy Chicago created the first feminist art program (at Fresno State in California) in 1970 and, most famously, the epic work known as *The Dinner Party*.* Miriam Schapiro created (among other innovations) "femmages," collages that incorporate domesticity and the traditions of overlooked female artists. A wide variety of art came out of this movement in the seventies. Much of it dealt with the female body, which had always been in art, but as an object—a nude, perhaps, painted by Gauguin. Carolee Schneeman created, for instance, *Interior Scroll*, which she unfurled from her vagina as she stood naked in an art space, using the familiar nude form, but in a context controlled by the "object" herself. Meanwhile, Yayoi Kusama covered her furniture sculptures in large penis-like projectiles, making men's intimate parts the object of scrutiny— and of beauty.

---

*After years of having no home, *The Dinner Party* is now permanently housed at the Brooklyn Museum of Art. Philanthropist and patron Elizabeth A. Sackler underwrote the resurrection and preservation of this historic work. She is also creating the Elizabeth A. Sackler Center for Feminist Art at the Brooklyn Museum.

The feminist art movement of the seventies "changed everything," wrote the *New York Times* art critic Holland Cotter in 2002. "It gave a new content to painting, sculpture and photography. It pushed performance, video and installation art to the fore." Until the advent of feminist art, much of the art created by women had been downsized to "craft." But feminism renamed as art those female folk traditions: from traditional quilters in Gee's Bend, Alabama, to "high art" star Faith Ringgold, who incorporated quilting techniques in her huge fabric paintings. As Cotter recounts, the feminist art movement claimed "high art and low art, and it put folk art, outsider art, non-Western art, not to mention so-called women's art (sewing, quilting, and crafts of all kinds) center stage." Embroidery and ceramics became a part of fine art, as in the case of *The Dinner Party* installation, with its decorated plates and hand-stitched table runners. "What art in the next 30 years will look like I don't know, but feminist influences will be at its source," Cotter concluded.

By the eighties, feminists were looking to have women included in art "institutions"—museums, academic faculties, and art magazines—rather than primarily focusing on creating a separate space for women. (Separate but equal was providing a space, but it was a marginalized space.) To fight for this space, the Guerrilla Girls hit the scene in 1985. They are an inside-the-art-world gang of artists and critics who don gorilla masks to invade big shows and raise awareness of the dearth of women represented there. They print huge, stylish posters with sarcastic comments like "Do women have to be naked to get into the Met Museum?" and a wry list of "The Advantages to Being a Woman Artist." (One advantage: "Not having to deal with the burden of success.") By 2004, they had produced more than eighty posters, print projects, and actions as well as developed a college tour.

Due in part to activist critics like the Guerrilla Girls, women and minority artists were more present in the nineties, a minor trend which continues today. By the nineties, "girl power" was on the rise and women artists were working with pink, symbols of girlie-girlhood, and laying claim to parts of traditional femininity that had been presumed mere vestiges of patriarchal conditioning and not authentic. In pop culture, formidable artists like Madonna and TLC deliberately embraced stereotypes of women as if to say these female tropes were no longer traps for women that were to be avoided at all costs. In 1994, there was New York City's New Museum's Bad Girls' show, described as "a smorgasbord of feminist expression from various sectors of contemporary culture." In the late nineties, artists like Lisa Yuskavage painted gauzy nude pinups and demonstrated that the role of voyeur was no longer off-limits to women. By the millennium, artists who had worked for several decades marveled at the changed terrain, the barrier had moved *and* had become harder to see. "I have no idea what it would be like to be 21 now, in a world with Madonna, J.Lo, and Buffy, Venus and Serena, the Frida Kahlo industry, grrrll this and that, kick ass female rock stars and thousands of other powerful, famous, talented, media-savvy women," wrote the artist Mira Schorr in *Gloria*, the catalog for a 2002 retrospective of feminist art at White Columns in New York City. "[Now,] when the glass ceiling is very high and made of verilux, transparent and invisible." In contrast to today's generation of emerging artists, Schorr noted that she came of age in a time when there were no female artists taught in schools or shown in museums. At that time she had few role models; it "seemed that to be a woman artist you had to live alone on a mesa in New Mexico."

Far from condemning one to a life of desert isolation,

feminist art today is often about coming together publicly, such as with the DIY (Do-It-Yourself) feminist art and music expo Ladyfest and performances and workshops at the National Women's Music Festival. Today, feminism is expressed in pop culture—Missy Elliott's raps and Reese Witherspoon's roles—and women are reaping the benefits of having had an activist feminist art scene for more than three decades. There are thousands of examples of feminist artists (self-identified and not) in music, art, film, poetry, comic books, comedy, and sculpture. In 2002 alone, there were three major feminist art retrospectives—Judy Chicago's *The Dinner Party* at the Brooklyn Museum of Art, the aforementioned Gloria: Another Look at Feminist Art in the Seventies, and Personal and Political: The Women's Art Movement, 1969–1975 at galleries in Easthampton, New York. There are also at least two national women's museums—the National Museum of Women in the Arts in D.C. and the more recently opened Women's Museum in Dallas. Two more are due to open in 2008—one in New York City and one in Washington, D.C.

The Women's Museum in Dallas isn't explicitly feminist, which points to the confusing fact that as women's inclusion is more commonplace, politics are more likely either to be left out altogether or to be implied but not stated. It could be argued that there is a de facto political nature to a lot of art by women—such as the gathering of women musicians on one bill with the Lilith Fair. Conversely, you can be a woman in the arts and support male chauvinism, by being the one woman who "paints like a man" or the one chick allowed into the boys' club. More positively, you can also be a feminist in your private life and work in the mainstream, like the photographer Annie Leibovitz, whose work is primarily for the magazine *Vanity Fair*, or you can do art that is specifically from a feminist perspective, as the comedian Margaret Cho does. Another problem is that since the inception of feminist art, there has been a corresponding movement to discredit it. This is one of the reasons why many individual artists don't rush to identify their work or themselves as feminist.

WHAT IS ACTIVIST ART?

What makes work activist? We posed this question to Helen Klebesadel, an artist and professor who teaches classes on art and activism (and creates activist art). She is the director of the Women's Studies Consortium for the University of Wisconsin system and Jennifer's former art professor at Lawrence University. Her answer included the following five elements: it is often collaboratively made, collectively run, doesn't *require* art training or a pedigree, is process oriented, and is accessible to the public. Given Helen's definition, we immediately thought about the self-described radical intergenerational women artists collective Women Empowered through Revolutionary Ideas Supporting Enterprise (WERISE) to help answer this. It was the brainchild of three emerging female vocalists-songwriters, including Rozz Nash, a Brooklyn-based singer who believed that women artists in New York needed a support network. Her style and talent conjure a female Stevie Wonder and she lives the typical eclectic life of a struggling artist, playing gigs that run the gamut from headlining at Joe's Pub to playing Hava Nagila at a thirteen-year-old's bar mitzvah. In 1999, she attended the third part of a three-level leadership course called The Forum, a process which challenged participants to create a project within an area or community in

their lives that could benefit from development. The catch
was that the project must be led by a team and include at
least twenty to twenty-five others previously unknown to
the participant.

Rozz didn't personally know Imani Uzuri (another vo-
calist) or hip-hop performer Tomasia Kastner, but she had
long admired their work and decided to reach out to them
about the event she envisioned in response to The Forum's
challenge. Soon after, WOMON—a showcase of the three
women's work that also reached out to and brought together a diverse community of women artists—was created.
Inspired by the support for this event, Rozz, Imani, and
Tomasia sat around the kitchen table and WERISE was
born. They secured a pro bono lawyer to incorporate them,
asked the Sister Fund to donate meeting space, and assembled a mailing list from their combined friends and contacts. They put out a call for their first meeting and thirty
women artists showed up. After the first two years (WERISE
is now beginning its sixth year) and more than six hundred
members later, they assembled a creative development
board of artists and decided that each of the seventeen
board members would design and chair one of the monthly
meetings, as well as help to develop programming. "We
want all members to feel ownership over the organization,"
says Rozz.

At meetings they can share skills or gain expertise, from
learning how to transfer one's portfolio to slides to better
understanding loan applications. WERISE envisions and
supports all of its artists becoming entrepreneurs. "We
want them to learn the business side of art," says Rozz, "so
that they aren't ripped off and, more important, so they
can develop their business acumen and turn their art into
financial profit." WERISE doesn't privilege one type of art

over any other. The board itself is composed of visual artists, actors, musicians, dancers, writers, filmmakers, and more. The work is accessible to the public, too. Their annual conference at Barnard College—the International Women Artists Conference—aims to show as much work by women artists in the northeast as possible and get as much of an audience as they can there to support it, too. Rozz hopes to carry this model over to youth and build a performing arts organization for young aspiring artists. She is now in graduate school at New York University for Performing Arts Administration.

THE POWER OF DOWN THERE

There is no greater example of putting art to political use by ordinary people than the phenomenon of *The Vagina Monologues*. In 1995, Eve Ensler was a successful but somewhat obscure feminist playwright. A random conversation with a friend going through menopause led Eve to ask other women about their vaginas. Why is "vagina" a word we whisper or use a euphemism like "down there" for? Why don't women talk about their vaginas? She decided to conduct a series of vagina interviews with diverse women and ask them serious questions about their first sexual experiences, whether they had orgasms, and if they were ever abused. She also threw in more creative, fun questions like, "If your vagina got dressed, what would it wear?" and "What do you call your vagina?" The questions were designed to get women to think about their "most core part," as Jane Fonda put it. After all, it's part of every woman, not some odd secret tucked away.

Inspired by these interviews Eve wrote a series of monologues, which she first performed solo in 1996 at a small theater in Soho called HERE. Eve was overwhelmed by the audience response—women buttonholed her after the show to tell this perfect stranger something they had never told anyone before: their vagina story. These stories were complex and often painful. After hearing women's stories of rape, incest, and abuse instead of stories about their great pleasure and sex, she realized that the play was striking a chord in women and allowing them to release their stories of violence. Given the UN statistic that one in three women in the United States and the world will experience violence in her lifetime, she wanted to use the play to end violence against women, and began talking to friends and colleagues about how to do this. Eve had experience with using her work to raise money for and awareness of issues. Her early works about homeless women were often performed as benefits, and her play *Necessary Targets* was performed at the Kennedy Center for the Performing Arts in Washington, D.C., for an audience that included prominent women's groups and leaders including Hillary Clinton (then the First Lady).

Her friend, the actress and comedian Kathy Najimy, orchestrated a meeting between Feminist.com and Eve. One night in 1997, Eve met with the six-member board of Feminist.com and proposed this outrageous idea she had of doing a celebrity benefit performance of the monologues to raise a million dollars to end violence against women. That was the first mention of what would become V-Day.

The board of Feminist.com got behind Eve, joining many other women Eve had contacted. The evolving plan was to have celebrities perform the show in New York City on Valentine's Day to raise awareness and as much money as possible for antiviolence work. They began developing the now well-known alphabet rubric: the V for Valentine, Violence, and Vaginas (and, as of 2004, Vote). The first V-Day came to fruition on February 14, 1998. Winona Ryder, Susan Sarandon, Shirley Knight, and Rosie Perez starred in the sold-out performance at New York's Hammerstein Ballroom. It was a huge success; people clamored for more.

Feminist.com board members were among the first people on the V-Day Benefit Committee that coordinated the event. Susan Swan and Lauren Horn, PR mavens, worked with Marianne Schnall to create and host the V-Day's Web site; Amy, also a board member, created the original resource guide with violence statistics; and Karen Obel handled ticket sales and managed production elements. Karen was thrilled with the Hammerstein event, but noticed how limited it was in terms of audience reach. "The tickets were expensive, the event was only in New York, and the venue's capacity was only two thousand," says Karen. "I began to think about how V-Day could more broadly spread the message and the urgency of ending violence against women." These were the seeds for the V-Day College Campaign she ultimately created and directed, which is arguably the most pervasive campus action since Oxfam began asking students to fast for a day and donate their unused lunch funds to hunger relief. "To me, young people are the leaders, shapers, and messengers of the future," says Karen. "While activism welcomes everyone and it's important that people get involved in efforts that matter to them, I think that young people are in a unique position to change our world and have more to offer and to gain from being activists."

Karen realized that what happened at the Hammerstein Ballroom could happen anywhere, should happen everywhere, and that it could be done on a grassroots level by reaching out to people on college campuses. Celebrities might have been the draw in New York City, but in Madison, Wisconsin, it could be anyone from the economics major to the school librarian performing such a powerful and accessible work as *The Vagina Monologues*. The V-Day College Campaign invites members of college and university communities around the world to present benefit productions of *The Vagina Monologues* on their campuses on or around V-Day (Valentine's Day) to raise money and awareness to stop violence against women.

Karen had a full-time job and wasn't a self-described activist, so becoming the director of the V-Day College Campaign wasn't on the surface an obvious choice for her, but the project became her heart and soul. Perhaps what made Karen the right person to oversee the project was her total (almost naïve) sense that it could work. (Not knowing what one is embarking on is a key characteristic of successful activist endeavors.) Karen sent letters to every person, theater department, and group at every school she could think of, describing the college campaign and inviting participation in it. "I was purposeful and specific about who I sent the letters to," meaning this was no mass e-mail campaign, but highly personal. "When I started, I really didn't know what to expect," Karen recalls. "Then I realized that if even one school participated, that would make a difference, that would be the beginning." The launch of the College Campaign coincided with Eve touring around the country performing *The Vagina Monologues*, stimulating interest in towns small and large. Eve waived her usual royalty fee, making the play free to any campus as long as they did it in its entirety and donated proceeds from the performances to local antiviolence groups and initiatives. The only other parameters were that schools could only present up to three benefit performances, and they had to run on or around V-Day—February 14.

"I believe that we at V-day 'headquarters' provide a good balance of structure and freedom for our organizers and their teams: they can feel grounded in the project, connected to us and their college campaign peers, and clear about their mission but also free to bring their own creativity and visions to their specific events," says Karen. "It is as important that people who organize or otherwise participate in V-Day College Campaign events have a valuable experience as much as they help further V-Day's mission to end violence against women."

In just seven years, the College Campaign became an annual event on campuses worldwide, all at the initiative of students drawn to its message. In 2004 alone there were 626 productions. The V-Day Web site, the College Campaign organizer's kit, and the V-Day staff provide information and see campus organizers through their events, from assembling a cast and renting a venue, to printing programs and soliciting advertising, to educating students and community activists about how to raise funds within their community. Through all the V-Day efforts, $25 million has been raised to stop violence against women and girls.

Since Karen has been involved in V-Day, she has also worked full-time in TV production. (She's a technical director—in real terms that means that she pushes the buttons that put the show on the air.) She often works long shifts in her television job, but in order for this V-Day mass dissemination to be effective, she decided that she had to be available "100 percent of the time" for the student activists. And Karen is one to meet her responsibilities. "I just didn't get much sleep," she recalls of her five seasons running the College Campaign. "I was devoted to my organizers. They are the reason that the College Campaign has been so successful. I dealt with every person who contacted me as if she was the most important person that I was dealing with that day," says Karen, "even if she was the hundredth." If every burgeoning activist got that kind of attention, there'd be no need for a book like *Grassroots*. Often the College Campaign was the first time students had done anything activist and Karen was there to walk them through the process. We've met hundreds of these students who have been changed into theater producers/fund-raisers/organizers—even feminists— by staging a V-Day production of *The Vagina Monologues* and can attest to its transformative power.

People who would never attend a NOW march not only flock to the show but purchase VIVA LA VULVA T-shirts, chomp on vagina-shaped chocolates, and chant "C-U-N-T!" We have personally attended two campus performances, at Drew University and at St. Olaf's, but we can't think of a single school that we have visited that hasn't yet had a V-Day. Some are doing it for their first time, some their fourth—but we think of it as the Starbucks of feminism: everywhere, progressive, popular.

V-Day's success is a victory for feminism, but you don't have to use the term feminist in order to do the play. In fact, many people don't. The most famous and lucrative V-Day was at Madison Square Garden in 2001 and it raised $2 million, featuring stars like Oprah Winfrey (just the mention of her name elicited a standing ovation) and Glenn Close, who led an audience of nineteen thousand in the "C-U-N-T!" chant. After the show, a *Village Voice* reporter, Sharon Lerner, asked the stars if they called themselves feminists. According to Lerner's ensuing article, many of the performers either did not or asked back, "What do you mean by feminist?" which Lerner construed as being afraid of or oblivious to the feminist implications. Simply being a part of such a radical, body-loving, pro-woman, controversially named theater piece could be assumed to be feminist—but the fact that they didn't immediately say "yes" or questioned what the writer meant doesn't take away from the activist and political achievement of the event.

Now that it's such a success, people (like the *Village Voice* reporter mentioned above) have begun to question its politics. While we could debate the content of the monologues (and we have—taking issue with the monologues "Under the Burqa," which some audience members have interpreted as implying that wearing one is inherently oppressive, and "The Coochie Snorcher," which contains sex between a minor and an adult but, because it's same-sex, is treated as humorous rather than illegal), the bottom line is that the play and the accompanying V-Day have exposed more people to feminism than any other entity in the last decade. Furthermore, it has raised millions of dollars in a grassroots fashion—all without even having an office. Its power is in its presence in so many communities, linked by a common cause of ending violence and saying the word "vagina." The latter has proved to be a more profound act than you might think. The play raises funds that keep local antiviolence initiatives alive and raises consciousness that antiviolence resources are available in a given community. Karen defines V-Day's success simply as "having increasing numbers of people join and support us each year and changing things for the better." It truly is a movement.

Sometimes art is the most effective way to express politics. For instance, the two of us have watched well-meaning adults attempt to do programs in high schools where the goal is to talk frankly about dating violence and domestic discord. The students tend to distance themselves from the presumption that there is violence in their lives, because they feel exposed, defensive, and embarrassed. By contrast, art can be very personal and affecting without requiring any "confession" from the students.

Kids at EBT, a public school in impoverished Bushwick, Brooklyn, for instance, are compelled to think more critically about sexual violence, teen pregnancy, and strategies for survival from reading Sapphire's novel *Push* than from any required appointment with a guidance counselor. Lectures have little success—we all remember our resistance to the "clueless" guest speakers who came to our high schools to talk earnestly about after-school special issues. When the progressive education training organization Facing History and Ourselves used the HBO film *The Laramie Project*,* it allowed the students to have their own emotional response to homophobia and hate crimes based on a real story, not a generic role-play slogan. In this way, it's no longer singling out kids to offer up their personal stories if they're not ready, making assumptions about their personal lives, or lecturing them. Art is an avenue to solutions and understanding that we wouldn't have gotten to any other way.

"In order to make art that isn't just copying others you have to be willing to have an opinion and make decisions," says Helen Klebesadel. "If you start to develop opinions for your art and make them visible, it is not too much of a step to having opinions about the world and beginning to raise your voice. Heck, from my perspective just doing art in this anti-art culture can be considered activist."

---

*Based on extensive interviews conducted by the actors of the Tectonic Theater Project, *The Laramie Project* dramatized the struggle of town residents to come to terms with the murder of Mathew Shepard, a young gay man who was brutally beaten and left to die in Laramie, Wyoming.

chapter 7 | The Revolutionary Next Door

"You must be the change you want to see in the world."

—Mahatma Gandhi, the leader of the India independence movement

JENNIFER

In college, it seemed I was always in a fight with the one virulently antifeminist philosophy major in the room, ignoring everyone else. At some point, he'd corner me and say something like, "If men *can* rape women, then provide me with the logical argument of why they should not." I'd sputter and, hysterical, resort to yelling, "*If I can shove this broomstick up your ass, explain to me why I shouldn't!*"

It's funny—I never have that conversation anymore. One of the main differences in my life now compared to when I was younger is that I no longer take the bait from people who just want to goad me. Earlier in the book, I talked about how important it was for me, as a feminist, to figure out what I authentically believe and separate it from the viewpoints I had simply inherited. Once I started doing that, I realized that my feminist problems with pornography, for instance, had more to do with the fact that it excluded me—it appeared to be for men only—and not that I found it fundamentally degrading. (Though it can be.) I also began listening when women told me that they are "pro-life, but they don't want to make that decision for another woman." Now I no longer say, "Oh, but that *is* pro-choice." I let her define herself and use her own words.

I guess I'd say that now I'm more firm and clear about what is true to me and, therefore, find other's opinions to be less threatening. Knowing what I believe is related to understanding who I am, which is related to my effectiveness as an activist. I don't force myself to get on board with a party line if I don't believe it, and I *know* that I can be an important feminist activist without abhorring porn or giving up shopping. This not only gives me peace—I think it helps keep the women's movement accessible. One anecdote that bears this out: I recently attended an Our Bodies Ourselves fund-raiser in a gorgeous Manhattan loft. Like many women who grew up post-1970s, *Our Bodies, Ourselves* was one of my adolescent totems, along with Judy Blume books and Love's Baby Soft. Judy Norsigan, part of the original collective and still one of its most vibrant spokespeople, addressed those attending the fund-raiser. She was great, as always, talking about how much progress we'd made on women's health and women's rights—identifying the moment when women realized that doctors weren't God and that they could check their own cervixes. But then Judy lamented the way that pop culture undermines those strides: "I mean, young people today are learning about sex and their bodies from *Sex and the City*!" she cried.

I loved *Sex and the City*. While it certainly had its irresponsible elements, they center on afternoon drinking and profligate spending. If anything, the characters Carrie, Miranda, Charlotte, and Samantha are very *Our Bodies Ourselves*-y—from their blithe acceptance (and know-how) of masturbation, contraception, and Sapphic relationships to their healthy sex drives. During the Q&A, I asked Judy what she thought was specifically dangerous about the show. "I like it," I offered. "I'd even say it reminds me of my friends and me." Judy admitted that she hadn't really watched the show, she was just interpreting that it was retrograde from the title and its style. As it turned out, this fund-raiser was filled with intense *Sex and the City* fans, ages twenty-five to seventy, and they piped up about their favorite episodes. There was a time when I would have heard a feminist criticize something I secretly liked and I would have remained silent. The *Sex and the City* moment made me realize how unproductive that silence is—it contributes to misinformation about what it means to be a feminist and encourages others to self-censor.

AMY

In the same way that Jennifer was a magnet for the antifeminist right-winger when she was in college, I still seem to attract the holier-than-thou leftie and end up in similar predicaments. Who knew that the grungy *Nation* reader could be just as oppressive as the Phi Delt? For example, shortly after *Manifesta* was published, Jennifer and I were giving our first big talk: San Francisco's City Arts and Lectures. Joining us were Michael Franti (of the band Spearhead) and Gloria Steinem. Activism was our topic. To augment what those onstage were saying, I invited young activists whom Jennifer and I respected to be in the audience as our guests so I could point them out as examples of Third Wave feminism. Taking it one level deeper, I even convinced the sponsor to make the event a fund-raiser for the Third Wave Foundation and to give away dozens of seats to young people who couldn't afford the $18 ticket price. In short, the whole night was designed less for promoting our book and more as an example of how to make an event accessible to the working poor and younger people, and how to turn any event into a fund-raiser.

I was accustomed to creating environments where I put either other people or the issues themselves in the spotlight. I anticipated that it would be uncomfortable for me to be the focus, which is another reason I asked these other activists to be in the audience. It didn't help that I was also nervous that something would go wrong; having organized countless events, I was well aware of this possibility. Still, I was excited and eventually thrilled that the evening went off without a hitch. People actually showed up, the audience asked questions, I got a few laughs. Elated after the talk, I traipsed off for a late dinner with some of the young activists I had pointed out in the crowd. I quickly felt deflated when one of the young women I had invited said, rather abruptly, "Amy, I have to say, I just don't understand what is activist about what you do." I would have interpreted this question differently if it was coming from someone who genuinely wanted to know more about what it was I did. But this was coming from someone with whom I'd worked for years. Her comment seemed designed to put me in my place, which was, apparently from her perspective, behind

the scenes doing hours of scut work, not anything pioneering that would lead to my being onstage being acknowledged as an activist. I was shocked and angry—and I felt
very vulnerable. To defend myself, I immediately listed my
recent activist efforts: the dramatic late-term abortion I had
raised funds for that same day; the twenty-five desperate
e-mails I had waiting for my reply at Ask Amy; my refusal to
participate in an event with only white panelists; and the
launching of Third Wave's I Spy Sexism campaign, which I
created but insisted (as with most of the work I did for Third
Wave) that it not be owned by me but by the foundation.

This exchange haunted me for years. I felt judged and
misunderstood, and I interpreted this woman as saying
that I was misrepresenting myself as a revolutionary when
I was clearly just a privileged white wonk. I made peace
with this conversation when I realized that any amount of
energy I spent defending myself only legitimized her assumption. Before coming to terms with this exchange, I felt
compelled to bring up the fact that I was raised by a single
mom or on welfare for part of my life in order to justify
myself as an activist or as more than the textbook entitled
white woman. Precisely because that is part of "my story," I
can relate to the power of assimilation and the value of the
mainstream. You can only safely reject something once you
have access to it.

This process has made me contemplate a fundamental
conflict of progressive organizing. Poor or otherwise oppressed people are perceived as natural allies. Conversely,
rich or otherwise privileged people are challenged before
they are welcomed as activists. While we should never gener-
alize that poor people are lazy, we shouldn't assume that
rich people are insensitive, clueless, and selfish. Most social
justice work is about providing resources so that people

who are poor or victimized can have comforts, education, basic health care—"privileges" that are currently available only to those who can afford them. The problem is that as soon as someone is successful, he or she is often accused of as being too privileged to be radical. I don't fall prey to that critique anymore because I know from my own experience that I am using what privilege I have to expand resources to others.

*   *   *

I am a 20-year-old woman who considers myself to be a feminist, yet I don't feel that I am making any sort of contribution to feminism. My friends feel the same way I do. Do you have ideas of things we can do or organizations we can help with to make us feel more a part of the "Third Wave"? Help please!!!!
> Stacey Yannacopoulos
> Windsor, Ontario

We began this book wondering if you even imagined yourself as an activist. In the preceding chapters, we analyzed the people who had asked us "What can I do?" We hope you saw yourself in at least a few of those scenarios, even if you aren't a high-school student desperate to start a club or an artist processing September 11. Maybe you are someone who took a friend along to go vote or asked a relative who supports the death penalty to go with you to *The Exonerated*, a play by Jessica Blank and Eric Jensen that tells the true stories of the wrongfully convicted on death row. Perhaps you took charge of recycling for your office or turned your mothers' group into an advocacy circle where the kids play while moms work the phone bank. The final frontier as an activist is having it be "in you"—so integrated into your life that it's instinctual, not premeditated. Your life no longer contains the question "What can I do?" because the way you lead your life is the answer. Once you try on the identity of an activist, it starts to feel . . . natural.

This is the sort of thing we are talking about: When you go to the dentist, you leave your copy of *Ms.*, *Colorlines*, or *Bust* in the waiting room next to—or on top of—*People* and *Town and Country*, introducing your fellow patients to a perspective that is missing from mainstream media. If you're shopping, you go into the Gap armed with cards identifying where and under what conditions their jeans were made—and you tuck the card into the back pocket of every pair. After all, you don't have to be an expert on child labor practices to inform other shoppers about Sweatshop Watch or their jeans' provenance. At the post office, you buy the more costly breast cancer stamps that donate a percentage to research or the Thurgood Marshall stamps to show that there is support for black heritage. Both stamps send a message of your values to your correspondents. Besides bringing your own bags to the grocery store, you bring back your returnables or put them directly into the hands of a bottle redeemer. Otherwise the five cents per bottle goes directly into the hands of the businesses—and they don't need your donations. If you are at a job interview, you ask about the policy on same-sex partner benefits and prescription birth control coverage, regardless of whether either issue affects you personally. In fact, it's sometimes better if it doesn't affect you personally, so it can't be written off as a selfish interest. Instead of the latest Hollywood movie, you go to the women's basketball games in your town to prove that they have an audience and that the professional players deserve to make a semi-comparable salary to men's basketball players. After your workout, you lobby the gym for towels that cover people who are larger than a size two. While reading the morning paper, you write a positive letter to the editor commending the newspaper for having a female sports columnist and their leadership in breaking out of the gender ghetto. If geopolitical events call for it, you stage an eat-in at the Middle Eastern restaurant in town or order the French wine.

Does the above list sound trivial? It shouldn't. Being an activist in the world doesn't have to be complicated and full of sacrifice; it can be as simple as influencing conversations around you. Saying "That's not funny" to a racist (or sexist, or homophobic) joke can be enough to provoke change—and there doesn't have to be a gay or black person in the room to point out bigotry. Maybe it's saying "I like Hillary Clinton" at the Junior League brunch or "I've listened to Eminem and, as an artist, he has something insightful to say about gender" at the NOW-NYC meeting. There are likely to be allies in your midst whom you didn't know existed until you bravely spoke your mind. Confront and name bigotry where you find it. You don't have to be righteously indignant, merely informative. Respectfully disrupting the status quo is eye-opening, as Jennifer's Our Bodies Ourselves example attests. Honesty alone can be transformative: for instance, disarming others by revealing that you have herpes or HPV or have had a miscarriage. This could lead to your being a resource for those who need advice about how to have a sex life after diagnosis or who need to know that they are not alone. Breaking the silence is often a welcome cue for others to do so—and comforting for those who are not yet ready to share their "shameful" secrets. Bringing your vulnerabilities to a conversation can be a contribution, too. You can admit that you're a feminist who doesn't have it all worked out, from your relationships with men to worrying about your weight.

These small organic forms of activism focus on what *you* can do, right now, right here. They fly in the face of history and common assumptions that traditionally define activist behavior as something that requires you to seek change outside of yourself or your community. Northern white students going down South to register black voters in the sixties, sixth-grade girls wanting to help girls in Somalia who are in danger of female genital mutilation: these are valid forms of activism—but they are not the *only* forms. Massive letter-writing campaigns do help curb human rights violations in other countries, but they also perpetuate perceptions that such atrocities only happen elsewhere. While we would never discourage this type of meaningful activism, the problem with looking outside of your community to change another's situation is that it involves "helping others" without understanding one's own stake in the issue. For instance, when Amy helped organize the Freedom Summer '92 cross-country voter registration drive, she thought that she was doing it to help poor people who didn't have access to voting. She eventually realized that she also wasn't served if she lived in a democracy where so few people participated.

The more profound reason to look closer to home is that everyone who is spurred to activism is really responding to a need inside himself or herself. It might be unacknowledged guilt over privilege. It might be empathy because you feel out of place and thus relate to other outcasts. It might be that sexism or racism damaged you, but you haven't yet realized it. Looking close to home can be threatening (and thus critically important), because then you have to admit that you are possibly part of the problem and confront people whom you actually know. Telling your Catholic father about your abortion is more dangerous than wearing a KEEP YOUR LAWS OFF MY BODY T-shirt at a march. The consequence is greater—you could be ostracized in your family or community for acting up—but the revolutionary potential is much greater, too.

When you yourself embody your activist values, then every space that you inhabit—from the ice-cream shop to the dentist's office to a seat on the subway—has the potential to become an activist space. After all, political realities intersect with every aspect of your life. Incorporating what you think and believe into what you do confirms that you are an activist. Doing this is challenging because you begin to question every decision, from the paper products you buy to the car you drive. When your activism is this instinctual, you stop asking "Am I good enough?" because you realize that you are doing something—you are always doing what you can.

SPONTANEOUS ACTIVISM

In 2002, a lawyer named Lois Abraham was just your normal concerned citizen. She cared about social justice issues, volunteered when she could, gave money to support her local (Taos, New Mexico) Planned Parenthood, and generally kept abreast of world politics by reading the paper and watching CNN, but she didn't consider herself above average in her activism. That is, until April 26th when she read a *New York Times* editorial called "Devastated Women." In it, the writer Nicholas Kristof detailed the impact of the United States withholding $34 million in funds promised to health care programs in some of the poorest countries in the world. The article criticized Bush's first action as President, which was to reinstate the "Mexico City Policy," commonly referred to as the "global gag rule." This policy refers to the U.S. government's refusal to release money to any international organizations that perform abortions or even mention abortion as an option, even if no U.S. money is used to pay for them.

Lois was particularly upset by a young girl Kristof reported on who was in obstructed labor for *three days* as a result of a fistula, an entirely preventable pregnancy-related rupture that can leave a woman permanently incontinent. Lois never thought that random funding battles would feel so urgent to her, but as she told us, "I became very angry about the coercion in the Bush administration." Besides, she thought, $34 million was a "pretty pitiful" contribution by the United States when you consider that it's the same amount pledged by considerably smaller countries such as Norway and Sweden. Unlike the United States, Norway and Sweden actually honored their financial commitment to the UNFPA. According to *The Economist*, America is consistently the biggest donor to poor countries in absolute terms but one of the stingiest relative to the size of its economy, spending only 0.12 percent of its GDP. Meanwhile, Denmark, Norway, and the Netherlands are the most generous, each giving more than 0.8 percent of their economies to developing nations. This isn't so surprising. Most progressives dream of taking refuge in Scandinavia with their year of required family leave for men and women, universal health care, and honest, comprehensive sex education.

Although it looked impossible to lobby a right-wing administration to fork over the $34 million, Lois had a flash of brilliance: What if there were another way to approach this goal? What if 34 million people who were in favor of family planning each gave *one* dollar?

Inspired, Lois called the UNFPA office in New York and left a message on the general voice mail outlining her plan to make up the $34 million through individual one-dollar contributions. "I told them to give me a call if they were interested," says Lois, "but I thought to myself, 'Well, now I'm off the hook, because no one's going to call and answer that message.'" To her surprise, someone at the UNFPA called back within an hour, saying, "We love the idea!" To create the campaign, Lois requested just two things from the UNFPA: that they read and edit the letter she intended to mass circulate on the Internet (which they did by the end of the day), and that they provide a mailing address for the donations (which they did). Then Lois called forty of her friends and colleagues and "got the commitment from them not to hit the delete button when they got the e-mail" and to forward it to everyone in their address books.

In an odd fluke of synchronicity, Jane Roberts, a retired French teacher and tennis coach in California, connected with the U.S. Committee for UNFPA the same day with essentially the same suggestion.* By August 2002, the two joined forces to create the 34 Million Friends of UNFPA campaign—the world's most effective chain e-mail. (When we each received the e-mail plea, we procrastinated for two months and then sent in our two dollars. Despite the delay, we can attest that this campaign was compelling, since neither of us had ever responded to a mass e-mail letter before.)

---

*Jane Roberts responded to news of the UNFPA funding cuts by writing a letter to the editor of her local paper, the San Bernardino *Sun*. In the letter she called on 34 million of her fellow citizens to join her in sending one dollar to the UNFPA.

Creating an e-mail campaign that attracts its members through personal relationships is the most effective way of doing an e-mail petition. First of all, friends are more likely to help you. If you can't even get people who know and like you to support your project, 34 million strangers probably won't either. Second, targeted campaigns mean you send the e-mail to people who would be interested in what you are doing—so you wouldn't send this e-mail to your uncle in North Carolina who loves Jesse Helms, but you would to your secretary who escorts at the Planned Parenthood on Saturdays. Finally, receiving an original e-mail from a friend about a campaign that she is spearheading guarantees its legitimacy.*

Further, Lois and Jane's request in the e-mail was both specific and pro-active: send $1 to UNFPA. The whole action takes less time and money than making a call to a politician's office. Plus, you never really know whether that message you left with the senator's intern had any impact. Three weeks after they began, fifty responses came to UNFPA all at once. By late fall of 2003, the two women had raised $1.5 million—most from one-dollar donations, although a few big hitters, like Ben Cohen of Ben and Jerry's, donated $10,000 in one pop.

Lois and Jane's project was a more formalized riff on a surprise success the year before, also protesting Bush's an-

---

*This is unlike the many forwarded, out-of-date calls to "Stop Dr. Hager's appointment to head the FDA!" (Dr. Hager, who believes prayer is as good a cure for fistula as adequate health care, was appointed to an FDA advisory panel, but he does not head it), or urban legends such as the one that claims that the U.S. Postal Service is discontinuing the Black Heritage series of stamps and destroying the remaining stock. When you get the un-personalized campaign e-mail, it's always wise to check it out at snopes.com before forwarding it.

tichoice policies. When *Los Angeles Times* writer Patt Morrison jokingly opined in her column that people who support abortion rights should make a Presidents' Day contribution to Planned Parenthood in honor of Bush, people forwarded the column all over the country. The next thing Planned Parenthood knew, they had received $500,000 and more than fifteen thousand cards to deliver to the White House in time for Presidents' Day.

Lois and Jane's approach is infinitely more effective than just complaining. For instance, the money raised by 34 Million Friends begins to make up for what the United States isn't paying, and the funds are free from the censorship and restrictions that come with U.S. federal aid. They can even use the money for abortions directly, which flies in the face of all governmental meddling on this issue. The campaign is still a long way from its financial goal, but beyond money, their efforts have kept the issue alive in the media and people's in-boxes. As a result, more people know about the health care struggles of women in developing countries and how manipulative aid from the U.S. government can be. Certainly, it helped prevent some of the 4,700 maternal deaths, serious illness in nearly 60,000 pregnant women, and some of the 2 million unwanted pregnancies—which is what the UNFPA funding was calculated to accomplish. There is one downside to this story: projects like these let the government off the hook. If women and feminists raise money (on our gender gap salaries) every time the Bush administration deems our health care too controversial, we are inadvertently propping up a terribly sexist policy.

Lois's evolution from your average citizen to an activist crusader shows how an individual's mundane lifestyle has political reverberations. Lois was just reading the *Times* when she had her "click." Lois and Jane are now models for feminist fund-raising. This is wonderful but tricky because the force of their idea comes from its uniqueness. If we received an e-mail plea every day asking us to give a dollar to help save the seals or fund a foster child, we'd stop giving and start deleting. This is called burnout. As activists, we can burn out in one of at least three ways: on a strategy, as an overwhelmed individual, and on the "stars." There are days when getting the seven MoveOn.org e-mails is not only uninspiring but irritating, and going to a Meetup is no longer urgent but a chore. The strategy—and its tactics—become stale. Further, unreachable standards of purity cause people to burn out. Sometimes we have to let ourselves off the hook. For instance, just because you were once a vegan or vegetarian in order to have a more holistic life or one that is consistent with your values, doesn't mean that if you decide to eat meat again this all goes out the window. The truth is that all of our lives are complex, and often conflicted. Who absolutely accepts her body, knows where and under what condition his food is grown, knows who stitched his sneakers? And who always recycles? Even the rare person who has successfully disavowed globalist consumer culture and lives in a hemp hut can most likely only afford to do so because of a trust fund.

Movements burn out on the superstars, too. They become overexposed and vulnerable to their own contradictions. On this note, one of the biggest enemies to activism is other activists, as Amy's experiences attest. The most undermining and critical people we have encountered are not right-wing ideologues like Rush Limbaugh or libertarian absolutists like Camille Paglia; it's the super-activists who act like they were imbued with the responsibility to decide who is radical enough. Activism brings its own elitism, clubs, and rules. One demoralizing moment for us was when a women's studies professor at a Wisconsin school stood up at our packed lecture and said, "I'm glad you're out there attracting young women to feminism, I guess, but where are your politics? What sort of message are you sending these *already apathetic* women?" This, at a lecture organized 100 percent by younger feminists who were staging *The Vagina Monologues* the next week and orchestrating a Take Back the Night demonstration. Another version of this kind of behavior is when people, usually white, take it upon themselves to point out how important it is to have a feminism that includes Asian, Native American, Latina, and black women and challenge us about what we are doing to ensure that it happens. We used to respond defensively and list our alliances, bring up the fact that Third Wave's entire staff is women of color, and point out the many, many women interviewed in *Manifesta* and *Grassroots* who *are* women of color. Now we don't take the bait—we know that we organize within a diverse community, and that diversity is actually more complex than simply seeing brown faces in a room. From experiences like these over the years we have learned our own valuable lesson and strive to give people who are self-described as activists the benefit of the doubt, rather than assuming that because they don't do things our way, they are against us, ineffectual, or uninformed.

Social justice movements will always produce stars, competition for resources, conflicts, splits, and trashing—but these problems involve a small number of activists. While the media focuses on the super-successful Eve Enslers and the MoveOn.orgs, it's the constant influx of new average people with new ideas attempting to make the world better who are the pillars of activism. Our friend Tara Brindisi has been a great inspiration for being a normal girl who incorporates her activism into everything—her conversations, her wardrobe, and her homework. Tara has two role models: Gloria Steinem and Marilyn Monroe. She speaks in a soft, babyish, Monroe-like voice and wears homemade T-shirts decorated with Steinem's quotes and visage. When we met her she was a sophomore in high school, and her e-mail address was the highly racy seductress69, which she changed to the slightly tamer SeDcTivE66 when others pointed out that the "69" reference might be partly to blame for the overtures she was getting in chat rooms. Now a fiercely feminist junior at NYU, Tara is vice president of her campus chapter of NOW and recently worked part-time in Gloria Steinem's office. Her current e-mail address is lueluestone. We assumed it was a reference to Lucy Stone, the nineteenth-century feminist and inspiration for the movement for women to keep their names after marriage. Actually, Tara told us, it's for Sharon Stone and, "I just like the name LueLue."

Years ago, when Tara was eleven, she was sexually molested by her fifth-grade teacher at Cliffside Park school in New Jersey. At the time, she didn't have a clear understanding that what he did to her was actually wrong—as in illegal—though it certainly felt wrong. As she grew older, she gained the political and feminist vocabulary to describe what had happened to her. Five years after she was molested, then age sixteen, Tara was in an e-mail chat room where the topic was rape. Girl after girl told stories of being molested or assaulted and almost all of the narratives ended with the same sentiment: "But . . . I'm okay now." Finally, one correspondent typed, "It doesn't matter if *you're* okay with what happened, how would you feel if your perpetrator did what he did to you to someone else?" Reading that question was enough to prompt Tara to call the police

about what had happened to her years earlier. As it turned
out, there had been several complaints against this same
teacher over the years, but after the girls would graduate to
middle school, the administration would let the individual
cases fall away. Coincidentally, the year Tara called the cops,
one current student of the molester—a ten-year-old girl—
finally took her case to the police rather than just to the
school. With this case, the teacher pleaded guilty and was
forced to leave his New Jersey teaching job, though he did
get to keep his pension. Having Tara's complaint on file with
the police contributed to the successful case against him.

Beyond personal injustices, Tara manages to follow up
on seemingly random things as a part of her daily life—
even if it's five years after the fact, she usually manages to
bring some justice to a situation. For instance, as a sophomore in college in 2002, she produced her campus's production of *The Vagina Monologues*. As producer, one of her
responsibilities was to put together the evening's brochure.
She scoured the Internet to find statistics to include, typing
in the search terms "rape" and "violence." Rather than feminist resources such as Rape, Abuse and Incest National
Network (RAINN) or even FBI crime statistics, she was led
to disgusting Web sites that detailed "how to rape a child"
or "how to sexually harass your student." She clicked on
one and was inundated with a barrage of porn pop-ups. By
the time she was able to close the graphic and offensive win-
dows, she had discovered numerous sites that depicted older
men raping boys, including one in Texas that featured a
man who was clearly over fifty sodomizing a prepubescent
boy. "I guess I was naïve," says Tara, "I didn't think there
would even be a market for looking at this sort of thing."

There was most definitely a market, but Tara began to

question why these blatantly violent sites were so easy to access. A professor encouraged her to call the New York Police Department. When Tara explained the sites to the "Director of Internet Crimes," he researched them and told her that most could not be shut down because they were either sufficiently "artistic" or, more often, they had been created in other countries over which the United States had no jurisdiction. There were, however, three that she was able to eliminate simply by following up on her own belief that child pornography shouldn't invade her computer screen as she researches schoolwork. Tara isn't the first feminist to be upset by the onslaught of porn, but she is possibly unique in that she did something very specific, small, and ultimately effective. Internet pornography ostensibly portraying rape and sexual harassment are common—even rampant—and there is no magical cure to abolish them.*

Tara's victory, though subtle, demonstrated that she had volition and that there was something she could do to help. She didn't create a new group or start a campaign, but she was effective. Lone individuals without affiliations are crucial because they aren't immersed in the politics of foundations. They don't use foundation-speak nor do they tailor their solutions to what is fundable. The danger with a passionate activist like Tara is that she doesn't leave any time when she isn't overscheduled and responsible. She hasn't learned to ever say no, because she fears it's letting down the movement. We encourage people like Tara to look beyond what they can accomplish right now and realize that

---

*In a similar vein, in 2004 a grandmother named Mary B. Conyers lobbied Congress to enact a law, the Obscene Internet Material Classification Act, requiring porn sites to end with the suffix ".XXX" rather than the innocuous .com, .org., or .net. At present, whitehouse.com is a porn site.

they have their whole lives to work on this. People who try to cram it into their college years or their twenties become overwhelmed.

YOU'RE WORTH MORE THAN YOUR NET WORTH

During the era of the dot-com millionaire, many of whom were barely old enough to drink, organizations from Safe Horizons to Amnesty International began to reach out to these and other young people as funders. They claimed they wanted to get young people involved, but the avenues were limited to donating money. Using the Natural Resources Defense Council as an example, the "junior committee" brought in a few new donors but the NRDC was disappointed by the lack of interest. When we were asked to assess what was behind this (their assumption was either apathy or stinginess—and as far as the so-called millionaires, no one seems to have taken into account that for many of them their fortunes existed entirely on paper), we suggested that young people recognized that they weren't being invited to change the environment; they were just being asked to write checks. What would have been equally if not more valuable is asking for the commitment of their lifestyle—especially while they are still young enough to change their lives easily. Rather than asking people to show up for an event or give money to a campaign, it would be more useful to have them demonstrate how their own lives can reflect their value system. If they had enough cash to contemplate a $1,000 gift, they could certainly afford to add solar panels to their home or to buy organic, locally grown food. If they had time to attend a black-tie event, they had time to refit the lamps in their house with energy-efficient bulbs. If more people's lifestyle was their activism, it might mean less of a need for social justice organizations and more dependence on our own ability to make significant change.

Unlike the people who pay $250 for the NRDC fundraiser but then drive there in their gas-guzzling SUV, the folk singer Amy Ray has made integrating activism into her every move an art form. She adapted her home and lifestyle to match her politics. Her primary cause is the environment but she is also devoted to reproductive freedom, gay rights, indigenous movements, and antiwar work. As a celebrity, she gets numerous daily requests to participate in urgent causes. By prioritizing the environment, she is able to pace herself and not become swallowed up in the specter of so many problems that need attention.

Amy's car is a hybrid, which gets forty-five to sixty miles to the gallon in town. Her floors are made from salvaged wood, the paint in her home is nontoxic, and the outside of the house is composed of a highly efficient heat and coolness-preserving stucco-like material. The landscaping consists of plants that are indigenous to the area and she composts on her property. Even the staples of running a household are purchased with political impact in mind. She won't buy GE lightbulbs, for example, because of the 109 superfund sites that they have created and refused to clean. Her paper products and cleaning supplies are made by the green Seventh Generation, Inc. It definitely takes more effort to live this way—and certainly costs more up front—but the act makes one's own home a part of the solution. In that way, she's the best ally an environmental group could ask for. The goal of these organizations is to pressure the government to in turn pressure the auto industry to make fuel-efficient cars, but the same effect is achieved when people like Amy create the demand. This doesn't mean that your checkbook is in no way a reflection of your values. One of the best fund-raising pitches we've heard is by Gloria Steinem. She asks you to imagine that you've just left a fabulous political event when you are hit by a Mack truck. Passersby look through your checkbook registry, trying to find clues about who you are. Would this be an accurate reflection of your values? Most people grimace and think, "No, it would reflect someone who loves J. Crew and pays their electric bill on time."

Activism should be of you, not outside of you. This is a critical message for readers of this book as well as for the representatives of organizations—the ones that are so anxious to get people involved. We can't always be looking to enact change through organizations or even movements; we have to look at ourselves and start with the individual.

We sometimes ponder what it would take to get people protesting and active the way they were in the "radical sixties." We used to think it would have to be some major world event—a war, for instance—something very public that would get us angry and scared and out of our homes. We have gone to the streets, amassed the masses—especially since September 11—and more and more we see that the last frontier is the individual. Therefore, it's not getting everyone in the United States to protest the war on the same day with the same point of view; it's getting everyone to do *something*. As Harleen Kaur Singh, a girl who attended our lectures at the University of Maryland, put it in a note she slipped to us, "I enjoyed your lecture and learned that I can do something small and be a feminist. Suggestions for a word for this: collective activism." She defined this as, "If everyone does a little, it adds up to a lot."

We hope by now you realize that you are already a potential activist. In a way, that's the most profound change you have to make: to see yourself as part of a revolutionary history. Then ask yourself a simple, but nonetheless important question: What opportunities for change does your life present?

Epilogue: A Day in the Life of an Activist

To underscore that you are part of the revolutionary process, we want to leave you with examples of how mundane the "lofty" calling of activism can be. The end of the book, therefore, is where you begin to look at your own life and see what you are already doing that might be activism. To get the ball rolling, here's a week in Amy's calendar and Jennifer's to-do list.

AMY'S WEEK

When people ask me what I do, I often freeze because I don't know how to explain my unconventional life in a way that makes sense—or even sound like I'm doing anything, despite how busy I always feel. Sometimes I think that I should just hand over my Palm Pilot in those moments and have the person take a look at my week. It not only clarifies my vague job as "activist" but demystifies activism. Here goes.

Monday, October 14: Estelle Freedman lecture at Barnard College's Center for Research on Women

As a Barnard alum, I try to attend events sponsored by the center. (I support the college in other ways, too—such as giving money and making calls for the annual phone-athon.) Estelle (Barnard class of 1969) is a professor of history at Stanford University in Palo Alto, California. She was in New York City to give a lecture at Barnard about her book *No Turning Back: The History of Feminism and the Future of Women*, which, I noted happily, shares many ideological and style points with *Manifesta*. Jennifer set up a coffee date with Estelle before the talk, so the two of us got a chance to hear what she was working on (which included a great Web site related to *No Turning Back*), and we got to tell her more about Soapbox, and some of the Third Wave Foundation's events.

I like Estelle's book because she clearly values her students. She recognizes that young people are indeed invested in finding out how feminism fits into their own lives. Her approach is far more effective than the all-too-familiar scenario in which the women's studies professor buys into the popular opinion that says that young women are scared of feminism and therefore don't see the feminists that are right in front of them—a self-fulfilling prophecy if you ask me.

At this event, I was also able to reconnect with Rosalind Rosenberg, a Barnard professor who taught my History of Women class back in 1991. After graduating, I read in an old issue of *Ms.* magazine that Rosenberg had defended Sears in a famous sex discrimination suit (*EEOC v. Sears, Roebuck and Co.*). The *Ms.* article roundly criticized her for taking the corporate side. I was an impressionable young feminist and thought that the *Ms.* perspective was the only legitimate opinion, thus Rosenberg must be an antifeminist. Seeing her there that night jogged my memory about the case and made me realize how much I used to toe an assumed feminist line, believing that there was only one genuine feminist point of view. It's only in recent years that I have learned to examine received wisdom—no matter what the source—and figure out my own opinion as a feminist. Articulating my opinion, especially when it is an unpopular one, can be a form of activism.

Tuesday, October 15, 5 P.M.: Third Wave Foundation conference call

Every Tuesday since 1999 I have had a call at five o'clock sharp with Third Wave's executive committee and staff. On this particular date we were planning our holiday art auction, one of our most significant fund-raisers of the year. The event evolved from our observation that many artists interested in supporting Third Wave might in lieu of a significant cash donation, contribute objects with a market value that exceeded what they could otherwise offer. We reached out to the artists we had some connection to—for instance, Jenny Holzer once gave us a $50 contribution, the choreographer Bill T. Jones appeared on a Why Vote panel Third Wave hosted, and the jewelry maker Heather Moore was close friends with one of our board members. After we secured donations from those three, we used their names to reach out to artists we didn't know, such as the photographers Annie Liebovitz and Cindy Sherman. This annual event now raises more than $10,000. Not only are these artists more willing to donate their work than cash, but the individuals who attend the auction spend more than they would if we relied just on the money from the door. They have the satisfaction of acquiring both good art and good politics.

Tuesday, October 15, 8 P.M.: *BETTY Rules* at the Zipper Theater

BETTY is a feminist pop trio—think the Bee Gees meets Margaret Cho. I first heard them in January of 1993 at a Voters for Choice concert during President Clinton's inauguration. They are ubiquitous at feminist events on the East Coast and a regular presence at the Michigan Womyn's Music Festival. This week, the trio was in the midst of a several-month run of their off-off Broadway show, *BETTY Rules*. Elizabeth Ziff, one third of the group, asked me to attend. I went, always excited to support a feminist cause, but was a bit daunted by the $40 ticket price. (The women of BETTY were aware that, for some, $40 is just too much, so they got the Zipper Theater to agree to a 10 p.m. show every Friday night for $10.) That night, the show was so fun and inspiring that my financial chagrin was replaced by the feeling that I had made a good investment—I was supporting feminist art, women's work, and having a better time than if I had rented a movie. It turned out that Elizabeth, a veteran of countless benefit concerts where she donated her time, was hurt that more people from the feminist community weren't repaying *BETTY* the favor by attending the show. I was relieved that I wasn't part of the problem, and I vowed to send out e-mails about the show's bargain night to all of my friends.

Wednesday, October 16: Gather donations and make calls for the Third Wave auction

The hardest part about gathering donations is getting over the embarrassment I have in asking. But since the prospect of a failed auction would also embarrass me, I steeled myself and began dialing. I called a yoga teacher who I had met at a party and never hit up before and asked if she would donate yoga "privates" (one-on-one classes that are worth $100 per session in Manhattan). I also went down to the little independent jewelry store on the ground floor of my building and asked if its owners would donate a necklace for the auction. They did, as did a jeweler colleague of theirs. I called the photographer Joyce Tenneson, with whom I was working on another project, and got her to donate an exquisite photograph. These four donations could bring in between $1,000 to $1,500 for Third Wave and took just under three hours to secure. Today there were no humiliating rejections, but that certainly isn't always the case.

Thursday, October 17: day off

I worked with Jennifer on this book, did yoga, and then had dinner with my boyfriend. Days off are crucial. Jennifer and I are frequently asked by campus activists how we avoid burnout. My answer is simple but true: I shop, have my hair cut, go running or to yoga, visit a museum, and indulge myself in other ways that allow me to feel rewarded for the work I do in the rest of my life.

Friday, October 18, 1 P.M.: Meet with Bill Wetzel in the Bronx

I read about Bill Wetzel's group, Students Against Testing, in a journal called *The Activist* and thought that he might be a good addition to *Grassroots*. Bill founded the group as a New Jersey high-school senior and helps high-school students interested in reforming standardized tests, especially with regard to the race and gender bias. He has organized dozens of students to stage walk-outs on the Regents exams (New York kids must pass them in order to graduate high school), devised a protest test (a "pro-test") for students to give to their teachers, and lobbied to get teachers to take standardized tests along with their students. Bill and I had been trading e-mails for the past two weeks, trying to set up a time to meet, and today was the day.

Part of the scheduling problem had to do with Bill's latest endeavor, in which he lives on the streets of New York with a sandwich board propped up next to him that says TALK TO ME. He wants to interact with people he wouldn't normally meet and uses the sign to invite strangers into conversation. His TALK TO ME sign had already provoked a huge range of responses, from younger people who challenged him ("What do you think you are trying to prove?") to people who had just lost their welfare benefits and wanted to know what to do next.

We had lunch at a Dominican restaurant. I treated, partly as a courtesy since I initiated the meeting and partly because he was, after all, homeless (albeit self-imposed). I left our meeting inspired by Bill's guerrilla approach to understanding individual New Yorkers' lives, and I also gained a deeper sense of how one can protest testing bias. I had only been exposed to strategies like redesigning the SAT or creating compensatory approaches, as Nancy Redd and Ron Foley did with their book *The Girls' Guide to the SAT*. Bill's approach included both a boycott and a testing alternative.

Friday, October 18, 6 P.M.: Meet Nicole Vandenberg

I had drinks with my friend Nicole, a Seattle-based publicist who specializes in progressive public relations. If you don't think there can be anything progressive about a PR job, Nicole will open your eyes. She advises the rock band Pearl Jam about how to give away their money and the income from that enables Nicole to do pro bono work for groups such as the Seattle-based self-defense group Home Alive. Nicole mentioned that one of Pearl Jam's largest beneficiaries is the Seattle Public Schools library system. "We started by visiting five schools, meeting with the librarians, and asking for their wish lists," Nicole told me. "We generally found it easiest to give money through the Northwest Literacy Foundation, because they cut checks directly to the librarians to buy the books they need for their libraries, avoiding the potential bureaucracy of the school system.

Meeting with Nicole is purely social, but given our shared passions, there is always a thread of work. This time I enlisted her to donate time and publicity skills to Scenarios USA, a group that creates sex education films that are written by high-school students and directed by established filmmakers such as Doug Liman (*Go* and *The Bourne Iden-*

tity) and Tamara Jenkins (*Slums of Beverly Hills*). Through the efforts of Nicole's firm, Vandenberg PR, Scenarios USA received coverage on *Salon.com* and in *USA Today*.

Saturday, October 19: Fly to Buffalo, speak at New York NOW annual conference

I didn't want to get up at 6 a.m. for my JetBlue flight to Buffalo, especially on this rainy, dreary Saturday, but I had committed to address the New York National Organization for Women on Third Wave feminism at their annual statewide conference. I arrived at the Adams Mark Hotel secretly amused and bemused that the NOW event was occurring there simultaneously with a beauty contest for girls age two to eighteen.

New York NOW has twenty-three chapters, all of which are struggling to keep up their membership. An obvious target for new members is young women—though perhaps not the ten-year-olds dolled up like J.Lo at the pageant. As an outsider to the organization, I could speak frankly. I said that it appeared the young women in NOW weren't visible or respected: young women weren't in leadership positions, their suggestions seemed to be met with suspicion, and it was clear to me that my presence fulfilled a token role. In fact, the whole concept of a Third Wave of feminism was absent, except as a private language among the few young women in the room.

From the outside, this trip looked like the most obviously political action of my week, but it actually felt like the least successful activist thing I did. I was very disheartened by the lack of communication among the generations, and doubtful that I had done much to bridge the divide present in that hotel banquet hall. Driving that feeling home was the fact that many of the older women in the NOW leadership talked to each other throughout my remarks. When I got home, though, I received an e-mail from one of the younger women at the meeting who thanked me, and I realized that my presence had the effect of making her feel validated about her own frustration with NOW. I reminded myself that there were a few older women who seemed grateful for the specific ideas I gave about working in a generational coalition, such as swapping jobs for a day (sort of a feminist *Freaky Friday*) or giving an intergenerational dinner party.

Saturday, October 19, 9 P.M.: Baby shower

For the baby shower, I gave my friend Becky a copy of *Breeders*, an anthology edited by Ariel Gore and Bee Lavender, the great feminist duo behind the Web site hipmama.com. I also bought the book at Bluestockings, the only feminist bookstore in New York City, thus supporting an independent business.

Sunday, October 20: Caught up on Ask Amy

Every week I receive about fifty e-mails to Ask Amy, the online activist advice column that I started in 1995. Some requests are simply for research tips or advice, but there is often a serious plea for help; for example, I recently received an e-mail from a woman named Sabah in Madison, Wisconsin, who wrote saying that she was being "forced to commit suicide." Obviously, an e-mail like that can't be ignored even if my instinct says that it may be a hoax. I called the National Coalition Against Domestic Violence and asked them if they had a shelter in Madison, then I called the shelter number they provided and asked them if they handled suicides. They didn't, and added that they weren't taking any new clients, probably the result of the nationwide problem of lack of funding. They referred me to the Department of Mental Health, where I serendipitously reached a doctor who had already encountered Sabah. He did believe she was in danger of committing suicide, and gave me the name of a local feminist therapist. When I called, she said that she would be able to see Sabah, so I e-mailed her infomation to Sabah and encouraged her to follow up.

Getting coffee later in the day, I ran into an acquaintance, Polly, who is a feminist therapist. Thinking of Sabah and how she kept slipping through the cracks of the mental health system, I told Polly that I frequently heard from people in need of a feminist therapist and asked if there was a national network. Polly knew of nothing formal, but suggested the Ackerman Institute for the Family, a not-for-profit in New York that was one of the pioneers of family therapy. Coincidentally, another Ask Amy came in later that day from a woman requesting resources for feminist therapy. After a few more calls and e-mails, I learned about the Feminist Therapy Referral Project in California and the Women's Therapy Centre Institute in New York.

Reading this over, I see that I accomplished quite a bit that week. Usually I focus only on what I *didn't* get done, so writing this had the bonus of making me realize just how effective I can be. It's critical to be able to see the impact one has as an activist and not only think about the millions of problems that are begging to be addressed. The next time I get a fund-raising e-mail proclaiming that by the time I finish reading its message, a woman will have died at the hands of her batterer, I'll think about what I have done and not just feel defeated that I haven't done enough.

JENNIFER'S TO-DO LIST

I've made "to-do" lists since I was about eleven. I love the planning, the paper products, and the gratifying feeling of crossing off a completed task. The older I get, the more dependent I am on lists just to remember what I have to do—not that my lists can't become unmanageable and time-wasters in themselves. Sometimes my list freaks me out (as when my "to-call" column is more than twenty names long or I see, "To do: Write bisexuality book"). But, usually, the list helps. It forces me to break down my goal into a series of practical bite-sized steps.

1. Figure out donations for NYAAF fund-raiser

The New York Abortion Access Fund raises money for women who need abortions but can't afford them. (For detailed information about how to start a fund, contact the National Network of Abortion Funds at www.nnaf.org.) Many women are in this position, so NYAAF's coffers are constantly in danger of depletion. The fund is local, meaning it's specifically for women who have procedures in New York, though it serves women from other states who have to travel to New York to get their abortions. In 1999, I met Lauren Porsch, founder of this fund, while I was writing a story on young people and abortion rights. She was an intern at Planned Parenthood and a student at Barnard where she had just restarted its Students for Choice group. When Lauren started

NYAAF, I knew I wanted to be a part of it. I don't have a lot of money to give, so I helped by hosting and organizing fund-raisers on their behalf. The first one (which Amy ended up having at her house) raised nearly $3,000 and spread the news about NYAAF to about eighty people. Three grand is a lot to NYAAF; the average grant they award is $100. I have a teeny apartment, so I asked my friends with bigger places to host. After the success of this first one, I asked Katha Pollitt, *The Nation* columnist and a friend, if she would have the next fund-raiser at her house. She said she would and offered to provide two cases of wine as a donation. I bought most of the food as my donation ($80), helped set up and clean up. (Buying wine or food is not only a good donation; it's still tax deductible as long as you get a receipt for the amount of goods purchased.)

The next fund-raiser they had planned was a silent auction. I thought about who I knew who might be able to make a donation and came up with Debbie Stoller (the editor of *Bust* magazine) who could offer a two-hour knitting lesson, and Katha Pollitt, who could auction "Lunch with Katha Pollitt." Katha threw in a poster of one of her poems signed by both her and the artist. I called an acquaintance who is a famous drummer to see if she would donate a drum lesson; but she didn't call back. I'll keep her in mind for next time—although after three calls with no response, I usually take that as "Please stop calling me. No really. Stop." Successful fund-raising means providing many opportunities for people to give—one event or cause might not speak to them, but the next thing could. Thinking ahead, I also asked Johnny Temple, the Girls Against Boys bass player and independent publisher of Akashic Books, to host the next fund-raiser for NYAAF in his brownstone in Fort Greene, Brooklyn.

2. Pick up dress for *Glamour* Awards

For fancy fund-raisers and formal events, I like to go in a dress made by a yet-to-be-famous female designer and fight the power in a small way against the Ralph Laurens and Calvin Kleins of the world. I'm definitely a shopaholic—most of my insecurities are sublimated into an irrational belief that if I am wearing the right outfit, my life will be better. I've tried to take the edge off of my consumerism by shopping almost exclusively from young female independent designers with small stores in my neighborhood. Not only do these businesses produce clothes that are in sync with my style but they give me a chance to support a female-owned business. Besides, they are sweatshop-free and they appreciate their loyal customers (so much so that I often get a 20 percent discount!). The first store I was obsessed with was Blue. When that became too bridal-atelier oriented, I turned to Anna, a Debbie-Harry-as-tomboy store about a block from my apartment.

3. Write letter of recommendation for Kathryn Welsh's business school application

When Kathryn was twenty-three (she's twenty-seven as of this writing) she opened the only feminist bookstore in New York City, on the Lower East Side—just blocks from where I live. She ran it cooperatively and named it Bluestockings after the Victorian-era feminists. Within months of its opening, the store became a center for some of the city's many disparate women's movements. New York Radical Cheerleaders held their meetings there, the Backdoor Boys (a drag-king ode to the Backstreet Boys) performed on Bluestockings' teeny platform stage, and Barbara Smith (who started the dearly departed Kitchen Table Press—an influential, if small, feminist press) read to a packed crowd. I am a huge fan of Kathryn's work, so when she decided she wanted to go to business school and asked me to provide a recommendation, I considered the day spent writing the letter a day of activism. I knew that she would infiltrate the business world with a goal of eventually bringing these mainstream success skills back to her queer feminist roots.

4. Host for Haven

When I first saw an e-mail outlining Haven's need for hosts for women and girls who have to travel to New York City for later-term abortions, I looked around my small East Village studio apartment and thought, "There is no way I can host a perfect stranger going through an intense personal moment here!" I had lunch with the founder of Haven anyway, and she convinced me that I could.

When I'm called by the coordinator to host, I pick up the client at the clinic after her first day of the procedure, buy or cook her some dinner, and then make up her Aerobed for the night (which is never more than ten feet from me, I might add). I take her back to the clinic early the next morning to finish her two-step procedure. Sometimes Haven doesn't need me to host overnight, but to Starbuck a woman; that is, I pick up the patient at the clinic, get coffee or a snack with her, and take her to the bus or train station to await her transportation back home. The hosting process has changed my perception of what women need regarding choice. I wish I *didn't* have to host—that there weren't financial restrictions that put women seeking abortions in a position where they have to spend the night with a perfect stranger. I'm more convinced than ever about the need for Medicaid to pay for abortions and the fact that restrictions cause women to get their abortions much later. Later abortions are harder financially, physically, and for some, emotionally.

5. Try to find contact info for Sapphire

My boyfriend Gordon works as a high-school English teacher in a low-income neighborhood in Brooklyn. Not only does his school have too few books for the kids he teaches but the photocopy machine works only sporadically and the computer lab is decidedly low-tech—despite the fact that it is supposedly a school for business and technology. The kids he teaches love *Push*, the wrenching first novel by Sapphire, and pass it around the class as if it were a comic book or favorite record. Since we live in New York, where Sapphire and so many famous artists and writers live, I decided to try to get her to visit his classes. I called Bluestockings, PEN (a writer's association with a program matching famous writers with school programs), and Sapphire's speaker's bureau. I eventually got an e-mail address for her, which I gave to my friend. He initiated a correspondence with her and persuaded the author to speak at a school assembly. By the time the reading was organized, he had collaborated with other high schools and managed to get $500 to pay Sapphire. The reading was incredible. After a performance by two talented student poets, Sapphire took the stage and held the (normally raucous) students rapt for forty-five minutes. Interestingly to me, it turns out that Sapphire used to teach in the Bronx at a school like Gordon's, and many of the characterizations in *Push* came from observing her students—their lives weighted down by missing parents, abuse, early childbearing, and poverty. This successful event spurred my friend to think of other ways to bring a little of the vast resources of New York to his students. The next frontier: a personal library campaign, where kids would get their own sets of half a dozen or so classic books, so they don't have to depend on the battered school copies that seem to invite doodling and often have broken bindings and missing pages. I helped him write a proposal and post it on Donors Choose, a Web site that matches people who want to fund education with individual teachers' initiatives. Sometimes my activism is midwifing someone else to do something activist.

6. Write article for *Roe v. Wade* anniversary

I make my living as a journalist, but I also see writing as a way to be an activist. If I write a story for *The Nation* (a progressive magazine that nonetheless uses predominantly white, older, male writers), my authorship is a statement in itself. In my opinion, *The Nation* is sympathetic enough to write a pro-choice story, but possibly biased enough to have the slant be "Why are young women so antichoice?"—an angle I think is overstated and puts the burden only on young women. This is why I jumped at *The Nation*'s request that I write its thirtieth anniversary of *Roe* story. In the end, my piece focused on the fact that the abortion rate had dropped for every demographic except poor black women. I framed the current atmosphere around choice as less a problem of young female apathy and more one of clear racism. I also could have written this story for a mainstream women's magazine, such as *Glamour*. I relish writing for popular women's magazines because I see it as injecting overt feminism into a magazine with a huge readership (and one with the longest and most consistently pro-choice viewpoint). In either context, I feel like I get to use writing as an activist tool to influence the media and readers.

I always strive to be accurate and to label anything that is opinion, but neither the facts nor the opinions are those that usually show up in the mainstream.

7. Post my response on History-in-Action Listserv about an article stating that young women need to roll up their sleeves and start fighting for abortion rights, which most Listserv members seemed to agree with

I co-founded this Listserv with dozens of Second Wave feminists, many of whom I recognize for their contributions to feminist theory and history. We created it in order to merge the lessons learned and gains made in the seventies with feminist activism today and it's a very lively discussion group. Ruth Rosen, a columnist for the *San Francisco Chronicle*, posts her columns to the Listserv. Her pieces are generally tremendous: progressive, upbeat, and on topics you are unlikely to see other columnists tackle. However, when she wrote a "wake-up call" to young feminists about the importance of abortion rights (I found it patronizing and inaccurate), I had to post a counter to her argument that young women aren't doing enough to preserve and increase choice. I cited the fact that most of the abortion funds were founded and are run by women in their early twenties, that, at the time, Haven is coordinated by a twenty-three-year-old, and that since young women are the people getting the abortions, we are the natural activists—just as Rosen's peers were thirty years ago. Before I hit Send, a part of me thought: Do I really want to publicly criticize Ruth

Rosen? But I decided that neither Ruth nor myself is served by perpetuating the stereotype of the clueless young woman who is letting abortion rights slip away.

We hope these snippets from our calendar and to-do list demonstrate that activism truly is in the details as much as in the huge visionary projects. Rather than being an extracurricular activity—something you do once a week from three to five—activism can be an organic, pleasurable, satisfying part of your daily life.

Appendix A:

A Glossary of the

Most Common

Forms of Activism

The point of *Grassroots* is to create new alternatives to traditional forms of activism. Of course, before we can do that, an understanding of the old approaches is necessary. These are some of the most common forms of activism, which are certainly still relevant today, but *Grassroots* prioritizes the less common forms.

Activist Trainings: Taking an interested body of people and giving them tools with which to organize or protest. Before the antichoice group the Lambs of Christ invaded Fargo in 1991, for instance, staffers from the Fargo Women's Health Clinic trained volunteer escorts in decoying (that is, pretending to be a woman coming into the clinic while the real patient was brought in through another entrance), nonviolent confrontation, and how to avoid getting arrested. Other activist trainings might be less about skills and more about building knowledge. For example, the School of Unity and Liberation teaches young people the history of the civil rights movement or the state of globalization, to prepare them for activism.

Boycotts: Regular people using consumer power to protest the practices of a large corporation, which would typically ignore individual comments. To cite one example, since the early seventies Nestlé has coercively distributed baby formula in developing countries with no sensitivity to the fact that the water used to mix the powdered formula is unclean and breast milk has proved to be an infinitely healthier choice. In 1977, activist groups called for a boycott of all Nestlé products, which has continued (with a short hiatus) until today and which led the World Health Organization to promote the benefits of breast feeding and to draft "The International Code on the Marketing of Breast Milk Substitutes."

Canvassing: Literally going door-to-door providing information and consciousness-raising. Canvassing might be pamphleting for a local candidate or getting out the vote or fund-raising for United Way by ringing doorbells in your neighborhood.

Petitions: A list of signatures in support of a certain issue or person. Some petitions are formally important—part of a structure to get a name on a ballot or a referendum. There are also online petitions, which are employed when there is a broad call for people to send their names individually to a central address, or to put the petition up at a site that hosts petitions, like petitionsonline.com.

Protests: Usually a gathering of people to disrupt the status quo or to erode support for an issue or institution. Protests can be walking out of meetings, organizing a buy-nothing day, National Smoke-out, National Meat-Free Day, etc. In 1903 Mary Harris (Mother) Jones rallied together children working in factories and marched with them for nearly two hundred miles, from city hall in Kensington, Pennsylvania, to President Theodore Roosevelt's house on Long Island, with their maimed fingers held high in the air to protest child exploitation.

Sit-ins: Activists take over spaces that need to be changed and just stay there—sitting tight—until demands are met, consciousness is raised, or the media catch on. In Alabama in the early sixties, the lunch counters at Woolworths were integrated by black men who had the guts to sit in white-only spaces. Similarly, the male-run *Ladies' Home Journal* was invaded by New York Women in Media in 1971. Before the activists left his office, John Mack Carter, then editor in chief, agreed to give the feminists a special section in a future issue to report on women's liberation.

Speak-outs: A public meeting or protest that features personal testimonials, such as often happens at a Take Back the Night march. Speak-outs are generally used to break silence about a taboo subject and to demonstrate the urgency of a particular issue. Thus, the abortion speak-outs of the late sixties were daring, making the point that women were getting illegal procedures and in huge numbers, challenging the idea that something so necessary to many was criminalized. Current speak-outs to legalize marijuana serve a similar purpose—uniting the vast numbers of people who use an illegal substance.

Street Theater: Using guerrilla art and acting to protest publicly. This might be performing *The Vagina Monologues* in the middle of Britain's House of Commons or throwing cherry pies at people who represent abuses of power, as pioneered by the Biotic Baking Brigade. This trio has pied former San Francisco mayor Willie Brown, Bill Gates, Pacific Lumber boss Charles Horowitz, and Keith Campbell, the geneticist who cloned Dolly the sheep. This form of activism tends to gather plenty of media coverage and makes a splash.

Tabling: Public education (pamphlets, handouts, or a person fielding questions at a table), usually taking place at some established event or space like a county fair, rock concert, or student union. Music for America has made a deal with many musicians to provide public education postcards at their concerts. The cards focus on the drug war, health care, and media consolidation—issues that are likely to get concert-goers to vote.

Teach-ins: Usually an informal crash course in a current and complicated political issue, making up for gaps or bias in the media coverage or one's education. After September 11, there were hundreds of teach-ins on college campuses that reflected how little most Americans knew about the Taliban until it directly affected us.

All of these traditional tools work in concert with one another. For instance, Rosa Parks attended activist trainings at the Highlander Folk School. In 1955, her refusal to give up her seat to a white guy—a protest—spawned the Birmingham bus boycotts, and marked the moment when the civil rights movement became visible to the world.

Appendix B: Chapter-by-Chapter Resource Guide

Prologue: Portrait of an Activist

The conflicts with Levi's aside, the Center for Third World Organizing (the publisher of *Colorlines*) is responsible for many great programs targeted toward organizing communities of color, including their national leadership training program, MAAP.

Center for Third World Organizing
1218 East 21st Street
Oakland, CA 94606
(510) 533-7583; fax (510) 533-0923
www.ctwo.org
e-mail: ctwo@ctwo.org

Chapter 1: Why the World Needs Another Advice Book

To keep up to the minute on recycling in New York:

www.nyc.gov/sanitation or www.nycwasteless.org

The National Coalition for the Homeless couldn't help with our recycling efforts, but they exist in many communities and provide clothing, food, and housing to homeless families. To get involved, contact the national office:

National Coalition for the Homeless
1012 Fourteenth Street NW, Suite 600
Washington, DC 20005-3471
(202) 737-6444; fax (202) 737-6445
www.nationalhomeless.org
e-mail: info@nationalhomeless.org

Those five-cent bottle deposits might seem like too little to bother with for you, but they provide income for many homeless and poor people. Perhaps WE CAN, the New York can and bottle redeemer, could be replicated in your town:

WE CAN
630 Ninth Avenue, #900
New York, NY 10036
(212) 262-2222

To find out about environmentally friendlier glass bottles:

Recycle America Alliance
448 Lincoln Highway
Fairless Hills, PA 19030

(215) 269-2100; fax (215) 269-2349
www.recycleamericaalliance.org

Besides publishing the *Democratic Left*, Democratic Socialists of America remains true to its mission of providing socialists with a place to hold on to their hope of a socialist
future:

Democratic Socialists of America
198 Broadway, Suite 700
New York, NY 10038
(212) 727-8610; fax (212) 608-6955
www.dsausa.org
e-mail: dsa@dsausa.org

With more than eight hundred affiliates, there is surely a
Planned Parenthood in your vicinity. Contact them for vol-
unteer information, birth control, or just to get a Pap smear.
The two of us actually live just a few blocks from the original
Planned Parenthood, located on Margaret Sanger Square.

Planned Parenthood New York City
Margaret Sanger Square
26 Bleecker Street
New York, NY 10012
(212) 274-7200
www.ppnyc.org
e-mail: choicevoice@ppnyc.org

For more about Dress for Success creator Nancy Lublin or
to help women transitioning to work check out

Dress for Success
32 East 31st Street, Suite 602
New York, NY 10016
(212) 545-3769; fax (212) 684-0021
www.dressforsuccess.org
e-mail: newyork@dressforsuccess.org

To follow Dr. Rebecca Gomperts's progress with her float-
ing abortion clinic (and her quest to perform procedures
for women in Catholic countries by doing the abortion itself
on international waters), contact

Women on Waves
P.O. Box 1800
1000 BV Amsterdam, The Netherlands
www.womenonwaves.org

Although we criticize major organizations like WEDO for
their generic answers to people's activist questions, we know
what important international work they do. To learn more
or support them, contact

Women's Economic Development Organization
355 Lexington Avenue, 3rd floor
New York, NY 10017
(212) 973-0325; fax (212) 973-0335
www.wedo.org
e-mail: wedo@wedo.org

Stop Hunger NOW
2501 Clark Avenue, Suite 301
Raleigh, NC 27607-7213
(888) 501-8440; fax (919) 839-8971

www.stophungernow.org
info@stophungernow.org

Bringing together local businesses into a neighborhood alliance need not happen only after a terrorist attack. To echo their model, contact

The Tribeca Organization
205 Hudson Street, 2nd floor
New York, NY 10013
(212) 966-0063; fax (212) 966-0276
www.tribecaorganization.org

Though Alice Paul proposed the ERA in 1923, it still hasn't passed. Sigh. To get the ball rolling on the three-state strategy (which is to get three states to ratify it and hope that using another precedent in which the time limit ran out won't be questioned), contact the ERA Campaign Network or the ERA Summit. You can also write your congressperson and ask him or her why the ERA is reintroduced with each new Congress but nothing comes of it:

ERA Campaign Network
www.ERAcampaign.net

ERA Summit
P.O. Box 113
Chatham, NJ 07928
(973) 765-0102; fax (973) 660-0766
www.equalrightsamendment.org
e-mail: era@equalrightsamendment.org

To call your U.S. representatives about issues that annoy you and also about those that elate you, the main numbers are

Senate: (202) 224-3121
House of Representatives: (202) 225-3121

Chapter 2: Of Minor Importance

Amy co-founded Third Wave Foundation in 1992 and Jennifer has been a supporter for nearly that long. We show up at events, give money, and initiate projects with them, but we're taking great pleasure in watching younger women bring the organization in new directions. The I SPY SEXISM T-shirt at Lauren's auction is part of a larger campaign Third Wave created to inspire people to act on the injustices they witness. However, there is a whole host of new and ongoing campaigns to support as well:

Third Wave Foundation
511 West 25th Street, Suite 301
New York, NY 10001
(212) 675-0700; fax (212) 255-6653
www.thirdwavefoundation.org
e-mail: info@thirdwavefoundation.org

There isn't an organization devoted to fighting sexist dress codes, but you can write to us for advice if you want to fight yours. In a nutshell: if teachers and administrators warn the girls but not the boys about attire, that can be used as evidence of unequal treatment. Request your school's dress code, read it carefully, and point out to students and administrators alike where the sexism is. Write to

jenandamy@soapboxinc.com

If you want to help get women's history into your school's history program, there are organizations to help fill that gap:

Matilda Joslyn Gage Foundation
Sally Roesch Wagner, Executive Director
P.O. Box 192
Fayetteville, NY 13066
(315) 637-9511
www.pinn.net/~sunshine/gage/mjg.html
e-mail: MJGageFoundation@aol.com

The National Women's History Project
3343 Industrial Drive, Suite 4
Santa Rosa, CA 95403
(707) 636-2888; fax (707) 636-2909
www.nwhp.org
e-mail: nwhp@aol.com

Shauna Shames was so successful at starting and sustaining her high school's club that we asked her to share suggestions for how to start a high-school feminist group:

Step 1: Find a teacher or staff person who will be your adviser. This can be a man or a woman, but it must be someone with an interest (and hopefully some experience) in feminism. A good way to find an adviser is to talk to any teacher or administrator or staff person who you think might be interested in feminism. If they say they don't have time or don't know enough about it, ask them who else would be good to talk to.

Step 2: You need other students to support you. Find at least one other student who can be your co-president, co-chair, vice president, vice-chair, or whatever you would like to call him or her. You'll need a right-hand person you can count on. If you can find a few other people who are willing to put in more time, it's good to assign roles, like secretary, treasurer, events planner, membership director, publicity or outreach director, and whatever other jobs you think you'll need.

Step 3: Decide what your main issues for the semester will be (that is, pro-choice activism, dealing with body image or eating disorders, re-educating your school about what "feminism" means, stopping sexual harassment on campus, creating intergenerational conversations about women and gender between students and faculty, educating about women's history, raising awareness about gay and lesbian issues or HIV/AIDS, or whatever you want to do). Meet with your co- or vice president and any other leaders you have, and make a plan for the club. Then talk about events you can do or actions you can take to work on those issues. Do you want to hold an assembly for the whole school for Women's History Month? Do you want to team up with some teachers and have a series of lunchtime discussions about women and gender and society? Do you want to raise money for your local Planned Parenthood clinic? Do you want to set up a ride service for students who need to get to the clinic for abortions or birth control or checkups? Do you want to raise money to attend a big march or protest? Think creatively!

Step 4: You're ready to go public. ADVERTISE YOUR-SELF! Put up fliers about your first meeting, talk to everyone you know, make all your friends come and have them bring their friends. Ask your teachers if you can make a quick announcement about your new club at the beginning of class. Have the meeting at a time when you know people can make it—we often did our meetings during lunchtime or study hall rather than after school, as lots of people in the club had after-school sports, theater practice, or other extracurricular pursuits. Find a time that works for a lot of people you know, find a room, and let the world know about it! Plan well for the first meeting, introduce your adviser and student leaders, make sure you present some ideas about what the club will do. You want to look organized and active, especially at the first meeting. Ask for suggestions from the people there, too, and if there is time, have everyone at least say their names and maybe a word or two about why they're there or what they would like to see the club do. You can get great ideas from your membership. Be sure to announce the time of the next meeting at the end of your first meeting!

Step 5: Get connected! Once you have had a few meetings and are feeling more comfortable in your role as leader, start to reach out to the feminist groups and organizations within the larger community. Every state and most big cities have a chapter of the National Organization for Women (NOW). Call them or go by their office if you can, and get to know them. They will help you get plugged into the larger feminist community around your high school. Many of these chapters have whole committees devoted to helping reach young feminists. They'll have ideas on good guest speakers for your group or events for you to join in, and they'll have a calendar of upcoming feminist protests and marches. Find out where your local Planned Parent-hood and battered women's shelters are, introduce yourself to them, offer to volunteer if they need help. If you are in-terested in gay and lesbian or HIV/AIDS issues, reach out to those groups in your community. Many of these groups will be official nonprofits, and you can probably find them online or in the phone book. NOW will also be able to give you a list of feminist groups in the area to talk to. Let people know you're there, and get to know the leaders and groups around you. You can bring them in as lunchtime or assembly speakers, or to strategize with your core group of leaders. They will be happy to hear from young activists, I promise.

Step 6: Get resources! Find books, articles, magazines, and Web sites about feminism in general and about any is-sue you have a particular interest in. Read some of the great feminist classics (see Jennifer and Amy's bibliography and Jackie and Jessica's Chick Lit Curriculum for starters) to get a sense of where feminism has been before you, and also read some of the newer books about and by young feminists to see where your generation is headed. *Ms.* magazine is still a great feminist publication you can subscribe to, and both NOW (www.now.org) and the Feminist Majority Foun-dation (www.feminist.org) have great Web sites with lots of informative and interesting links. Get to know the issues that interest you. You can search your local paper's Web archives to find out what's happening or has happened in your area on these topics, too, and get in touch with the people the articles talk about to get active on the issues. For instance, if you want to raise awareness about HIV/AIDS, check for articles in your local papers about any groups working on this, and call them and ask what you can do on your campus.

Above all, know your issues, work with people you trust, and have fun while you learn and organize!

The gay rights group that Wendy Brovold started at Fargo South High is still going today. We asked her to tell us specifically what she did so others could use her example to start a club in their school:

Step 1: Assess why there is a need for a group and what kind of group it should be. At FSH there were plenty of queer students but none of the faculty and only two of the students were openly gay. This didn't stop queer students from being harassed and isolated, and [Wendy's] school atmosphere meant that information and support were most urgent. For your school, it might be educational events (National Coming Out Day, a drag ball, or a screening of *The Laramie Project*) or political organizing about the issue of gay Boy Scouts or "don't ask, don't tell" policies.

Step 2: Build an alliance. Find an adult who has the authority to give you what you want and who is on your side, ideally a faculty or staff member who will be an ally. Parents can also be influential, especially in small areas where school boards can have the final say. Connect with established LGBT student groups, such as the Gay, Lesbian and Straight Education Network and Advocates for Youth, for support and legitimacy. (You should also check out www.bagly.org.)

Step 3: Put some serious thought into what you want to achieve with this group. Do you want to raise the visibility of gay people and challenge homophobia? Do you want to change school policies? Is it enough to simply have a social group and to make queer students feel safer?

Step 4: Research. You have to be ready to deal with

tough questions. People will ask you, "Why do you need this group?" Find statistics about suicide rates, kids coming out at different ages, why queer kids have to be around kids like themelves, and what the students perceive as "normal" and "not normal."

Step 5: Go public. Announce your group using flyers (post them in coffee shops, bookstores, around the school, on telephone poles), listings in the paper (most local mainstream and alternative papers have free listing sections), e-mails (including students who you think might be gay even if they aren't out).

Step 6: Be ready for the ethical bombardment. You will be accused of being immoral, deviant. You will hear, "God created Adam and Eve, not Adam and Steve. Although it's good to have answers to all questions, even to what you perceive to be the dumbest question in the world, keep in mind that the rights of gay people to exist and live with respect and dignity are not being put forth for dispute. You can say, 'Whether or not you agree with my existence, that's your problem, but I'm not up for debate.'"

Wendy's group is like the sixty-five or so others started through the Gay, Lesbian and Straight Educational Network, known as GLSEN

Gay, Lesbian and Straight Educational Network
121 West 27th Street, Suite 804
New York, NY 10001
(212) 727-0135; fax (212) 727-0254
www.glsen.org
e-mail: glsen@glsen.org

Allison Sparkuhl's feminist group was named after the Le Tigre song "Keep on Living." Like many bands with a young feminist following, Le Tigre is more than a band—it's a movement. They were on the great lesbian-owned record label Mr. Lady, but Mr. Lady recently shut down. Now Le Tigre is on Touch and Go Records. Check out their tour schedule to support or be inspired by their politics:

Le Tigre
www.letigreworld.com
e-mail: info@letigreworld.com

Allison's group raised money for Revolutionary Association of the Women of Afghanistan (RAWA) and for a feminist group in India. There are many groups in India, but the Self Employed Women's Association (SEWA) can always use support, and provides a good model for organizing that could be replicated in the United States. SEWA is an organization of poor, self-employed women laborers whose work tends to be under the radar of the formal economy (and which doesn't qualify for worker benefits). SEWA's main goals are to organize women laborers to obtain work security, income security, food security, and social security (and at a minimum, health care, child care, or shelter).

Revolutionary Association of the Women of Afghanistan
P.O. Box 374
Quetta, Pakistan
U.S. fax: (760) 281-9855
www.rawa.org
e-mail: rawa@rawa.org

Self Employed Women's Association
SEWA Reception Centre
Opp. Victoria Garden
Bhadra, Ahmedabad, 380 001. India
(91-79) 5506444 or 5506477; fax (91-79) 5506446
www.sewa.org
e-mail: mail@sewa.org

Keep on Living connected with men who were working to
end rape. To hook up with men's groups working on this
front, contact

Men Against Sexual Violence
www.menagainstsexualviolence.org

Men Can Stop Rape
P.O. Box 57144
Washington, DC 20037
(202) 265-6530; fax (202) 265-4362
www.mencanstoprape.org
e-mail: info@mencanstoprape.org

National Organization for Men Against Sexism (NOMAS)
P.O. Box 455
Louisville, CO 80027-0455
(303) 666-7043
www.nomas.org
e-mail: info@nomas.org

If independent folk star Ani DiFranco is your hero, you
aren't alone. Learn what she is up to or support her at

Righteous Babe Records
P.O. Box 95, Ellicott Station
Buffalo, NY 14205-0095
(716) 852-8020; fax (716) 852-2741
www.righteousbabe.com
e-mail: info@righteousbabe.com

Melody realized that vegetarian food was her route to activism. Perhaps that could be your path, too:

Feminists for Animal Rights
P.O. Box 41355
Tucson, AZ 85717-1355
(520) 825-6852
www.farinc.org
e-mail: far@farinc.org

Antonia Demas's vegan curriculum is available at

newcentury.vegsource.com/public_html/nutrition/chefs/
Antonia_Demas/overview.html

We don't believe that Title IX and women athletes will just disappear, but you can learn how to strengthen the rights gained by Title IX by contacting

Women's Sports Foundation
Eisenhower Park
East Meadow, NY 11554
(800) 227-3988; fax (516) 542-4716
www.womenssportsfoundation.org
e-mail: wosport@aol.com

Radical Cheerleaders don't cheer for sporting events; they expand what cheerleading can mean:

Radical Cheerleaders
www.radicalcheer.org

If you want to re-create Jackie Arcy and Jessica Hatem's Chick Lit Curriculum, here's what they did:

The required texts were *YELL-Oh Girls!*, by Vicki Nam; *Slut! Growing Up Female with a Bad Reputation*, by Leora Tanenbaum; *Cunt: A Declaration of Independence*, by Inga Muscio; *Manifesta: Young Women, Feminism, and the Future*, by Jennifer Baumgardner and Amy Richards; *The Vagina Monologues*, by Eve Ensler; excerpts from *Backlash: The Undeclared War Against American Women*, by Susan Faludi; and *Transforming a Rape Culture*, edited by Emilie Buchwald, Pamela R. Fletcher, and Martha Roth. They supplemented those texts with articles from *Ms.*, *Bust*, *Off Our Backs*, and other relevant newspaper stories. They also watched videos and popular TV shows such as The Man Show to critique the sexist behavior therein. Students were graded on class participation; projects (debate, art projects, music, sexism); papers (reflections, reports); and given extra credit for attending *The Vagina Monologues*, Take Back the Night, or the local lecture that the two of us gave.

The curriculum:

Week One: What is feminism, including the history of feminism, First Wave, suffrage, Second Wave, and Third Wave
Week Two: Feminist stereotypes

Week Three: Gender roles

Week Four: Sexism (in media, roots of sexism);
    introduced the I Spy Sexism campaign

Week Five: Sexual double standard

Week Six: Feminist music versus pop music

Week Seven: Women in the military—including the
    Tailhook scandal

Week Eight: "Cunts" and menstruation

Week Nine: Abortion, birth control, NARAL, being
    pro-choice

Week Ten: Health issues, insurance

Week Eleven: Feminist organizations and the
    perennial question "Is Feminism Dead?"

Week Twelve: Female genital mutilation

Week Thirteen: Rape

Week Fourteen: Domestic violence shelters

Week Fifteen: African American/Asian/Indian/Native
    American feminisms

Week Sixteen: Religion and feminism (feminist
    interpretations of religion; also, "Can I be a
    feminist and religious?")

Linworth Alternative High School has seniors participate in
a walkabout program that encourages students to become
independent and learn about what sort of life they might
want as adults. For advice on setting up such a program at
your school, contact

Linworth Alternative Program
2075 Dublin-Granville Road
Worthington, OH 43085
(614) 883-3700
www.linworth.org/walkabout.htm

Bust and *Bitch* (see contact information on pages 247–48) started as photocopied and stapled homemade zines; now they are found on many newsstands right next to the glossies—and *Blackgirl* magazine is on the newsstand, too, proving that the world doesn't have to look like *Seventeen* magazine. Or learn about creating your own zine:

Blackgirl Magazine
P.O. Box 90729
Atlanta, GA 30364
(404) 762-0282; fax (404) 762-0283
www.blackgirlmagazine.com
e-mail: editor@blackgirlmagazine.com

Francesca Lia Block and Hillary Carlip, *Zine Scene: The Do It Yourself Guide to Zines* (Los Angeles: Girl Press, 1998).
Veronika Kalma, *Start Your Own Zine, Everything You Need to Know to Put into Print*. New York: Hyperion Books, 1997).

Christi Stieffer was a member of several social justice organizations. These national offices can connect you with more local affiliates:

American Civil Liberties Union
125 Broad Street, 18th floor
New York, NY 10004
(212) 549-2585
www.aclu.org
e-mail: info@aclu.org
(The Web site can connect you to a local branch in your area.)

Human Rights Campaign
1640 Rhode Island Avenue NW

Washington, DC 20036-3278
(202) 628-4160; fax (202) 347-5323
www.hrc.org
e-mail: hrc@hrc.org

National Organization for Women
733 15th Street NW, 2nd floor
Washington, DC 20005
(202) 628-8669; TTY: (202) 331-9002; fax: (202) 785-8576
www.now.org
e-mail: now@now.org

Carissa Trenholm worked with SAGE to create a zine:

Senior Action in a Gay Environment
305 Seventh Avenue, 16th floor
New York, NY 10001
(212) 741-2247; fax: (212) 366-1947
www.sageusa.org
e-mail: sageusa@aol.com

Lisa Holt utilized the sadly shrinking network of independent bookstores to help distribute her book. Because these stores support emerging authors in ways that corporate bookstores just don't, we support them. The NewPages Guide to Independent Bookstores lists indie booksellers by state:

www.newpages.com/NPguides/bookstores.htm

Chapter 3: Rebels with Causes

To find out more about what Van Jones believes in:

The Ella Baker Center for Human Rights
1230 Market Street
PMB # 409
San Francisco, CA 94102
(415) 951-4844; fax (415) 951-4813
www.ellabakercenter.org
e-mail: jakada@ellabakercenter.org

An annual Take Back the Night march is a staple on many college campuses. If it isn't yet in your community, perhaps it can be:

Take Back the Night
109 Summer Hill Lane
St. Davids, PA 19087
(610) 989-0651; fax (610) 989-0652
www.campusoutreachservices.com/tbtn2.htm

The campus-based Feminist Majority Leadership Alliance is just one of the many arms of the Feminist Majority Foundation. An FMLA branch is a good way to jump-start feminist organizing at your college.

Feminist Majority Foundation
1600 Wilson Boulevard, Suite 801
Arlington, VA 22209
(703) 522-2214; fax (703) 522-2219
www.feminist.org

If you want to run for office and have no idea what it entails, consider training at places like

The Women's Campaign School at Yale University
P.O. Box 3307
New Haven, CT 06515-0407
(800) 353-2878 or (203) 734-7385; fax (203) 734-7547
www.wcsyale.org
e-mail: wcsyale@wcsyale.org

In the seventies feminists did an excellent job of creating hundreds of women's studies departments and also women's centers, but if your school is still without one, contact

National Women's Studies Association
University of Maryland
7100 Baltimore Boulevard, Suite 500
College Park, MD 20740
(301) 403-0525; fax (301) 403-4137
www.nwsa.org
e-mail: nwsaoffice@nwsa.org

Emily Feldman learned that working with like-minded groups was her best bet for building alliances. That is a great first step. Other than the groups listed in this book, there is also

Amnesty International
322 8th Avenue
New York, NY 10001
(212) 807-8400; fax (212) 627-1451
www.amnestyusa.org
e-mail: admin-us@aiusa.org

Greenpeace USA
702 H Street NW, Suite 300
Washington, DC 20001
(800) 326-0959
www.greenpeaceusa.org

To see what schools qualify as this year's most activist, *Mother Jones* seems to have its finger on the pulse:

Mother Jones
731 Market Street, 6th floor
San Francisco, CA 94103
(415) 665-6637; fax (415) 665-6696
www.motherjones.com
e-mail: backtalk@motherjones.com

Students at Harvard were successful in getting that university's employees a living wage. These campaigns are happening in most urban areas across the country. To undertake one in your area, here's where to go for an approach:

Living Wage Campaign
Living Wage Resource Center
1486 Dorchester Avenue
Boston, MA 02122
(617) 740-9500; fax (617) 436-4878
www.livingwagecampaign.org

If you want to learn what those students at Yale were thinking or what the outcome of their Middle East role-play action was, contact

Students for Justice in Palestine
www.justiceinpalestine.org
e-mail: info@justiceinpalestine.org

Students at Duke convinced their university to agree to a
strict code of conduct to ensure that their gear was made
under fair conditions. You could ask the same of your university or even of your favorite clothing store. To get the
Code of Conduct for Sweatshops, contact

Worker's Rights Consortium
5 Thomas Circle NW, 5th floor
Washington, DC 20005
(202) 387-4884; fax (202) 387-3292
www.workersrights.org
e-mail: wrc@workersrights.org

Both *Bust* and *Bitch* bring feminists much more than vibra-
tor ads, offering great insight into what young women and
men are thinking and doing. While you're at it, pick up
Fierce, created by Tara Roberts. A subscription is also a way
of supporting independent, women-owned media:

Bust
P.O. Box 1016
Cooper Station
New York, NY 10276
www.bust.com
e-mail: Debbie@bust.com

Bitch Magazine
1611 Telegraph Avenue, Suite 515
Oakland, CA 94612

(510) 625-9390
www.bitchmagazine.com
e-mail: bitch@bitchmagazine.com

Fierce
595 Piedmont Avenue
Suite 320–331
Atlanta, GA 30308
(404) 412-8000
www.fiercemag.com
e-mail: info@fiercemag.com

Rape remains a severe problem on virtually all campuses. There are many avenues to solutions. SAFER provides a model of one promising and evolving program and can be adapted for your campus or alma mater:

Students Active for Ending Rape
28 East 35th Street
New York, NY 10016
(212) 725-3710
www.safercampus.org
e-mail: organizers@safercampus.org

Among Harvard professor Diane Rosenfeld's many accomplishments is a film she co-produced that breaks down what rape is. It's informative and suggests ways to combat sexual assault on your campus or in your town. Find the film at

www.rapeis.org/activism/prevention/menagainstrape.html

Professor Rosenfeld is also working to make links and networks among campus sexual assault policies and programs. She recommends these two groups:

Security on Campus Inc.
133 Ivy Lane, Suite 200
King of Prussia, PA 19406-2101
(610) 768-9330 or (888) 251-7959; fax (610) 768-0646
www.securityoncampus.org
e-mail: soc@securityoncampus.org

www.stopcampusrape.org

Women's eNews reports on all news stories through a feminist lens. Even if this isn't your priority perspective, it's an interesting complement to the daily news:

Women's eNews
135 West 29th Street, Suite 1005
New York, NY 10001
(212) 244-1720; fax (212) 244-2320
www.womensenews.org
e-mail: editors@womensenews.org

To find out how much your professors are paid and to begin to use this information to reform your school's pay structures, check out

Academe
American Association of University Professors
1012 Fourteenth Street NW, Suite 500
Washington, DC 20005

(202) 737-5900; fax (202) 737-5526
www.aaup.org/index.htm

Professors at MIT asked themselves "Where are the women?"
and undertook an adventure in working within the system
to change the system. It's a great model for other organizing endeavors. You can also use this kind of investigation as
a model to investigate your workplace or any other area in
your life that might be in need of pay equity reform. The
MIT study is available at

http://web.mit.edu/fnl/women/women.html

Rather than binging at the Olive Garden or frying in Day-
tona Beach, students can take alternative spring breaks, giving them a chance to gain a new perspective or leave the
world a better place. The groups with whom these programs work get an infusion of energy and a chance to know
what young people are thinking about:

Habitat for Humanity International
121 Habitat Street
Americus, GA 31709-3498
(229) 924-6935, ext. 2551 or 2552
www.habitat.org
e-mail: publicinfo@hfhi.org

Pipeline Project
University of Washington
Gateway Center, MGH 191G
Box 352805
Seattle, WA 98195-2805

(206) 616-2302; fax (206) 685-8299
www.washington.edu/uwired/pipeline
e-mail: pipeline@u.washington.edu

Taco Bell Truth Tour
Food First
Institute for Food and Development Policy
398 60th Street
Oakland, CA 94618
(510) 654-4400; fax (510) 654-4551
www.foodfirst.org/ciw
e-mail: foodfirst@foodfirst.org

Reaching Out Across Movements (ROAMs), created by the
Third Wave Foundation, is no longer officially happening
through the organization, but it's easily replicable and
could make a great model for a spring break tour. See page
230 resources for Third Wave's contact information.

Like Kate Palmer, you could take our advice and contact
these groups for help with organizing in D.C.:

Choice USA
1010 Wisconsin Avenue NW, Suite 410
Washington, DC 20007
(888) 784-4494 or (202) 965-7700; fax (202) 965-7701
www.choiceusa.org
e-mail: info@choiceusa.org

Emmaus Services for the Aging
1426 9th Street NW
Washington, DC 20001

(202) 745-1200; fax (202) 745-1246
www.emmausservices.org/index.html
e-mail: emmaus@emmausservices.org

Kate discovered groups that she hadn't previously worked
with in the planning of her alternative spring break. It's always a good idea just to go out on a whim with new organizations, even if you only end up learning that they exist:

Bread for the City
1525 Seventh Street NW
Washington, DC 20001
(202) 265-2400; fax (202) 745-1081
www.breadforthecity.org
e-mail: info@breadforthecity.org

Community for Creative Non-Violence
425 Second Street NW
Washington, DC 20001
(202) 393-1909; fax (202) 783-3254

Christ House
1717 Columbia Road NW
Washington, DC 20009
(202) 328-1100; fax (202) 232-4972
www.christhouse.org

We highly recommend interning—especially if it's paid—as
a way to figure out what you want to do with your life. If
you are in a position to offer someone an internship, do it—
it could be crucial to nurturing that person's potential.
Don't worry about fanciness—the two of us work out of our

homes and regularly host interns—just working on a great project is enough. We are frequently asked if we know of any internships for budding or already-blossomed feminists. We developed this response:

Yes. Our suggestions are mainly in New York, because that is where we live.

1. The Third Wave Foundation offers internships. Interns work in the Chelsea office on a range of projects from coordinating regional training workshops to organizing a poetry slam. Regular tasks such as answering the phone and filing show up in this internship, too. Contact Third Wave—www.thirdwavefoundation.org—for more information.

2. *Ms.* offers an editorial internship in their Los Angeles office. It's *unpaid*, but you get to see the magazine in action, participate in editorial meetings, learn to fact-check articles, read the slush pile, and do all the regular clerical tasks such as faxing, photocopying, and phoning. Jennifer had an internship at *Ms.* when she was twenty-two and it was life-changing for her—in fact, it led to a job at the magazine. E-mail info@www.msmagazine.com and ask for the "intern coordinator" for more information. As of 2004 the coordinator was Michelle Kort. Contact her directly at mkort@msmagazine.com.

3. *The Nation* (the lefty weekly magazine) has a very good editorial internship program. There is a small stipend that comes with it, you learn to fact-check, and some interns end up writing small pieces (www.thenation.com).

4. The major women's rights, gay rights, civil rights, environmental, abortion rights, etc., organizations tend to

need interns. Try Planned Parenthood, NOW, Feminist Majority Foundation,* Voters for Choice, National Gay and Lesbian Task Force, Honor the Earth, PETA, the ACLU . . . and other organizations listed in this resource guide.

Loews proved to be a decent corporation to work with and if you want to take them up on getting tickets donated to a good cause, fax your request to (646) 521-6292.

Clearview Cinemas, of course, isn't the first mega-company to turn down a good cause. They are certainly entitled to their policies, but as consumers we are also entitled to boycott or to in other ways express our discontent. If you want to write them and ask for a better sense of community responsibility, contact

Clearview Cinemas
97 Main Street
Chatham, NJ 07928
(908) 918-2000
www.clearviewcinemas.com

Liz Masuhr and Anna Davies were able to get movie theater tickets donated to a local shelter. It doesn't have to be movie tickets nor does it have to benefit a shelter, but here's their recipe for replicating something along those lines:

*In 2002, the Feminist Majority Foundation acquired *Ms.*, so FMF also provides *Ms.* magazine internships.

Step 1: Find an outreach program (battered women's shelter, disadvantaged kids tutoring program) in your community.

Step 2: Think of something that might be useful or helpful for the shelter recipients (for example, Liz and Anna decided to get a movie theater to donate tickets).

Step 3: Call the directors of the program and bounce your idea off them. (If they say that they don't need movie tickets, ask them what would be useful.)

Step 4: Call various movie theaters until you get a real person on the phone. If you are in voice-mail hell, punch in any extension to get a real person.

Step 5: Nicely and politely explain your request, underscoring how it would benefit the community and be very little trouble (ideally) for the business itself.

Step 6: Make follow-up calls until you are successful.

Chapter 4: The Real World

Jennifer's abortion campaign (the film, the resource cards, and the re-casting of the *Roe* anniversary as I'm Not Sorry Day) is one attempt at ensuring that women and men can be "out" about their own procedures and feelings. Sometimes just telling your story can be liberating and many pro-choice activists (like Patricia Beninato of imnotsorry.net) are starting to create space for these stories to be documented:

www.imnotsorry.net

Abortion Conversation Project, Inc.
908 King Street, Suite 400W
Alexandria, VA 22314

(703) 684-0055; fax (703) 684-5051
www.abortionconversation.com

To find out how to screen the abortion stories documentary, write to

jennifer@manifesta.net or check out www.soapboxinc.com

In the San Francisco Bay Area, contact Exhale for non-
judgmental after-abortion counseling:

866-4EXHALE
www.4exhale.org

Ask Amy is only one of many things provided at feminist.com.
Check out excerpts from feminist books and an extensive
antiviolence resource guide. There are also links to most
feminist groups, including many that got their first Web-
presence through feminist.com:

Ms. Foundation for Women
120 Wall Street, 33rd Floor
New York, NY 10005
(212) 742-2300; fax: (212) 742-1653
www.ms.foundation.org
e-mail: info@ms.foundation.org

Equality Now
P.O. Box 20646
Columbus Circle Station
New York, NY 10023
www.equalitynow.org
e-mail: info@equalitynow.org

Girls Inc.
120 Wall Street
New York, NY 10005-3902
(800) 374-4475
www.girlsinc.org
e-mail: communications@girlsinc.org

National Committee on Pay Equity
1925 K Street NW, Suite 402
Washington, DC 20006-1119
(202) 223-8360 ext. 8; fax (202) 776-0537
www.pay-equity.org
e-mail: fairpay@patriot.net

9 to 5, National Association of Working Women
152 West Wisconsin Avenue, Suite 408
Milwaukee, WI 53203
(414) 274-0925; fax (414) 272-2870
www.9to5.org
e-mail: 9to5@9to5.org

If you don't yet have a knitting group and want one, Debbie Stoller, of *Bust* fame, has a new book to help—*Stitch 'n Bitch: The Knitter's Handbook*. Better yet, there's a Web site listing the one hundred or so stitch 'n bitch groups that have popped up in the last few years:

www.stitchnbitch.org

One-stop shopping for your reproductive health needs—from basic gynecological care to how to yell at Congress for the antiwomen legislation they passed this week:

Planned Parenthood Federation of America
434 West 33rd Street
New York, NY 10001
(800) 230-7526 or (212) 541-7800; fax (212) 245-1845
www.plannedparenthood.org
e-mail: communications@ppfa.org

What Meredith O'Neill Hassett, Louise Rexer, and Kristy
Irvine Ryan started is replicable for anyone with a few extra dollars and hours a month. These graceful gestures of
activism are often the most rewarding. They aren't formalized and are unexpected—like offering someone a seat on
the subway—but can have a big impact:

Secret Smiles
233 Wall Street, #213
Huntington, NY 11743
phone/fax: (631) 673-3918
www.secretsmiles.org
e-mail: secretsmiles@att.net

Nancy Lublin left Dress for Success to become executive
director of Do Something, an organization committed to
helping young people change the world:

Do Something
24–32 Union Square East
4th Floor South
New York, NY 10003
www.dosomething.org

We met Karin Heisecke at the November 2001 New Girl
Order conference in London, England. This conference

was a great gathering of feminist academics and activists from around the world. Conferences are often bureaucratic and expensive, but the idea behind them—bringing like-minded people together—is something valuable:

www.newgirlorder.org

To buy organic Muskrat coffee, support the Wild Rice Campaign, or find out more about what White Earth Land Recovery Project is working on:

White Earth Land Recovery Project
32033 East Round Lake Road
Ponsford, MN 56575
(888) 779-3577 or (218) 573-3448; fax (218) 573-3444
www.welrp.org
e-mail: info@welrp.org

Haven requires an open mind, a few hours, and a couch. It could be replicated in your town, not only to help women who need abortions but to host activists who travel for marches, people who are lobbying, or any individual who can't afford a hotel. The current coordinators can give advice about how to become a haven or use the following recipe to replicate their work:

(917) 371-2035
e-mail: Havencoalition@yahoo.com

We asked Catherine to condense what she told us about starting Haven so we could make it widely available to others. Here's what she said:

Step 1: Assess whether the clinic in your area needs hosts and, if so, make an appointment with the clinic administrator.

Step 2: Tailor your activism to what the clinic's needs are. Most towns don't do later-term abortions that would attract women from out of town who need to stay for several days. Many states, however, do have twenty-four-hour waiting periods and only one clinic in the entire state, meaning clients may have to drive great distances and stay overnight, which might precipitate a need for hosting. Madison, Wisconsin, for instance, has three clinics and a waiting period. One clinic there organized with the local Red Roof Inns to provide rooms for women traveling for abortions. In other places, at Planned Parenthood New York City, for instance, they don't need hosts, but they do need people to pick up clients and accompany them to their neighborhoods or to public transportation.

Step 3: Once you have gotten the go-ahead from a clinic that they need your help, form a solid relationship. Develop a formal structure for doing intake and communicating that is appropriate to both their needs and time constraints.

Step 4: Get to know media, press, and publicity in your area. "There are so many people who want to help," says Shauna Shames, the second coordinator of Haven. "But they need to know what you are doing."

Step 5: If you are doing hosting, Starbucking, or escorting, screen the interested recruits. During the interview with prospective hosts, discuss why the person wants to be a host—are they approaching it from an activist side, personal side, etc. Shauna told us that she screens for the people who are pro-choice, but not exactly pro-abortion. The idea of helping someone is very attractive to most people, but in two interviews, she had to turn people down due to their ambivalence about abortion.

The National Abortion Federation is a network of abortion providers such as those at Westside Women's Clinic and Eastern Women's Clinic, the two clinics in New York City that Haven works with. Their hotline directs individuals to the nearest NAF-approved abortion provider. They also have statistics related to abortion, should you need to make a case:

National Abortion Federation
1755 Massachusetts Avenue NW, Suite 600
Washington, DC 20036
(202) 667-5881 or (800) 772-9100
www.prochoice.org

Besides the New York Abortion Access Fund (NYAAF), there are nearly one hundred abortion funds across the country—and new funds are created each year. We still need more, in case you want to start one or support an existing one—or need one:

National Network of Abortion Funds
c/o CLPP
Hampshire College
Amherst, MA 01002-5001
(413) 559-5645; fax (413) 559-6045
www.nnaf.org
e-mail: info@nnaf.org

New York Abortion Access Fund
P.O. Box 7569, FDR Station
New York, NY 10150

(212) 252-4757
www.nnaf.org/nyaaf
e-mail: nyaaf@nnaf.org

When Catherine Megill needed to get the word out about
Haven, she approached the Brooklyn Pro-Choice Network.
Every issue needs a network—this means easy access to in-
dividuals for marches or protests, or to celebrate a victory.
It's also comforting to individual members to know that
they aren't alone:

Brooklyn Pro-Choice Network
172 Fifth Avenue, #122
Brooklyn, NY 11217
www.brooklynprochoicenetwork.org
e-mail: brooklynprochoicenetwork.org

Aradia Women's Health Center took reproductive health
care to a political level by advertising voter registration in
their clinic. Other progressive organizations should make
this link between what happens in their offices and on Capitol Hill. Even the price of milk is affected by who is in office—and if you don't vote, you lose your right to complain:

Aradia Women's Health Center
1300 Spring Street, Suite 500
Seattle, WA 98104
(800) 644-9389 or (206) 323-9388; fax (206) 323-0120
www.aradia.org
e-mail: aradiawhc@aradia.org

The League of Women Voters has long been a great resource for voting. When Amy was organizing Freedom

Summer '92, she was dependent on them for the latest information about how each state conducted its elections. The organization could also use an infusion of younger participants—as could voting:

The League of Women Voters
1730 M Street NW, Suite 1000
Washington, DC 20036-4508
(202) 429-1965; fax (202) 429-0854
www.lwv.org
e-mail: lwv@lwv.org

No matter how much bitching about the media's impact we do, eating disorders won't go away. Though seemingly intractable, we have to keep challenging ourselves to look beyond the media for solutions:

Eating Disorders Coalition for Research, Policy and Action
611 Pennsylvania Avenue SE, #423
Washington, DC 20003-4303
(202) 543-9570
www.eatingdisorderscoalition.org
e-mail: manager@eatingdisorderscoalition.org

Chapter 5: The Activist at Work

Indigenous people remain the world's most marginalized group. There is hope that with land rights, self-governance, and some means of being economically self-sufficient, they can move from this oppressed place and return to their goal of living in balance with the earth. There are many groups working with this population, including

First Nations Development Institute
2300 Fall Hill Avenue, Suite 412
Fredericksburg, VA 22401
(540) 371-5615; fax (540) 371-3505
www.firstnations.org
e-mail: info@firstnations.org

Soapbox is our first official business venture. So far it has
proved to be a success and has helped to connect students
with feminist speakers:

Soapbox, Inc.
106 Suffolk Street #2A
New York, NY 10002
(646) 486-1414; fax (212) 674-4930
www.soapboxinc.com
e-mail: jenandamy@soapboxinc.com

We aren't the only progressive speaker's bureau; among
others is

Circle of Life
P.O. Box 3764
Oakland, CA 94609
(510) 601-9790; fax (510) 601-9788
www.wetheplanet.org
e-mail: info@circleoflife.org

We were thankful to finally be in a financial position to be
able to pay the Handy Design Company for the work they
do. They still do pro bono ventures for us and we are always looking for other graphic designers to share their expertise. Most organizations need design help—in fact, most

depend on it to get their information out in a digestible format. If you can afford to pay for it, consider Handy Design, or if you are a designer, consider donating your creativity:

The Handy Design Company
(530) 566-1157
www.handydesignco.com
e-mail: erin@handydesignco.com

The Guerrilla Girls are waking people up on several campuses. There are actually three Guerrilla Girls groups—Broadband, On Tour, and the original. All tackle the issue of feminist art and the lack of mainstream representation of women artists. They are inspiring as speakers or as a model for how to turn your town's museum into a feminist inclusive one:

Guerrilla Girls
www.guerrillagirls.com
e-mail: gg@guerrillagirls.com

The YWCA was doing community organizing before there was even a term for it. They exist in most towns and magnetize many disparate groups through their wide-ranging programming. We reached out to them when we first started traveling around the country to see what groups they were working with and what types of issues they were addressing. The Y is often overlooked when it comes to undertaking projects—and they shouldn't be:

YWCA
1015 18th Street NW, Suite 1100
Washington, DC 20036

(202) 467-0801; fax (202) 467-0802
www.ywca.org
e-mail: info@ywca.org

Even the most conservative workplaces concede that they
have certain kinds of activism available to their workers.
Adopting a highway and walking, riding, or dancing for
AIDS should be the *minimum* that a workplace can provide:

AIDS Walk
P.O. Box 10
Old Chelsea Station
New York, NY 10113
(212) 807-9255; fax (212) 807-6429
www.aidswalk.net
e-mail: awnyinfo@aidswalk.net

Adopt a Highway
3151 Airway Avenue, Suite F-110
Costa Mesa, CA 92626
(800) 358-0231; fax (800) 358-0230
www.adoptahighway.com
e-mail: info@adoptahighway.com

Planned Parenthood has made it easy for employees to ask
that their employers cover birth control as a part of their
comprehensive health coverage. (They've been successful,
too. In the last decade three times as many group insurance
plans purchased by employers cover contraceptives, in large
part due to campaigns spearheaded by Planned Parenthood to change state laws.) This model could be adopted
for other issues that employers should be providing:

Fair Access to Contraception
Cover My Pills
(800) 727-2996
www.covermypills.org

In an ideal world, none of us would ever have a need to file a sex discrimination case. If you do, though, contact the Equal Employment Opportunity Commission to figure out if you have grounds for a suit and what steps you need to take in order to properly file a claim:

Equal Employment Opportunity Commission
1801 L Street NW
Washington, DC 20507
(202) 663-4900; fax (202) 663-4494
www.eeoc.gov

If you don't want to deal with the waiting time at the EEOC or if you know there is a case and need legal advice, there are lots of nonprofits devoted to helping. For starters, check out these two:

Legal Momentum
395 Hudson Street
New York, NY 10014
(212) 925-6635; fax (212) 226-1066
www.legalmomentum.org
e-mail: peo@legalmomentum.org

Equal Rights Advocates
1663 Mission Street, Suite 250
San Francisco, CA 94103

(415) 621-0672; fax (415) 621-6744
www.equalrights.org
e-mail: info@equalrights.org

Boycotts mean that consumers can expect the companies
they support to be accountable to a larger good. These
protests need not be large; you could just refuse to patron-
ize a business whose practices you don't agree with.

Boycott Action News
Co-op America
1612 K Street NW, Suite 600
Washington, DC 20006
(800) 584-7336
www.boycotts.org or www.coopamerica.org
e-mail: boycotts@coopamerica.org

Businesses can be socially responsible and profitable. It's a
challenge for business owners to present new models, but
those that do are likely to earn a loyal customer base. We
mention these unique, morally adept businesses—and there
are many more:

Daemon Records
P.O. Box 1207
Decatur, GA 30031
www.daemonrecords.com
e-mail: hello@daemonrecords.com

Bluestockings
172 Allen Street
New York, NY 10002
(212) 777-6028; fax (212) 777-6042

www.bluestockings.com
e-mail: info@bluestockings.com

Akashic Books
P.O. Box 1456
New York, NY 10009
(212) 433-1875; fax (212) 414-3199
www.akashicbooks.com
e-mail: akashic7@aol.com

Jane Lockett found a group in her community and asked
the best question: What do you need?

Laura's House
California Domestic Violence Center
27129 Calle Arroyo, Suite 1822
San Juan Capistrano, CA 92675
(949) 361-3775; fax (949) 361-3548
www.laurashouse.org
e-mail: laurashouse@laurashouse.org

Rani Chattergee began her career at the New York Civil
Liberties Union, which is a part of the American Civil Liberties Union. This particular chapter has a teen health initiative, a great resource for teens' rights generally but most
expert, obviously, on New York state laws:

New York Civil Liberties Union
125 Broad Street
New York, NY 10004
(212) 344-3005; fax (212) 344-3318
www.nyclu.org
e-mail: DeSilver@aclu.org

Rani was involved in many organizations, including the Third Wave Foundation and SAKHI for South Asian Women. We already told you about Third Wave, so

SAKHI for South Asian Women
P.O. Box 20208
Greeley Square Station
New York, NY, 10001
(212) 714-9153; fax (212) 564-8745
www.sakhi.com
e-mail: sakhiny@aol.com

You don't have to be a hotel executive to influence your workplace to offer its resources to those in need. Project Debby could, in fact, exist wherever there is a domestic violence shelter.

Project Debby, Inc.
(262) 240-0400
www.projectdebby.com
e-mail: info@projectdebby.com

Chapter 6: Creating Activism

The zine *Bamboo Girl* is Sabrina Margarita's contribution to art and feminism—and a great expression of her activism:

Bamboo Girl
Sabrina Margarita Alcantara-Tan
P.O. Box 507
New York, NY 10159-0507
www.bamboogirl.com
e-mail: bamboogirl@aol.com

The ethic of Punk Planet combines art and social justice, interviewing activists like Winona LaDuke, and pointing out the connections between punk rock and creating a revolutionary new world:

Punk Planet
4229 North Honore
Chicago, IL 60613
(773) 248-7172; fax (773) 248-7189
www.punkplanet.com
e-mail: punkplanet@punkplanet.com

Films like Nisha's are available at local video stores and through places like Women Make Movies and Joanie 4 Jackie, a distribution group founded by Miranda July:

Women Make Movies, Inc.
462 Broadway, Suite 500WS
New York, NY 10013
(212) 925-0606; fax (212) 925-2052
www.wmm.com
e-mail: info@wmm.com

Joanie 4 Jackie
c/o The Bard College Film Department
P.O. Box 5000
Annandale-on-Hudson, NY 12504
www.joanie4jackie.com
e-mail: info@joanie4jackie.com

For those who want to get involved in politics as usual, here is one of the places that can help direct your energies:

Women's Campaign Fund
734 15th Street NW, Suite 500
Washington, DC 20005
(202) 393-8164 or (800) 446-8170; fax (202) 393-0649
www.wcfonline.org
e-mail: deputy@wcfonline.org or rachel@wcfonline.org

The Feminist Majority Foundation created Rock for Choice to attract more people to the issue of reproductive choice. Their goal with these concerts is to raise money and consciousness:

Rock for Choice
www.feminist.org/rock4c/book/intro.html

The program that Judy Chicago created at Fresno State is still going strong:

The Feminist Art Symposium
(559) 278-2153
www.fresnostate.net/femart/welcome.htm
e-mail: feministart@email.com

As a patron of the arts, Elizabeth A. Sackler resurrected Judy Chicago's *The Dinner Party* and gave it a permanent home at the Brooklyn Museum of Art. Chicago's piece will become one of many aspects of the newly minted Elizabeth A. Sackler Center for Feminist Art:

Elizabeth A. Sackler Center for Feminist Art
The Brooklyn Museum of Art
200 Eastern Parkway
Brooklyn, NY 11238

(718) 638-5000; fax (718) 501-6136
www.brooklynmuseum.org
e-mail: information@brooklynmuseum.org

Ladyfest began as a one-time event in Olympia, Washington, and each year adds new cities, in the United States and abroad, to its web of affiliations. No one owns it and you can do it your own way in your community:

LadyFest
www.ladyfest.org
e-mail: info@ladyfest.org

Musician Jenny Toomey first helped artists put out their own records by co-authoring the Simple Machine's "Mechanics Guide" with Kristin Thompson. More recently, she is helping other artists to both fight the FCC and educate artists about "music, technology, public policy and intellectual property law." Like her work on the "Mechanics Guide," the FMC also promotes innovative business models "that will help musicians and citizens to benefit from new techologies." You can get the guide online at www.indiecentre.com/info/guide.cfm.

Future of Music Coalition
c/o Michael Bracy
1615 L Street NW
Suite 520
Washington, DC 20036
(202) 429-8855; fax (202) 429-8857
www.futureofmusic.org

In 2004, the National Women's Music Festival celebrated its thirtieth anniversary. We have no reason to believe it won't be around for thirty more:

National Women's Music Festival
P.O. Box 1427
Indianapolis, IN 46206-1427
(317) 713-1144; fax (317) 916-1212
www.wiaonline.org
e-mail: wia@wiaonline.org

The art world has begun to prioritize women and feminists have begun to prioritize art correspondingly. There are now two national museums devoted to women and two are in development (the two that are pending don't have contact information yet, but are slated for New York City and Washington, D.C.):

National Museum of Women in the Arts
1250 New York Avenue NW
Washington, DC 20005-3990
(800) 222-7270 or (202) 783-5000
www.nmwa.org

The Women's Museum
3800 Parry Avenue
Dallas, TX 75226
(214) 915-0860; fax (214) 915-0870
www.thewomensmuseum.org
e-mail: Bea.Bourne@thewomensmuseum.org

Rozz Nash developed her vision of a community for women artists into reality. To create your own WERISE, contact

Women Empowered through Revolutionary Ideas
Supporting Enterprise
111 East 14th Street, #392
New York, NY 10003
(212) 561-9746
www.werise.org
e-mail: werise@hotmail.com

The Sister Fund can't give free office space to everyone, but it's likely that there is a generous leaseholder somewhere in your area. Beyond free space, the Sister Fund is a source for funding and learning about innovative projects:

The Sister Fund
116 East 16th Street, 7th floor
New York, NY 10003
(212) 260-4446; fax (212) 260-4633
www.sisterfund.org
e-mail: info@sisterfund.org

The Vagina Monologues is performed in more than a thousand communities annually, and V-Day is a great organizing model:

Vagina Monologues/V-Day
www.vday.org
e-mail: info@vday.org

Oxfam pioneered a form of activism that was adapted widely on college campuses, asking students to fast for a day and give the money that would have been spent on food to the cause of ending world hunger. Some students gave the money but ate anyway, eliminating the empathy part of the mission but still raising money. It became a great model for low-impact organizing:

Oxfam America
26 West Street
Boston, MA 02111
www.oxfamamerica.org
e-mail: info@oxfamamerica.org

Fighting racism, anti-Semitism, and homophobia are the priorities of Facing History and Ourselves, an organization that supplements high-school curricula. They do this mostly through training middle- and high-school teachers who then go out and impart this information to their students. Their philosophy focuses on the power of the bystander. Even as observers, we contribute to crime, racism, and bigotry. Their message is: you have to act and interrupt these passively transmitted evils. *Grassroots* tries to give you the tools to act, so we feel a complementary kinship with Facing History and Ourselves:

Facing History and Ourselves
16 Hurd Road
Brookline, MA 02445
(617) 232-1595; fax (617) 232-0218
www.facinghistory.org

Chapter 7: The Revolutionary Next Door

Though perhaps not entirely current with pop culture, *Our Bodies, Ourselves* is always up-to-date on women's health needs. You can read the book and contact the organization:

Our Bodies Ourselves
34 Plympton Street
Boston, MA 02118
(617) 451-3666; fax (617) 451-3664
www.ourbodiesourselves.org
e-mail: office@bwhbc.org

Even if you don't go so far as to leave your copy of *Colorlines*
or *Ms.* at the dentist's office, we at least recommend that
you read them:

Colorlines
PMB 319
4096 Piedmont Avenue
Oakland CA, 94611-5221
(510) 653-3415; fax (510) 653-3427
www.colorlines.com
e-mail: colorlines@arc.org

Ms. Magazine
433 S. Beverly Drive
Beverly Hills, CA 90212
(310) 556-2515; fax (310) 556-2514
www.msmagazine.com
e-mail: info@msmagazine.com

To oppose sweatshop labor and other negative repercussions of globalization:

Sweatshop Watch
310 Eighth Street, Suite 303
Oakland, CA 94607
(510) 834-8990

www.sweatshopwatch.org
e-mail: sweatinfo@sweatshopwatch.org

If you haven't yet sent your $1 to UNFPA, they are still at-
tempting to make up for the $34 million shortfall precipi-
tated by the U.S. government's refusal to release funds:

34 Million Friends of UNFPA
c/o The U.S. Committee for UNFPA
3800 Arapahoe Avenue, Suite 210
Boulder, CO 80303
www.unfpa.org or www.34millionfriends.com
e-mail: info@34millionfriends.org

For information on Moveon.org or Meetup, go to

www.moveon.org and www.meetup.com

RAINN has current rape statistics and also offers a great
support network to survivors of sexual assaults:

Rape, Abuse and Incest National Network
635-B Pennslyvania Avenue SE
Washington, DC 20003
(800) 656-4673, ext. 3 or (202) 544-1034; fax (202) 544-3556
www.rainn.org
e-mail: info@rainn.org

NRDC does great work, even if they occasionally miss the
mark when it comes to bringing in new recruits:

National Resources Defense Council
40 West 20th Street

New York, NY 10011
(212) 727-2700; fax: (212) 727-1773
www.nrdc.org
e-mail: nrdcaction@nrdc.org

To begin to make your lifestyle reflect your values, here are
a few places to start:

Bradley Berman's general information Web site about hybrid cars:

www.hybridcars.com
e-mail: brad@hybridcars.com

Seventh Generation, Inc.
212 Battery Street, Suite A
Burlington, VT 05401-5281
(800) 456-1191 or (802) 658-3773; fax (802) 658-1771
www.seventhgeneration.com

The Rebuilding Center of Our United Villages
3625 North Mississippi Avenue
Portland, OR 97227
(503) 331-1877
www.rebuildingcenter.org/deconstruct

Epilogue: A Day in the Life of an Activist

Estelle Freedman keeps her Web site current:

http:noturningback.stanford.edu

BETTY's calendar is rarely empty, but contact them to play at your event, or if you are a musician/activist, be inspired by their tireless efforts:

BETTY Rules
www.bettyrules.com
e-mail: BETTY@hellobetty.com

Recently merged with Planned Parenthood Action Fund, Voters for Choice was one of the first organizations committed to figuring out who is honestly a pro-choice candidate. You can give them your money or your time, or learn their model of quizzing candidates to get to the root of their position:

Voters for Choice
c/o PPAF
434 West 33rd Street
New York, NY 10001
(212) 541-7800; fax (212) 245-1845
www.ppaction.org
e-mail: actionfund@ppfa.org

There are several women's music festivals, but the Michigan Womyn's Music Festival is the mother of them all. It's also the site of an evolving understanding of transgenderism and feminism:

Michigan Womyn's Music Festival
P.O. Box 22
Walhalla, MI 49458
(231) 757-4766
www.michfest.com

You can easily copy Bill Wetzel's TALK TO ME sign. It's a bit more difficult to create an organization to protest standardized tests. Join already existing ones like Students Against Testing to protest these outdated exams:

Students Against Testing
615 Little Silver Point Road
Little Silver, NJ 07739
www.nomoretests.com
e-mail: discuss@nomoretests.com

Like Nicole Vandenberg, you can support Home Alive:

Home Alive
1415 10th Avenue
Seattle, WA 98122
(206) 323-4663
www.homealive.org
e-mail:selfdef@homealive.org

If you are inspired by Pearl Jam's example and want to start a campaign in your city to strengthen your school's libraries, start by following this model:

Northwest Literacy Foundation
Fill the Shelves Campaign
P.O. Box 3514
Seattle, WA 98214
www.nwliteracy.org
e-mail: nwl@nwliteracy.org

Filmmakers can give their time to Scenarios USA, as can educators and students interested in combining political messages with filmmaking:

Scenarios USA
80 Hanson Place Suite 305
Brooklyn, NY 11217
(718) 230-5125
www.scenariosusa.org
e-mail: info@scenariosusa.org

Ariel Gore and Bee Lavender not only wrote a book, but run a great Web site for mothers who want to be more than cupcake-makers and lullaby-singers:

www.hipmama.com

Kathryn Welsh, the founder of Bluestockings, is now fully immersed in business school. With new owners, this radical (rather than solely feminist) bookstore has continued to serve the young progressives of New York City. (See address on p. 268.)

The National Coalition Against Domestic Violence is a great resource for connecting with local shelters and also with other groups working to end violence against women:

National Coalition Against Domestic Violence
P.O. Box 18749
Denver, CO 80218
(800) 799-7233 or (303) 839-1852; fax (303) 831-9251
www.ncadv.org
e-mail: mainoffice@ncadv.org

If you are a feminist in need of therapy or are looking to create better referral services for therapists, these places are a great start:

Ackerman Institute for the Family
149 East 78th Street
New York, NY 10021-0405
(212) 879-4900, ext. 100; fax (212) 744-0206
www.ackerman.org
e-mail: ackerman@ackerman.org

Feminist Therapy Referral Project California
(510) 843-2949
www.feministtherapy.org
e-mail: feministtherapy@mail2woman.com

The Women's Therapy Centre Institute
562 West End Avenue, Suite 1A
New York, NY 10024
(212) 721-7005; fax (212) 721-5554
www.wtci-nyc.org
e-mail: wtcinyc@aol.com

Looking to connect with your favorite writer? PEN might be able to help—and specifically to help teachers like Gordon who want to bring their students' role models into the classroom. (It's also a good idea to contact writers through their publishing house, which is listed in the book itself.) Meanwhile, Donors Choose connects funders with one-time projects initiated by public schoolteachers:

PEN American Center
568 Broadway 4th floor

New York, NY 10012
(212) 334-1660; fax (212) 334-2181
www.pen.org
e-mail: pen@pen.org

Donors Choose
347 W. 36th Street, Suite 503
New York, NY 10018
(212) 239-3615; fax (212) 239-3619
www.donorschoose.org
e-mail: ilana@donorschoose.org

Notes

Prologue

xix *Lois Weisberg from Chicago, Illinois*: Malcolm Gladwell, "Six Degrees of Lois Weisberg," *The New Yorker*, January 11, 1999.

xxiii *Al Sharpton took Republican funding*: Wayne Barrett, with special reporting by Adam Hutton and Christine Lagorio, "Sleeping with the G.O.P.," *The Village Voice*, February 5, 2004.

xxiii Colorlines *magazine*: Ryan Pintado-Vertner, "From Sweatshop to Hip-Hop," *Colorlines*, Summer 2002, Vol. 5, #2. The letters from Levi's, underscoring their commitment to social justice, including funding *Colorlines*, appeared in the Fall 2002 issue, Vol. 5, #3.

Chapter 1

3 *"How do we bring . . .":* "Special Report 2000," *The Crisis*, Nov./Dec. 2000.

12 *much of the millions of dollars*: Nick Paumgarten, reporting in the February 18, 2002, issue of *The New Yorker*, revealed that: "The Red Cross was offering Tribeca residents the equivalent of three months' mortgage and maintenance payments

(or rent), along with money for utilities, groceries, transportation, and medical expenses, if applicable. In a building like the ones on Hudson Street, some victims could expect more than fifteen thousand dollars." Paumgarten went on to report that these residents weren't in fact victims of a heinous crime, but rather exploiters of a poorly run system.

12 *"Regardless of whether our listeners . . ."*: Malveaux wrote this in the October 25, 2002, issue of *USA Today*.

Chapter 2

25 *"I mean to resist the hatred . . ."*: June Jordan, *On Call: New Political Essays 1981–85*, South End Press, 1985.

30 *Egalitarian society*: To learn more about how equality is possible because it did exist among Native American tribes, consult the work of Sally Roesch Wagner, including *Sisters in Spirit: Haudnosaunee (Iroquois) Influence on Early American Feminists*, Summertown, TN: Native Voices, 2001.

36 *"Among women . . ."*: The *Ms.* poll was reported on in the Spring 2003 issue of the magazine, which also included an article by Lorriane Dusky titled "Feminist Tide Sweeps In as the 21st Century Begins."

Chapter 3

58 *"Boomers grew up drunk . . ."*: For more on Brooks's assessment of the boomer generation, see "The Transformer: Is Tony Blair What Bill Clinton Should Have Been?" *The Atlantic Monthly*, July/August 2003.

58 *"apolitical"*: From Meredith Bagby's *We've Got Issues* (2000).

65 *Only 37 percent . . .* This is according to the Spring 2003 issue of *Ms.*, quoting a report released by Congress in Fall 2002.

70 *"insisting victims turn over"*: From Gretchen Cook, "Campuses May Be Developing Tactics to Hide Rapes," *Women's eNews*, May 25, 2003.

76 *Within five years, the number of women on the School of Science faculty increased*: For the full story on how MIT approached gender, see http://mit.edu.fnl/women/women.html.

Chapter 5

127 *"Activism should be directed at achieving . . ."*: Jonathan Schnell, "No More unto the Breach," *Harper's Magazine*, April 2003, pp. 41–55.

Chapter 6

155 *"[F]or me it's just very obvious . . ."*: Jessica Gary and Janine Lidell, "Bamboo Girl: Sabrina Margarita Alcantara-Tan," *The Matrix: The Humboldt State University Magazine of the Women's Center*, Spring 2003.

160 *"To insist that they're opposite . . ."*: Daniel Sinker, ed., *We Owe You Nothing*, New York: Akashic Books, 2001.

163 *"I believe the American culture is so infused . . ."*: Matt Dellinger, "Redeemers," www.newyorker.com, April 21, 2003.

166 *"What art in the next 30 years . . ."*: Holland Cotter, "Two Nods to Feminism Long Snubbed by Curators," *The New York Times*, October 11, 2002.

167 *"a smorgasbord of feminist . . ."*: Roberta Smith, "A Raucous Caucus of Feminists Being Bad," *The New York Times*, January 21, 1994.

167 *"Seemed that to be a woman artist . . ."*: From "Gloria," the official catalog of the exhibition. Published by White Columns, the sponsoring gallery, 2002.

189 *According to* The Economist . . . : "Gauging generosity: Which rich countries do most to help poor countries?" *The Economist*, May 3, 2003.

196 *Having Tara's complaint on file*: This story was reported locally in a December 6, 2002, 1010wins.com story.

Appendix B

266 *They've been successful, too* . . . : According to a 2004 Alan Guttmacher Institute Study (www.guttmacher.org/pubs/journals/3607204.html).

Bibliography

Bagby, Meredith. *We've Got Issues: The Get Real, No B.S., Guilt-Free Guide to What Really Matters*. New York: Public Affairs, 2000.

Bartlett, John. *The Future Is Ours: A Handbook for Student Activists in the 21st Century*. New York: Owl Books, 1996.

Baumgardner, Jennifer, and Amy Richards. *Manifesta: Young Women, Feminism, and the Future*. New York: Farrar, Straus and Giroux, 2000.

Blaustein, Arthur I. *Make a Difference: Your Guide to Volunteering and Community Service*. Berkeley, CA: HeyDay Books, 2002.

Bornstein, David. *How to Change the World: Social Entrepreneurs and the Power of New Ideas*. New York: Oxford University Press, 2004.

Brumberg, Joan Jacobs. *The Body Project: An Intimate History of American Girls*. New York: Vintage, 1998.

Buchwald, Emilie, Pamela R. Fletcher, and Martha Roth. *Transforming a Rape Culture*. Minneapolis, MN: Milkweed Editions, 1995.

Chideya, Farai. *The Color of Our Future*. New York: Willian Morrow, 1999.

———. *Don't Believe the Hype: Fighting Cultural Misinformation About African Americans*. New York: Plume, 1995.

Collins, Joseph, Stefano DeZerega, and Zahara Heckscher. *How to Live Your Dream of Volunteering Overseas*. New York: Penguin Books, 2002.

Costello, Cynthia B., Vanessa R. Wight, and Anne J. Stone. *The American Woman 2003–2004: Daughters of a Revolution—Young Women Today*. New York: Palgrave, 2003.

Coupland, Douglas. *Generation X: Tales for an Accelerated Culture*. New York: St. Martin's Press, 1991.

Cowan, John, and Rob Nelson. *Revolution X: A Survival Guide for Our Generation*. New York: Penguin Books, 1994.

Demas, Antonia. *Hot Lunch: A History of the School Lunch Program*. New York: Food Studies Institute, 2000.

Ducombe, Stephen. *Notes from Underground: Zines and the Politics of Alternative Culture*. London: Verso, 1997.

Edut, Ophira, ed. *Body Outlaws: On Body Image and Identity*. Seattle, WA: Seal Press, 2004.

Ehrenreich, Barbara. *Nickel and Dimed: On (Not) Getting By in America*. New York: Owl Books, 2002.

Ensler, Eve. *The Vagina Monologues: The V-Day Edition*. New York: Villard, 2000.

Faludi, Susan. *Backlash: The Undeclared War Against American Women*. New York: Anchor, 1992.

Findlen, Barbara, ed. *Listen Up: Voices from the Next Feminist Generation*, revised edition. Seattle, WA: Seal Press, 2001.

Fine, Michelle, and Lois Weis. *The Unknown City: The Lives of Poor and Working-Class Young Adults*. Boston: Beacon Press, 1998.

Freedman, Estelle. *No Turning Back: The History of Feminism and the Future of Women*. New York: Ballantine Books, 2003.

French, Marilyn. *The Women's Room*. New York: Ballantine Books, 1988.

Gore, Ariel, and Bee Lavender, eds. *Breeders: Real-Life Stories from the New Generation of Mothers*. Seattle, WA: Seal Press, 2001.

Hernandez, Daisy, and Bushra Rehman. *Colonize This!: Young Women of Color on Today's Feminism* (Live Girls Series). Seattle, WA: Seal Press, 2002.

Heywood, Leslie, and Jennifer Drake, eds. *Third Wave Agenda: Being Feminist, Doing Feminism*. Minneapolis: University of Minnesota Press, 1997.

Holt, Lisa, Adam Krause, and Tim Shea, eds. *Lit Kids: An Explosion of Youth Writing*. Minneapolis, MN: Porchlight Press, 2002.

hooks, bell. *Killing Rage: Ending Racism*. New York: Owl Books, 1996.

———. *Teaching Community: A Pedagogy of Hope*. New York: Routledge, 2003.

Kim, Jee, Mathilda De Dios, Pablo Caraballo, Manuela Arciniegas, Ibrahim Abdul-Matin, and Kofi Taha. *Future 500: Youth Organizing and Activism in the United States*. New Orleans, LA: Subway & Elevated Press, 2002. (To order copies of this book visit www.future500.com or www.newmouthfrom thedirtysouth.com, or send $12 per book to: New Mouth from the Dirty South, P.O. Box 19742, New Orleans, LA 70179.)

Klein, Naomi. *No Logo: Taking Aim at the Brand Bullies*. Toronto: Knopf Canada, 2000.

Labaton, Vivien, and Dawn Lundy Martin, eds. *The Fire This Time: Young Activists and the New Feminism*. New York: Anchor, 2004.

Lappe, Frances Moore. *Diet for a Small Planet* (20th Anniversary Edition). New York: Ballantine Books, 1992.

Lappe, Frances Moore, and Anna Lappe. *Hope's Edge: The Next Diet for a Small Planet*. New York: J. P. Tarcher, 2002.

Malveaux, Julianne, and Deborah Perry. *Unfinished Business: A Democrat and a Republican Take on the 10 Most Important Issues Women Face*. New York: Perigee, 2003.

Mankiller, Wilma, Gwendolyn Mink, Marysa Navarro, Barbara Smith, and Gloria Steinem, eds. *The Reader's Companion to U.S. Women's History*. New York: Houghton Mifflin, 1998.

McAllister, JoAnn, Bill Moyer, Mary Lou Finley, and Steven Soifer. *Doing Democracy: The Map Model for Organizing Social Movements*. Gabriola Island, BC: New Society Publishers, 2001. (To order directly from the publisher, please add a $4.50 shipping and handling fee to the price of the first copy, and $1.00 for each additional copy [plus GST in Canada]. Send check or money order to New Society Publishers, P.O. Box 189, Gabriola Island, BC V0R 1X0, Canada.)

Mitchell, Michelle. *A New Kind of Party Animal: How the Young Are Tearing Up the American Political Landscape*. New York: Simon & Schuster, 1998.

Muscio, Inga. *Cunt! A Declaration of Independence*. Seattle, WA: Seal Press, 1999.

Nafisi, Azar. *Reading Lolita in Tehran: A Memoir in Books*. New York: Random House, 2003.

Nam, Vicki. *YELL-Oh! Girls!: Emerging Voices Explore Culture, Identity, and Growing Up Asian American*. New York: Quill, 2001.

Prokosch, Mike, and Laura Raymond. *The Global Activist Manual: Local Ways to Change the World*. New York: Nation Books, Thunder Mouth Press, 2002.

Redd, Nancy, and Ron Foley. *The Girls' Guide to the SAT: Tips and Techniques for Closing the Gender Gap*. Princeton, NJ: Princeton Review, 2003.

Rosen, Ruth. *The World Split Open: How the Modern Women's Movement Changed America*. New York: Penguin, 2001.

Salomon, Larry R. *Roots of Justice: Stories of Organizing in Communities of Color*. Berkeley CA: Chardon Press, 1998.

Sapphire. *Push*. New York: Knopf, 1996.

Sen, Rinku. *Stir It Up: Lessons in Community Organizing and Advocacy*. Berkeley, CA: Chardon Press, 2003.

Seo, Danny. *Be the Difference: A Beginners Guide to Changing the World*. Gabriola Island, BC: New Society Publishers, 2001.

Shah, Sonia, ed. *Dragon Ladies: Asian American Feminists Breathe Fire*. Boston: South End Press, 1997.

Sinker, Daniel, ed. *We Owe You Nothing: Punk Planet, the Collected Interviews*. New York: Akashic Books, 2001.

Steinem, Gloria. *Revolution from Within: A Book of Self-Esteem*. New York: Little, Brown & Company, 1993.

Stoller, Debbie. *Stitch 'n Bitch: The Knitter's Handbook*. New York: Workman Publishing Company, 2003.

Tanenbaum, Leora. *Catfight: Rivalries Among Women—from Diets to Dating, from the Boardroom to the Delivery Room*. New York: Harper Perennial, 2003.

Thompson, Becky. *A Promise and a Way of Life: White Antiracist Activism*. Minneapolis: University of Minnesota Press, 2001.

Wagner, Sally Roesch. *Sisters in Spirit: Haudenosaunee (Iroquois) Influence on Early American Feminists.* Summertown, TN: Native Voices, 2001.

Walker, Rebecca. *Black, White and Jewish: Autobiography of a Shifting Self.* New York: Riverhead Books, 2002.

Walker, Rebecca, ed. *To Be Real: Telling the Truth and Changing the Face of Feminism.* New York: Anchor Books, 1995.

Werbach, Adam. *Act Now, Apologize Later.* New York: Cliff Street Books, a Division of HarperCollins Publishers, 1997.

Wimsatt, William Upski. *Bomb the Suburbs.* St. Louis, MO: Left Bank Books, 1995.

———. *How to Get Stupid White Men out of Office,* edited by Adrienne Maree Brown and William Upski Wimsatt. New York: Soft Skull Press, 2004.

———. *No More Prisons.* New York: Soft Skull Press, 1999.

Wolf, Naomi. *The Beauty Myth: How Images of Beauty Are Used Against Women.* New York: William Morrow, 1991.

Index